RUNAWAYS

TRUE BELIEVERS

Writer: Brian K. Vaughan
Penciler: Adrian Alphona
Inker: Craig Yeung

Colorist: UDON's Christina Strain
Letterers: Virtual Calligraphy's Randy Gentile & Dave Sharpe
Cover Artist: Jo Chen
Editors: MacKenzie Cadenhead & C.B. Cebulski

Collection Editor: Jennifer Grünwald
Assistant Editor: Michael Short
Senior Editor, Special Projects: Jeff Youngquist
Director of Sales: David Gabriel
Book Designer: Carrie Beadle
Creative Director: Tom Marvelli

Editor in Chief: Joe Quesada
Publisher: Dan Buckley

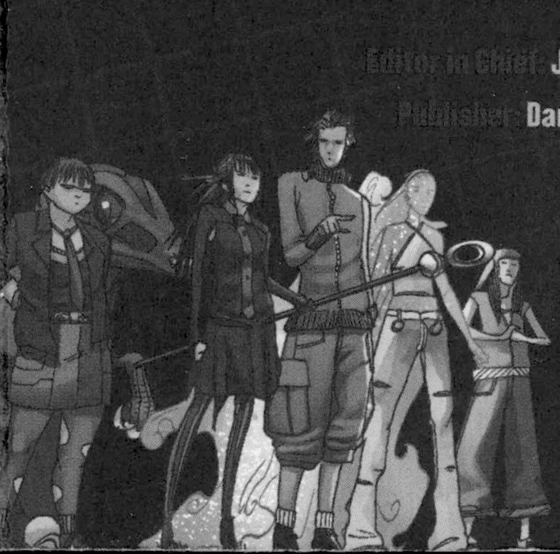

Runaways created by Brian K. Vaughan
& Adrian Alphona

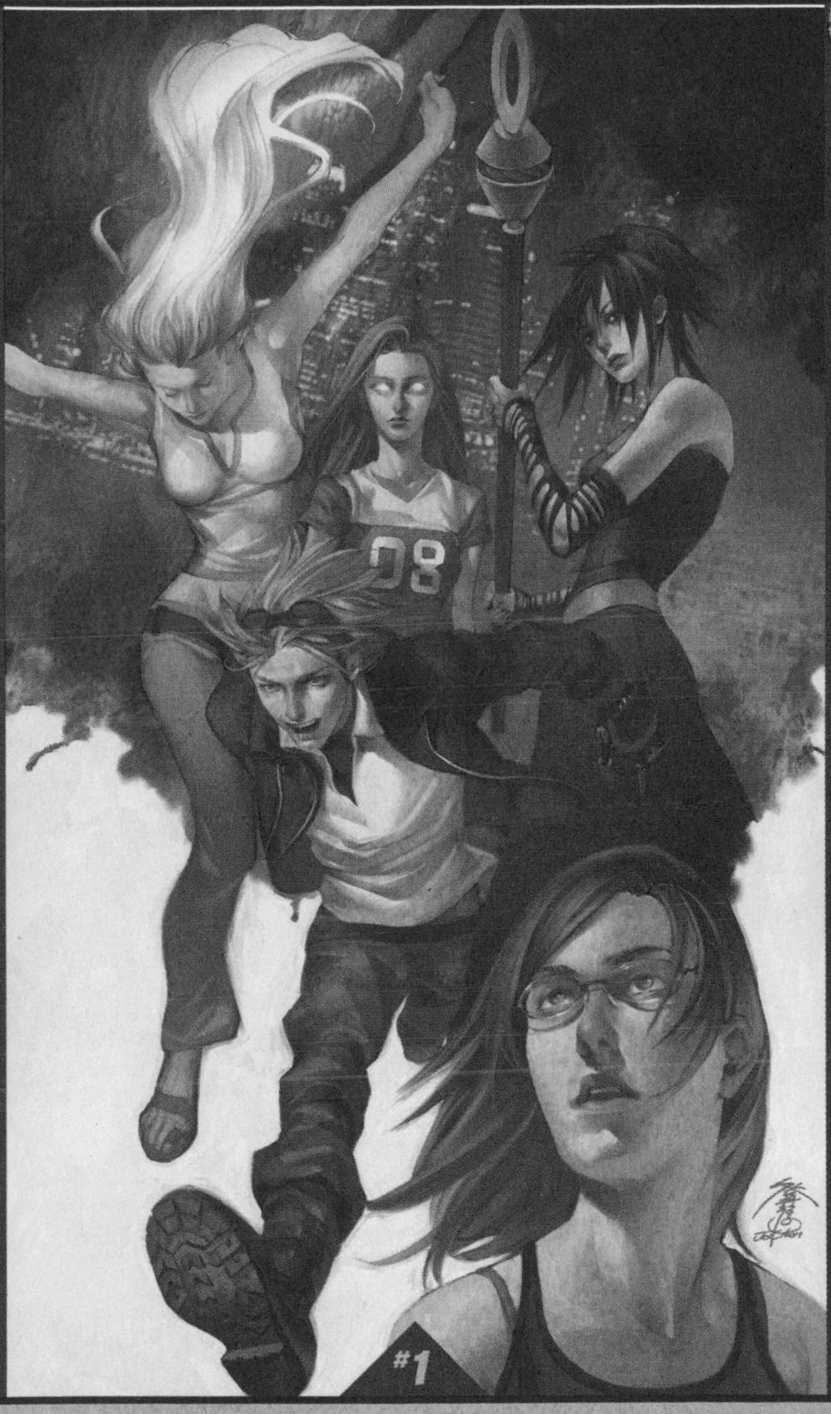
#1

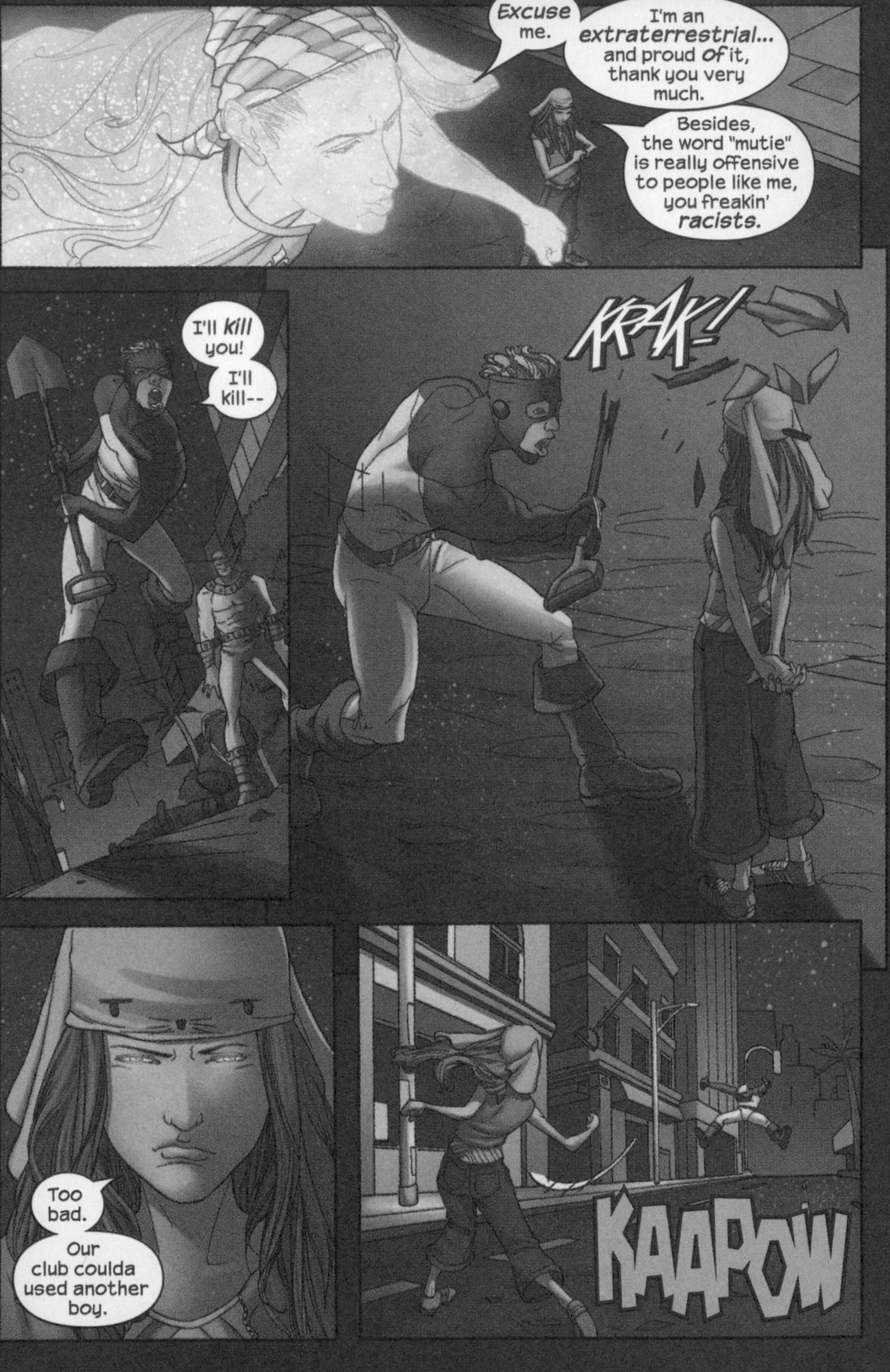

Excuse me.
I'm an extraterrestrial... and proud of it, thank you very much.
Besides, the word "mutie" is really offensive to people like me, you freakin' racists.
I'll kill you!
I'll kill--
KRAK!
Too bad.
Our club coulda used another boy.
KAAPOW

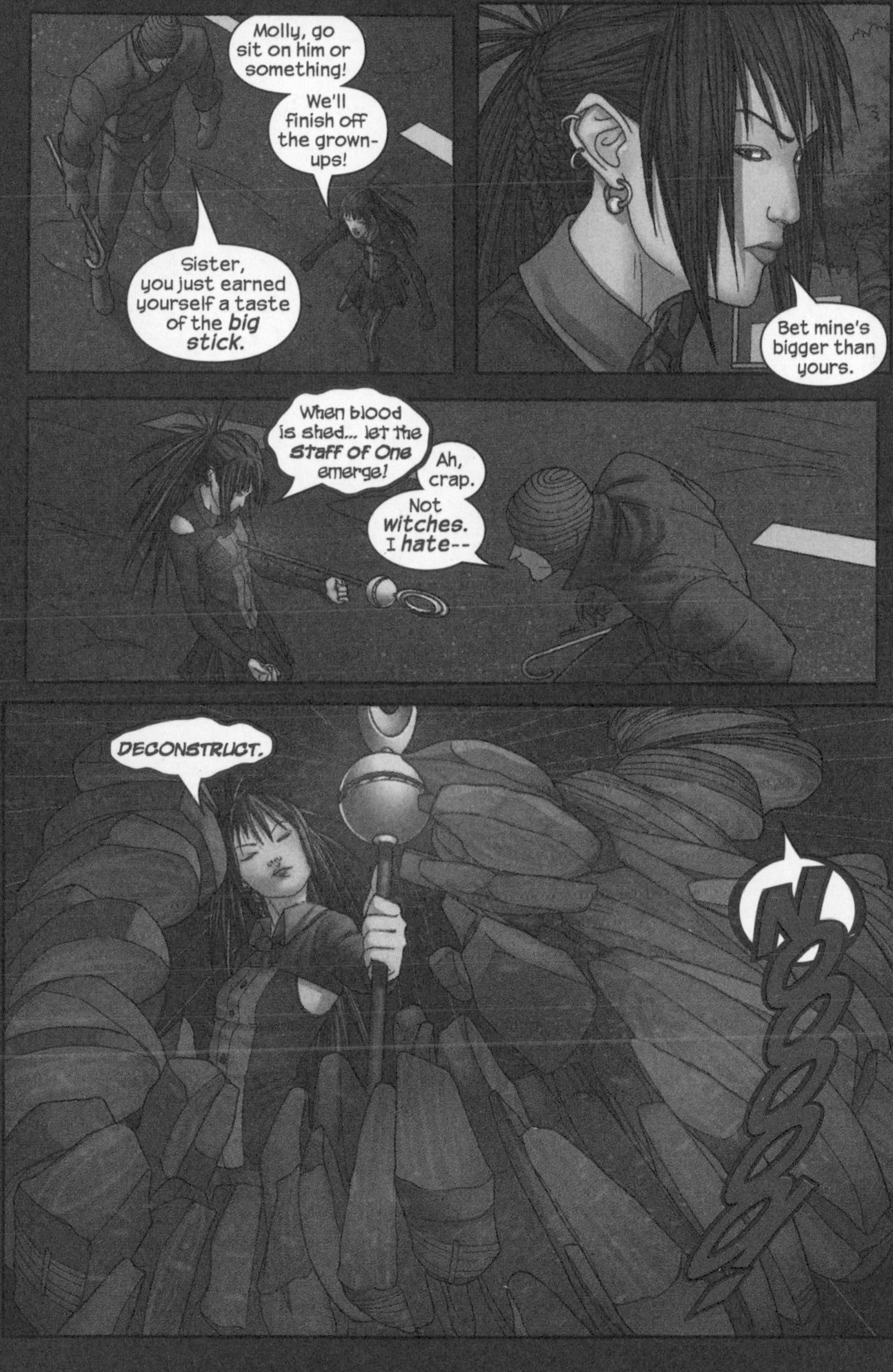
Molly, go sit on him or something!
We'll finish off the grown-ups!
Sister, you just earned yourself a taste of the *big stick.*
Bet mine's bigger than yours.
When blood is shed... let the *Staff of One* emerge!
Ah, crap.
Not *witches.* I *hate*--
DECONSTRUCT.
NOOOOOOOW

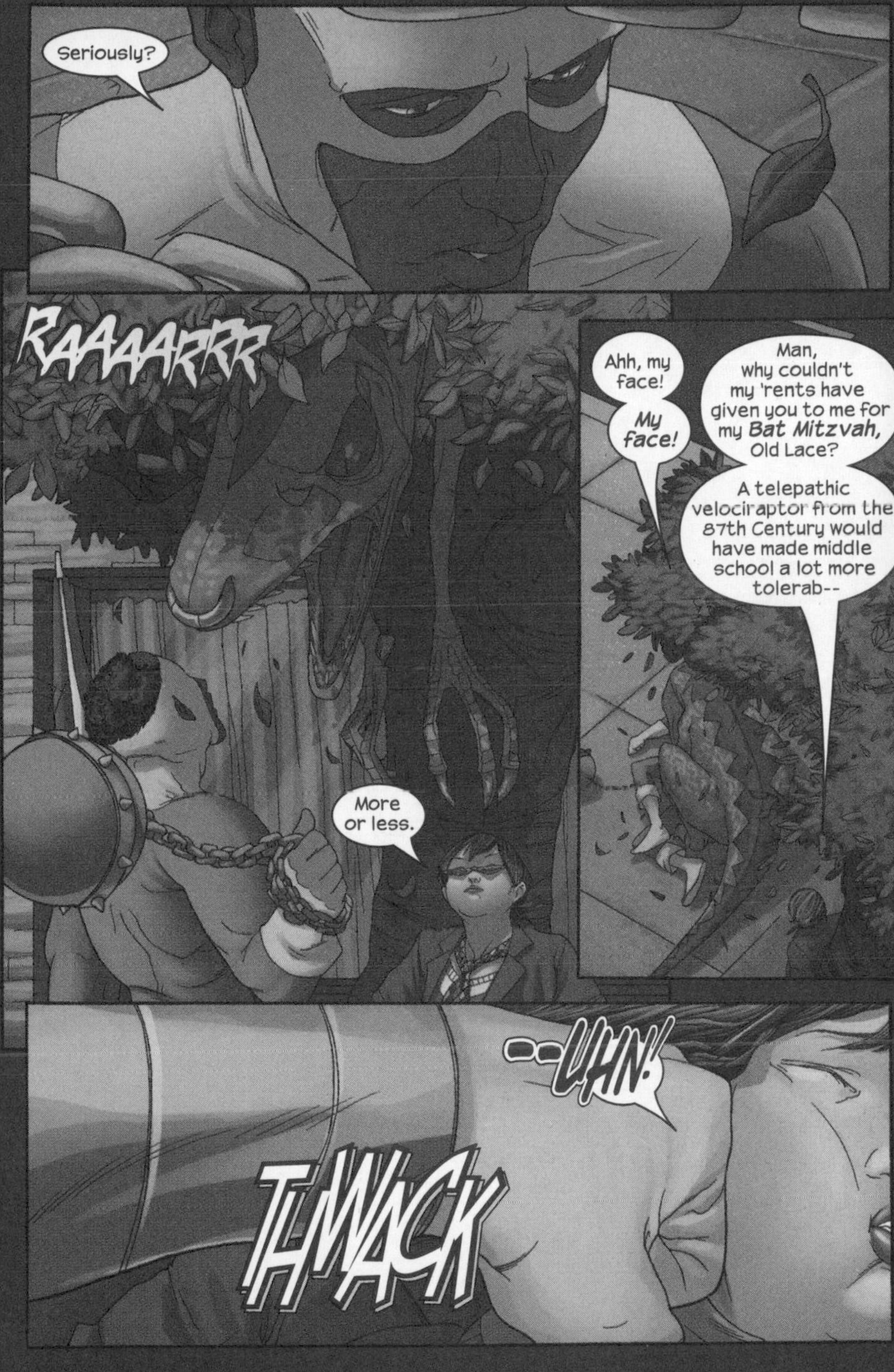
Seriously?
RAAAARRR
Ahh, my face!
My face!
Man, why couldn't my 'rents have given you to me for my Bat Mitzvah, Old Lace?
A telepathic velociraptor from the 87th Century would have made middle school a lot more tolerab--
More or less.
--UHN!
THWACK

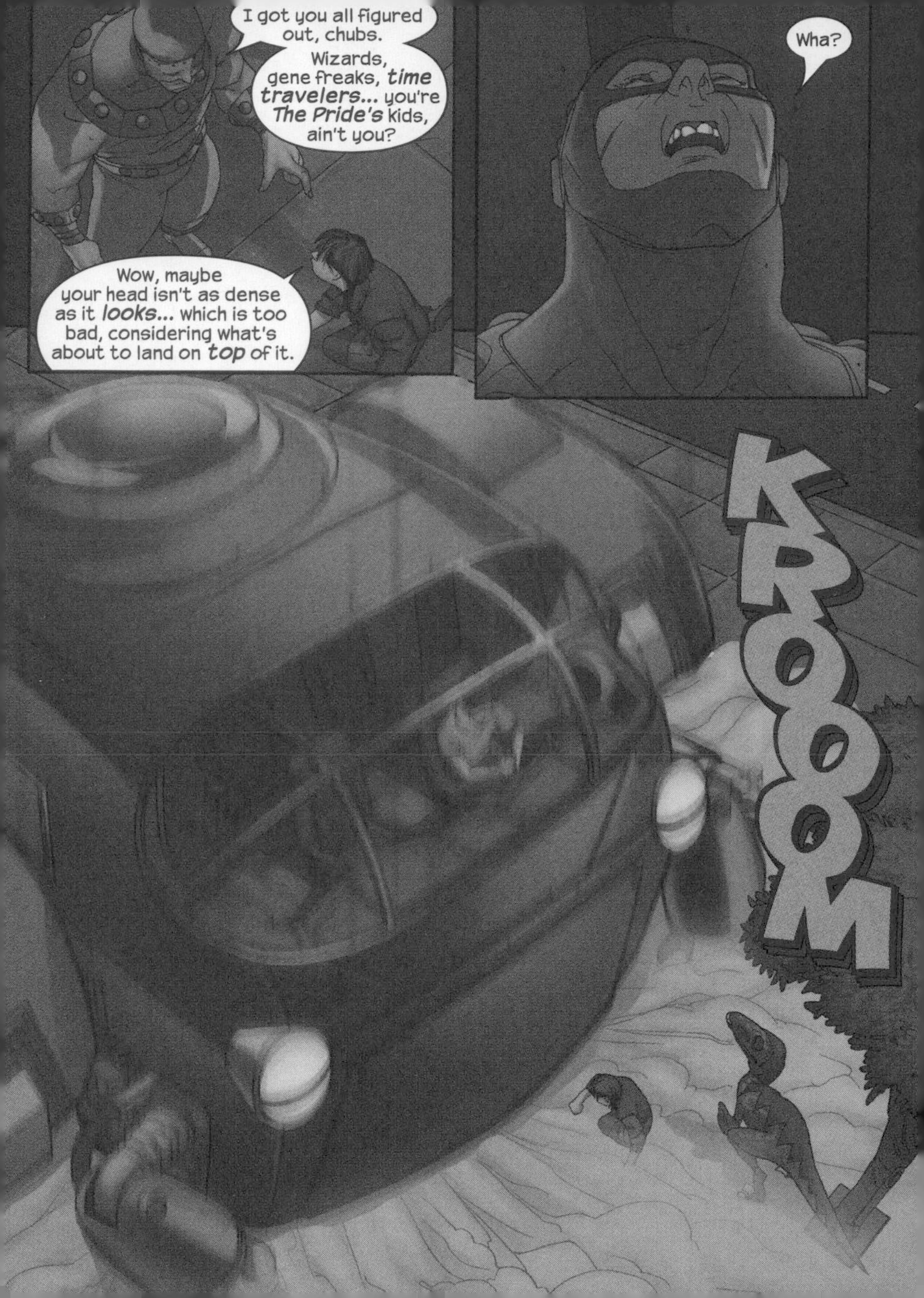
I got you all figured out, chubs.
Wizards, gene freaks, time travelers... you're The Pride's kids, ain't you?
Wha?
Wow, maybe your head isn't as dense as it looks... which is too bad, considering what's about to land on top of it.
KROOOM

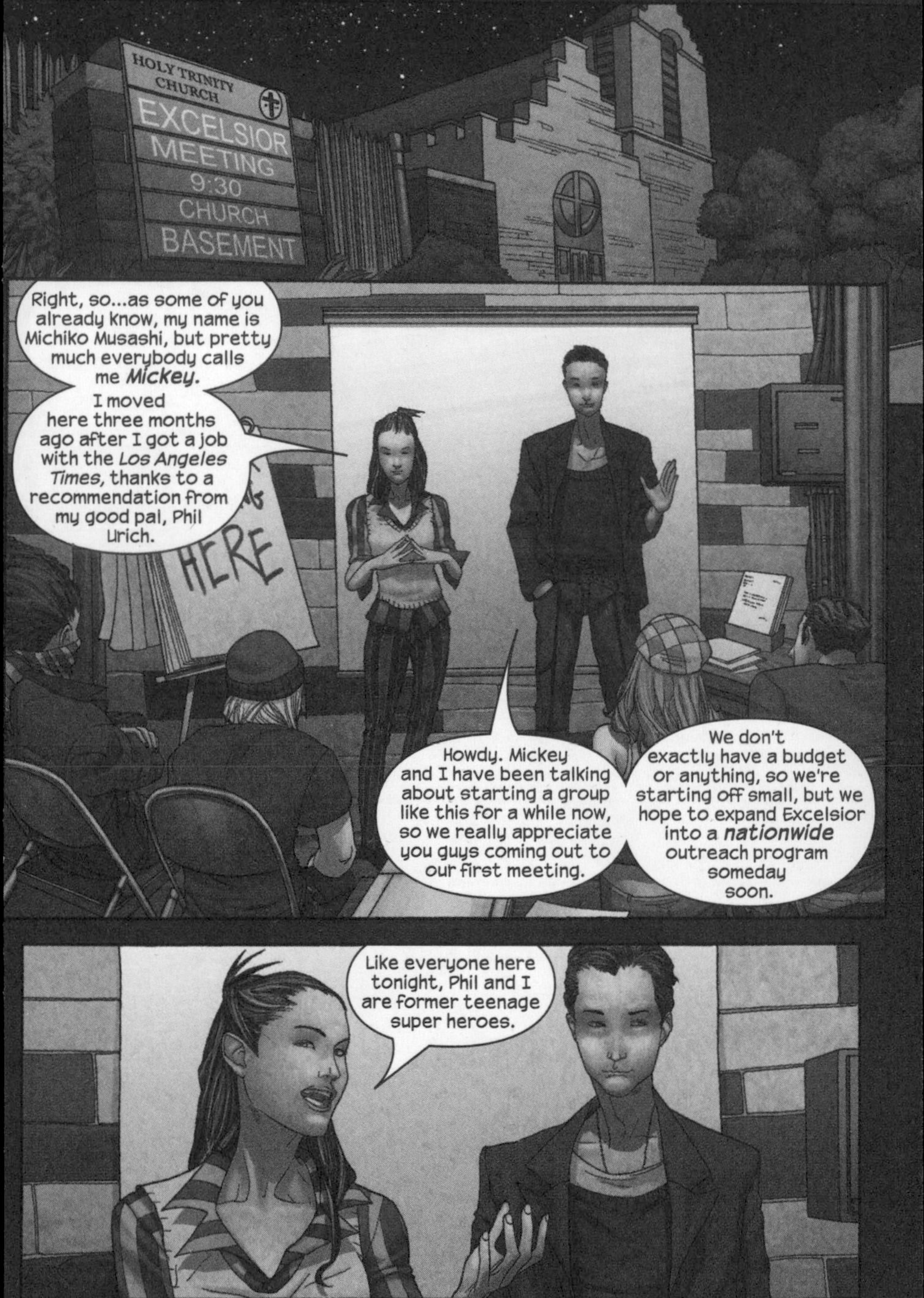
HOLY TRINITY CHURCH
EXCELSIOR MEETING 9:30 CHURCH BASEMENT
Right, so...as some of you already know, my name is Michiko Musashi, but pretty much everybody calls me *Mickey.*
I moved here three months ago after I got a job with the *Los Angeles Times,* thanks to a recommendation from my good pal, Phil Urich.
HERE
Howdy. Mickey and I have been talking about starting a group like this for a while now, so we really appreciate you guys coming out to our first meeting.
We don't exactly have a budget or anything, so we're starting off small, but we hope to expand Excelsior into a ***nationwide*** outreach program someday soon.
Like everyone here tonight, Phil and I are former teenage super heroes.

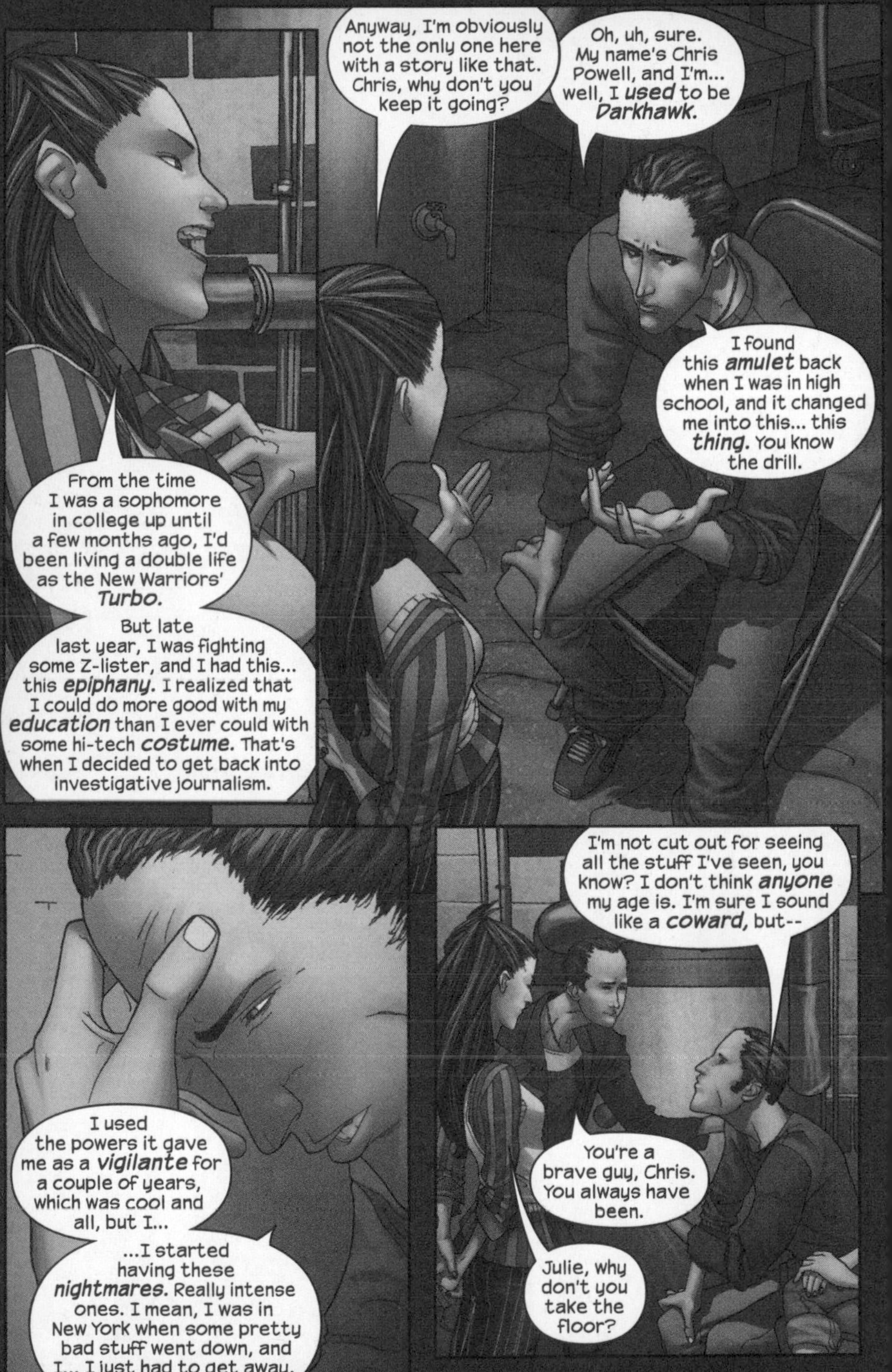
From the time I was a sophomore in college up until a few months ago, I'd been living a double life as the New Warriors' *Turbo.*
But late last year, I was fighting some Z-lister, and I had this... this *epiphany.* I realized that I could do more good with my *education* than I ever could with some hi-tech *costume.* That's when I decided to get back into investigative journalism.
Anyway, I'm obviously not the only one here with a story like that. Chris, why don't you keep it going?
Oh, uh, sure. My name's Chris Powell, and I'm... well, I *used* to be *Darkhawk.*
I found this *amulet* back when I was in high school, and it changed me into this... this *thing.* You know the drill.
I used the powers it gave me as a *vigilante* for a couple of years, which was cool and all, but I...
...I started having these *nightmares.* Really intense ones. I mean, I was in New York when some pretty bad stuff went down, and I... I just had to get away.
I'm not cut out for seeing all the stuff I've seen, you know? I don't think *anyone* my age is. I'm sure I sound like a *coward,* but--
You're a brave guy, Chris. You always have been.
Julie, why don't you take the floor?

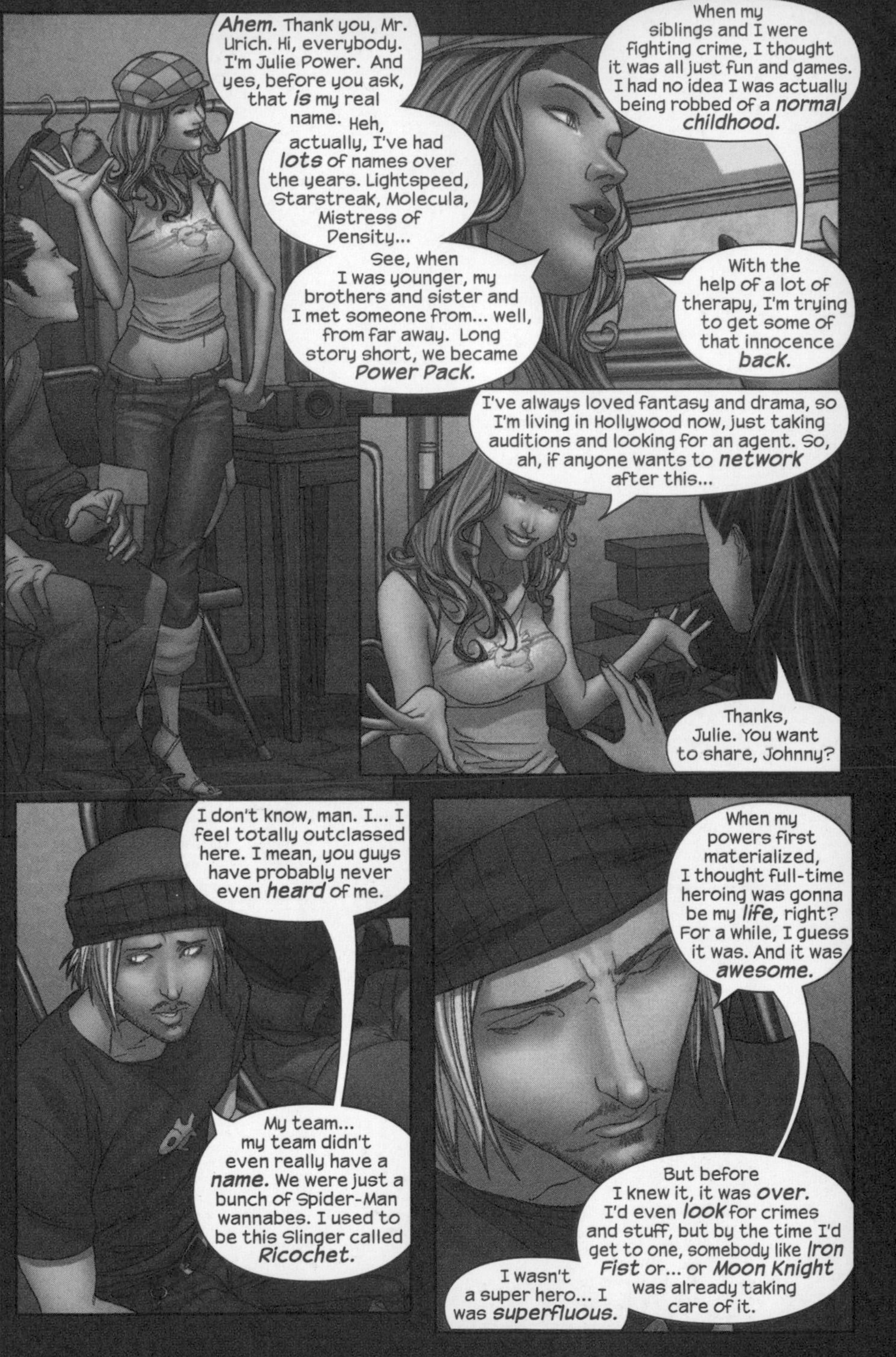
Ahem. Thank you, Mr. Urich. Hi, everybody. I'm Julie Power. And yes, before you ask, that is my real name. Heh, actually, I've had lots of names over the years. Lightspeed, Starstreak, Molecula, Mistress of Density...
See, when I was younger, my brothers and sister and I met someone from... well, from far away. Long story short, we became Power Pack.
When my siblings and I were fighting crime, I thought it was all just fun and games. I had no idea I was actually being robbed of a normal childhood.
With the help of a lot of therapy, I'm trying to get some of that innocence back.
I've always loved fantasy and drama, so I'm living in Hollywood now, just taking auditions and looking for an agent. So, ah, if anyone wants to network after this...
Thanks, Julie. You want to share, Johnny?
I don't know, man. I... I feel totally outclassed here. I mean, you guys have probably never even heard of me.
My team... my team didn't even really have a name. We were just a bunch of Spider-Man wannabes. I used to be this Slinger called Ricochet.
When my powers first materialized, I thought full-time heroing was gonna be my life, right? For a while, I guess it was. And it was awesome.
But before I knew it, it was over. I'd even look for crimes and stuff, but by the time I'd get to one, somebody like Iron Fist or... or Moon Knight was already taking care of it.
I wasn't a super hero... I was superfluous.

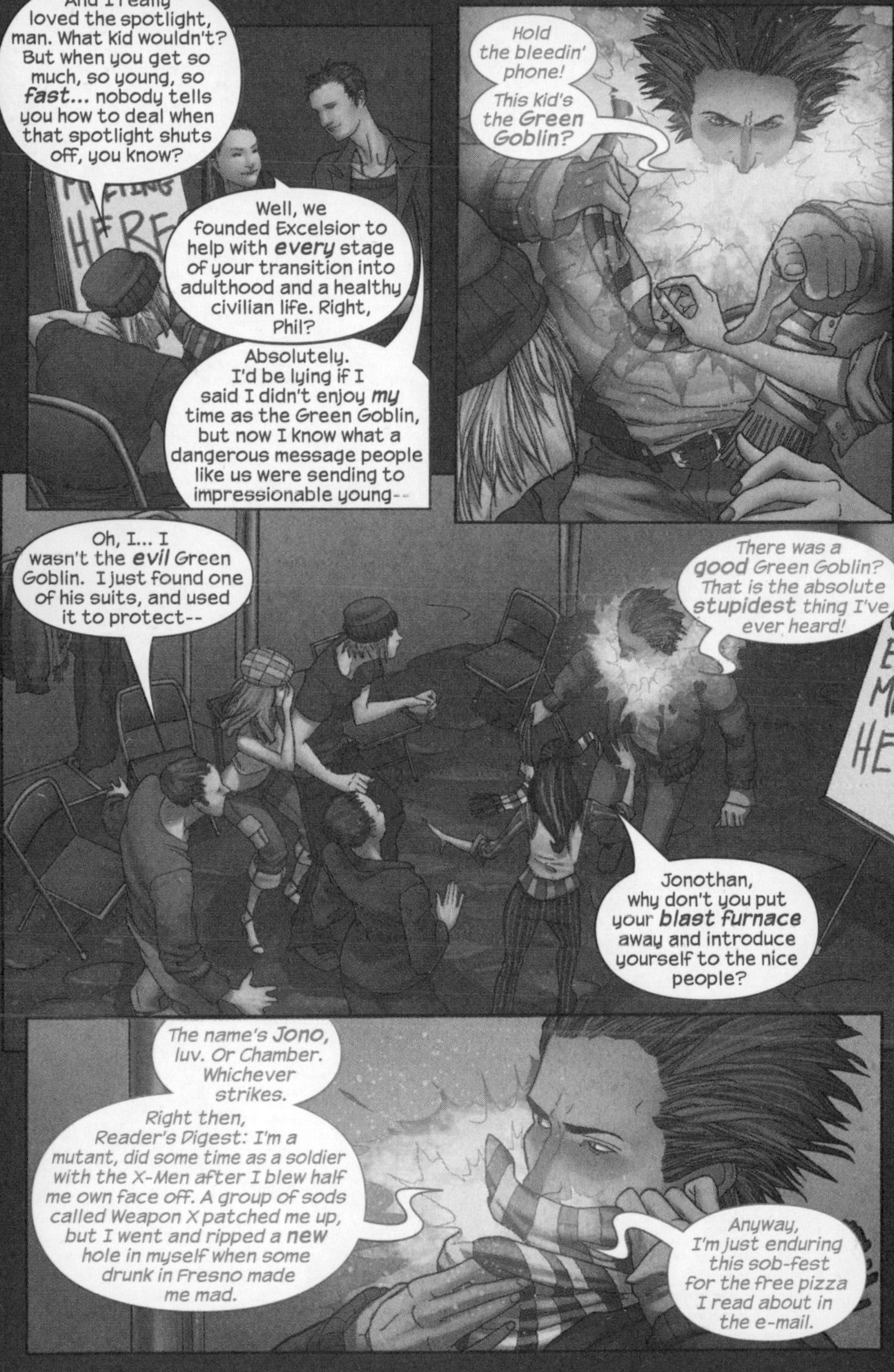
And I really loved the spotlight, man. What kid wouldn't? But when you get so much, so young, so fast... nobody tells you how to deal when that spotlight shuts off, you know?
Well, we founded Excelsior to help with every stage of your transition into adulthood and a healthy civilian life. Right, Phil?
Absolutely. I'd be lying if I said I didn't enjoy my time as the Green Goblin, but now I know what a dangerous message people like us were sending to impressionable young--
Hold the bleedin' phone!
This kid's the Green Goblin?
Oh, I... I wasn't the evil Green Goblin. I just found one of his suits, and used it to protect--
There was a good Green Goblin? That is the absolute stupidest thing I've ever heard!
Jonothan, why don't you put your blast furnace away and introduce yourself to the nice people?
The name's Jono, luv. Or Chamber. Whichever strikes.
Right then, Reader's Digest: I'm a mutant, did some time as a soldier with the X-Men after I blew half me own face off. A group of sods called Weapon X patched me up, but I went and ripped a new hole in myself when some drunk in Fresno made me mad.
Anyway, I'm just enduring this sob-fest for the free pizza I read about in the e-mail.

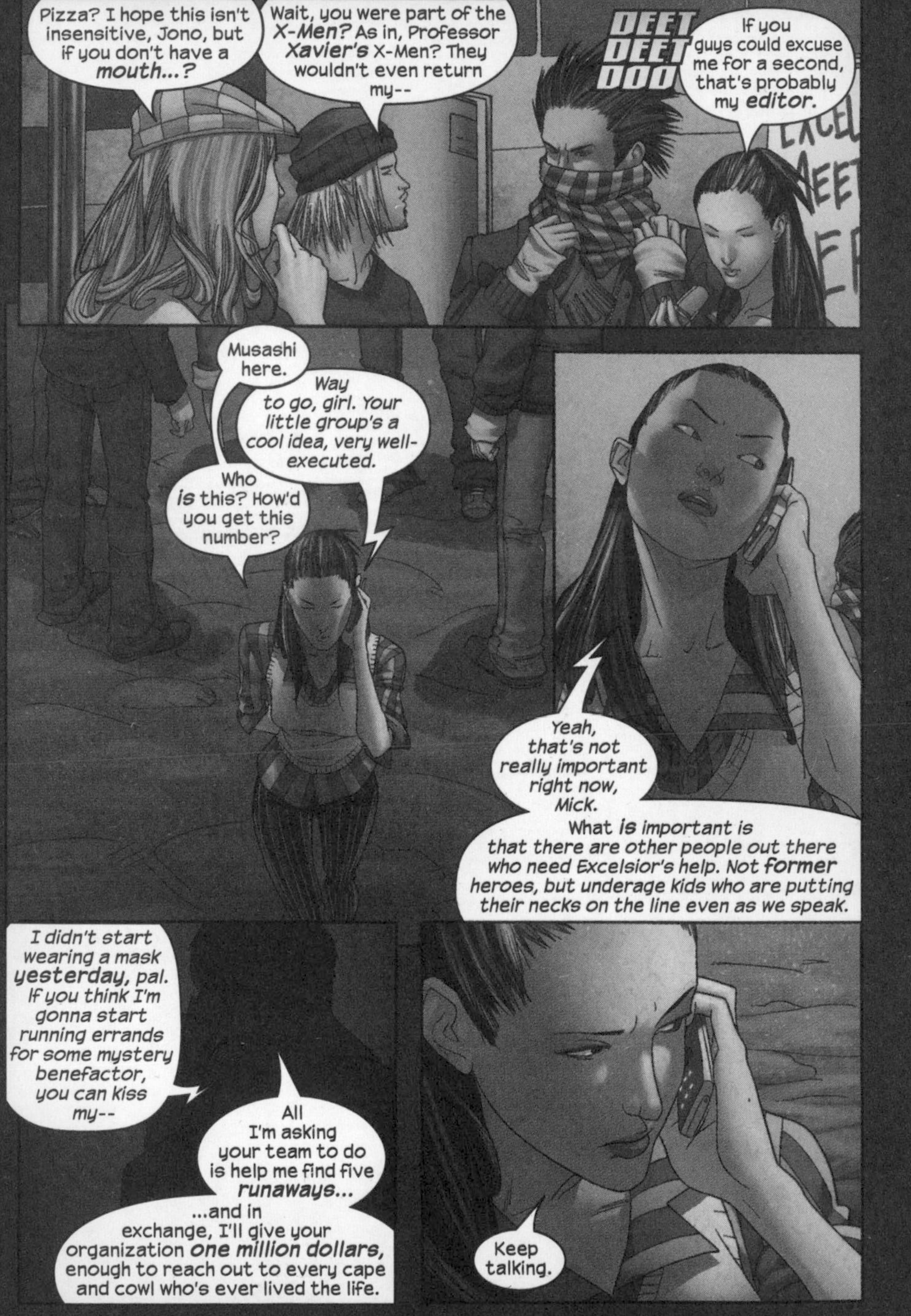

Pizza? I hope this isn't insensitive, Jono, but if you don't have a mouth...?
Wait, you were part of the X-Men? As in, Professor Xavier's X-Men? They wouldn't even return my--
DEET DEET DOO
If you guys could excuse me for a second, that's probably my editor.
Musashi here.
Way to go, girl. Your little group's a cool idea, very well-executed.
Who is this? How'd you get this number?
Yeah, that's not really important right now, Mick.
What is important is that there are other people out there who need Excelsior's help. Not former heroes, but underage kids who are putting their necks on the line even as we speak.
I didn't start wearing a mask yesterday, pal. If you think I'm gonna start running errands for some mystery benefactor, you can kiss my--
All I'm asking your team to do is help me find five runaways...
...and in exchange, I'll give your organization one million dollars, enough to reach out to every cape and cowl who's ever lived the life.
Keep talking.

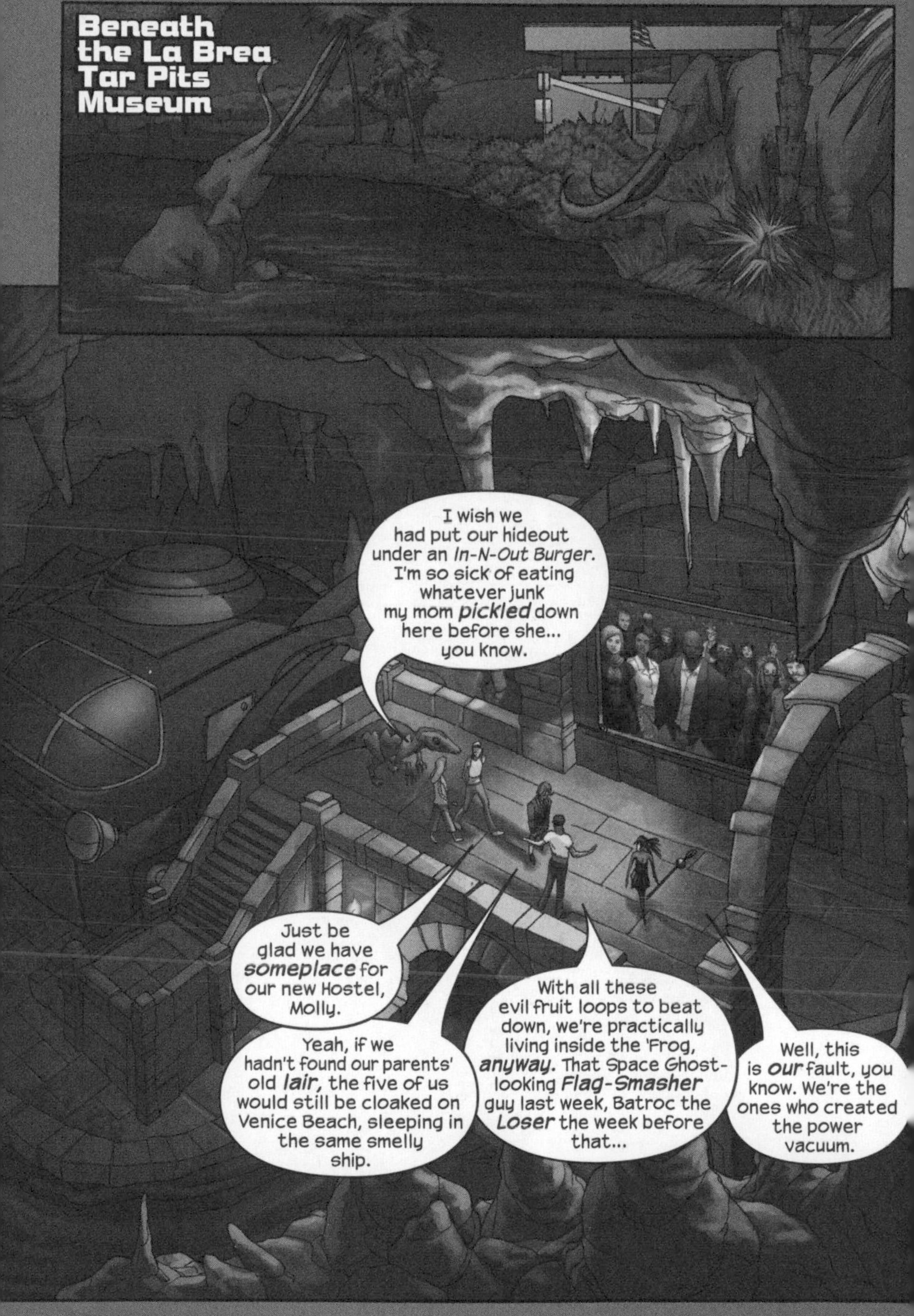

Beneath the La Brea Tar Pits Museum
I wish we had put our hideout under an In-N-Out Burger. I'm so sick of eating whatever junk my mom pickled down here before she... you know.
Just be glad we have someplace for our new Hostel, Molly.
Yeah, if we hadn't found our parents' old lair, the five of us would still be cloaked on Venice Beach, sleeping in the same smelly ship.
With all these evil fruit loops to beat down, we're practically living inside the 'Frog, anyway. That Space Ghost-looking Flag-Smasher guy last week, Batroc the Loser the week before that...
Well, this is our fault, you know. We're the ones who created the power vacuum.

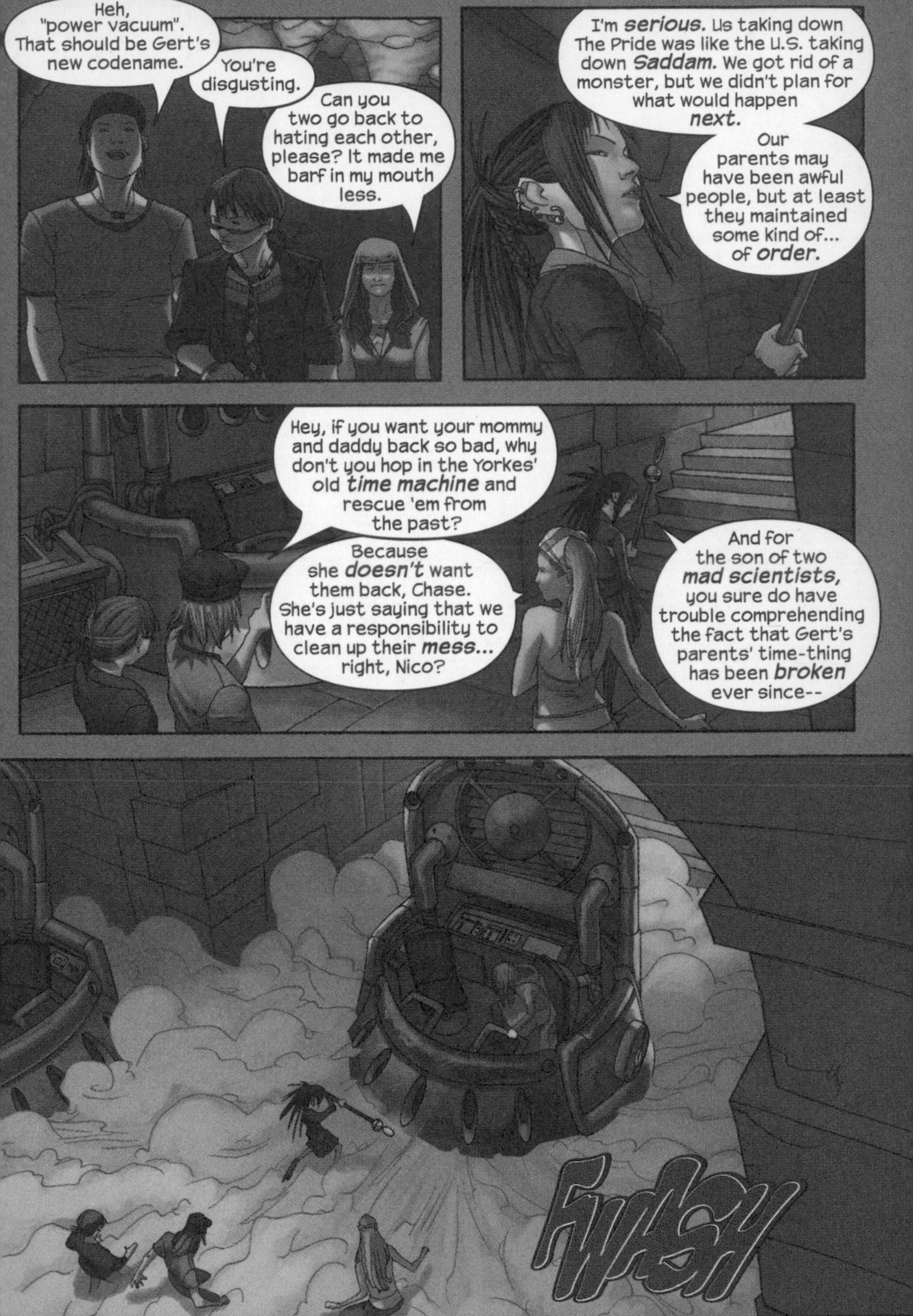

Heh, "power vacuum". That should be Gert's new codename.
You're disgusting.
Can you two go back to hating each other, please? It made me barf in my mouth less.
I'm serious. Us taking down The Pride was like the U.S. taking down Saddam. We got rid of a monster, but we didn't plan for what would happen next.
Our parents may have been awful people, but at least they maintained some kind of... of order.
Hey, if you want your mommy and daddy back so bad, why don't you hop in the Yorkes' old time machine and rescue 'em from the past?
Because she doesn't want them back, Chase. She's just saying that we have a responsibility to clean up their mess... right, Nico?
And for the son of two mad scientists, you sure do have trouble comprehending the fact that Gert's parents' time-thing has been broken ever since--
FWOOSH

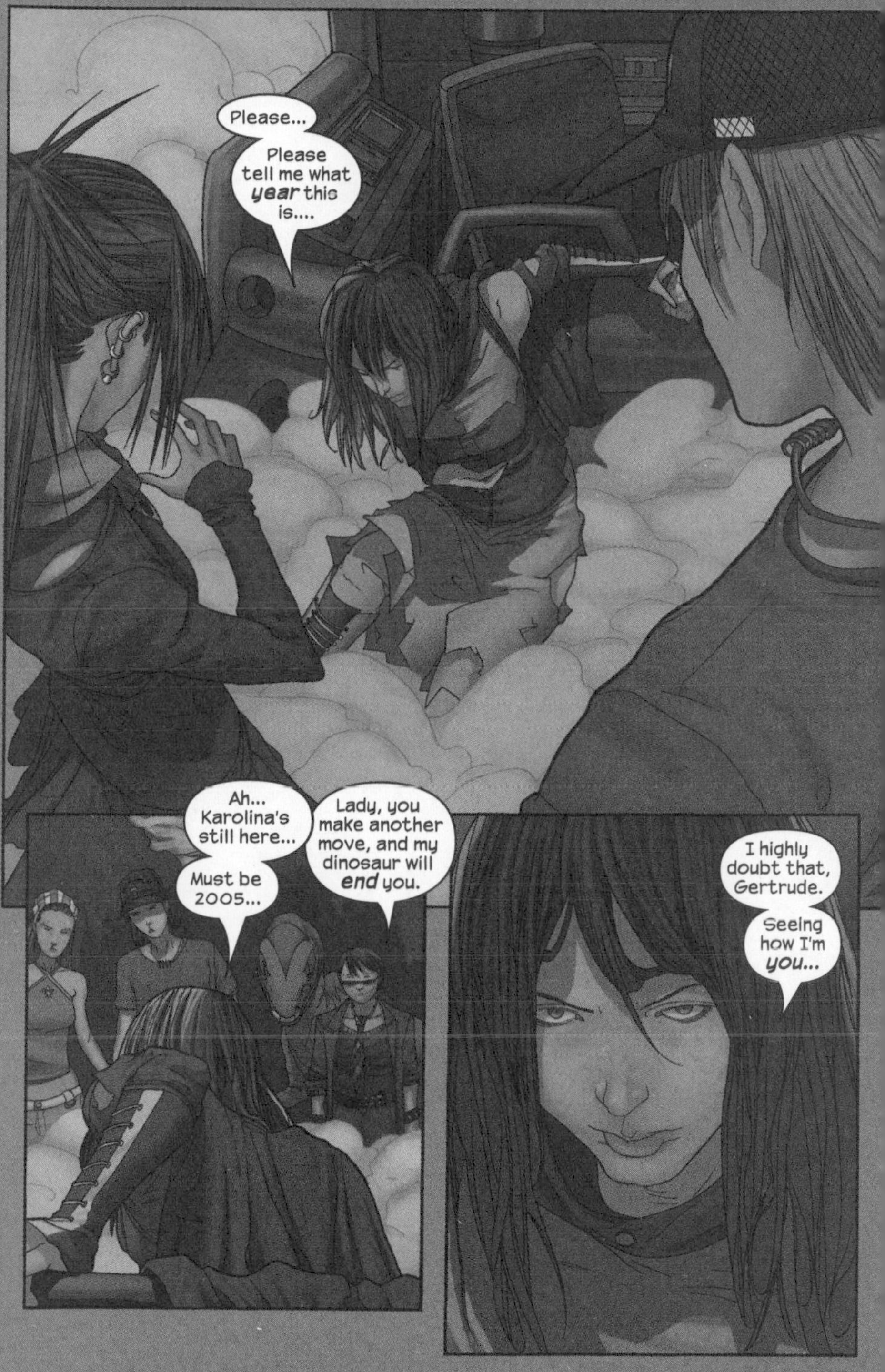
Please...
Please tell me what year this is....
Ah... Karolina's still here...
Must be 2005...
Lady, you make another move, and my dinosaur will end you.
I highly doubt that, Gertrude.
Seeing how I'm you...

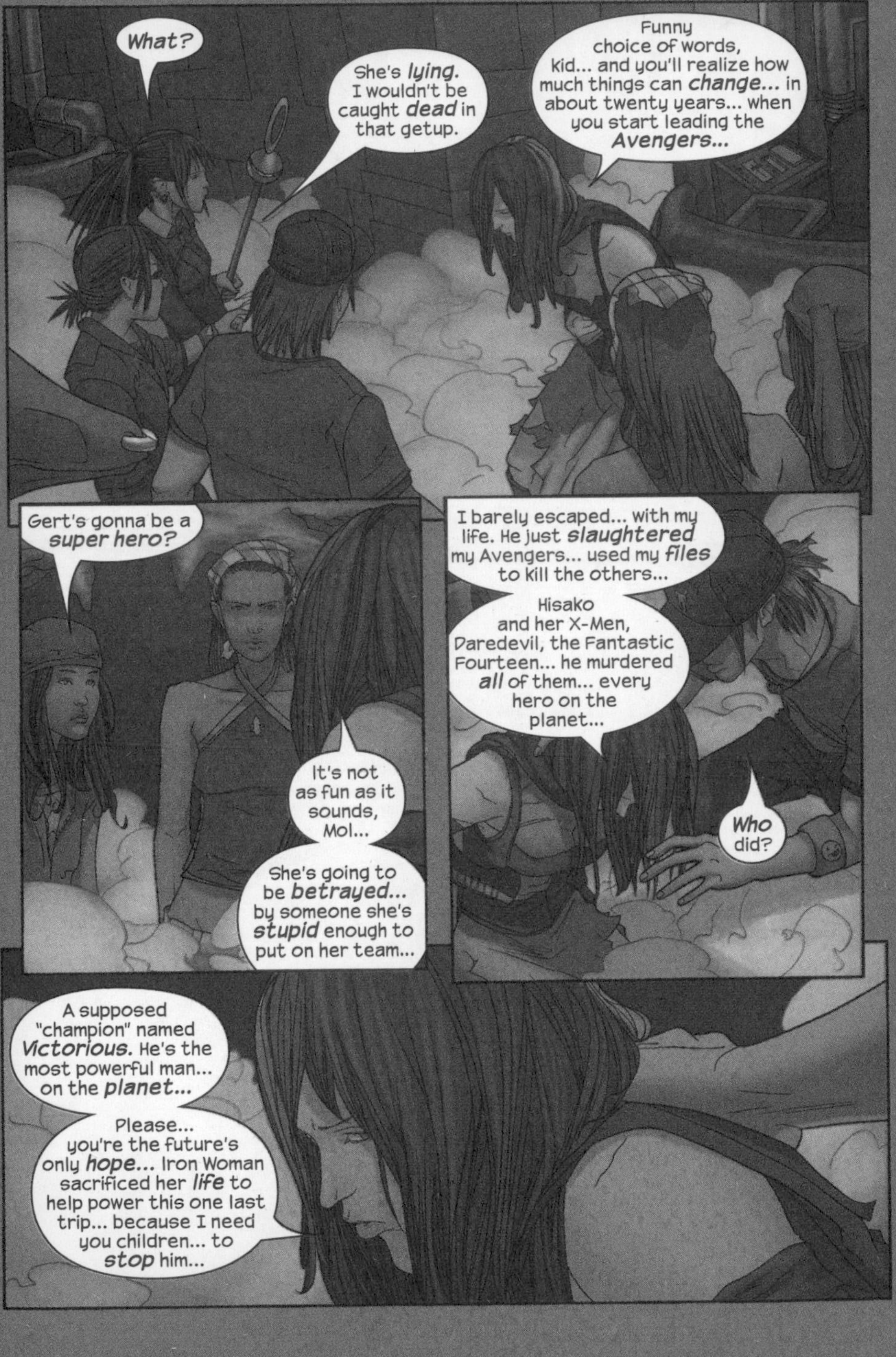
What?
She's lying. I wouldn't be caught dead in that getup.
Funny choice of words, kid... and you'll realize how much things can change... in about twenty years... when you start leading the Avengers...
Gert's gonna be a super hero?
It's not as fun as it sounds, Mol...
She's going to be betrayed... by someone she's stupid enough to put on her team...
I barely escaped... with my life. He just slaughtered my Avengers... used my files to kill the others...
Hisako and her X-Men, Daredevil, the Fantastic Fourteen... he murdered all of them... every hero on the planet...
Who did?
A supposed "champion" named Victorious. He's the most powerful man... on the planet...
Please... you're the future's only hope... Iron Woman sacrificed her life to help power this one last trip... because I need you children... to stop him...

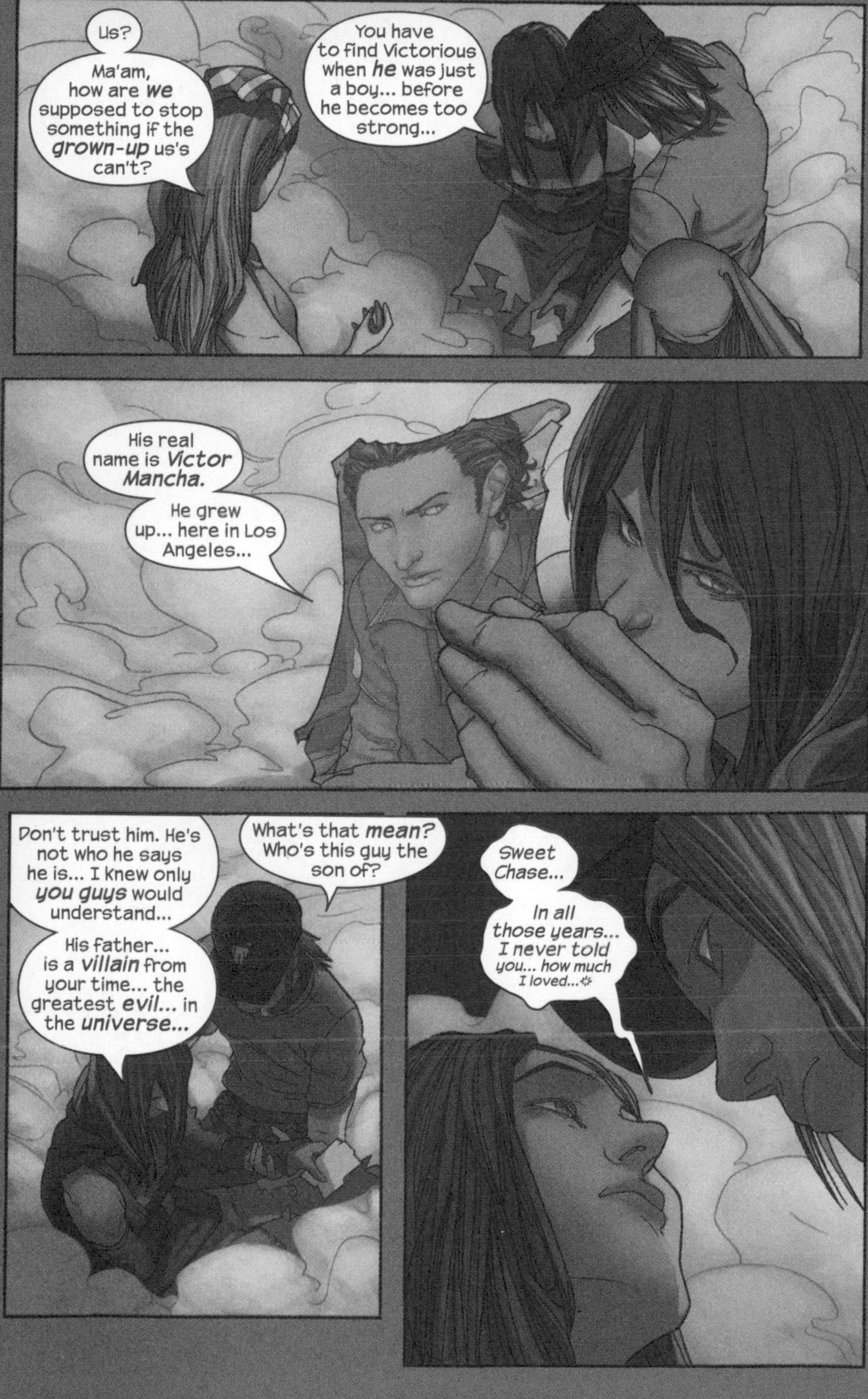
Us?
Ma'am, how are **we** supposed to stop something if the **grown-up** us's can't?
You have to find Victorious when **he** was just a boy... before he becomes too strong...
His real name is *Victor Mancha.*
He grew up... here in Los Angeles...
Don't trust him. He's not who he says he is... I knew only **you guys** would understand...
His father... is a **villain** from your time... the greatest **evil...** in the **universe...**
What's that **mean?** Who's this guy the son of?
Sweet Chase...
In all those years... I never told you... how much I loved...

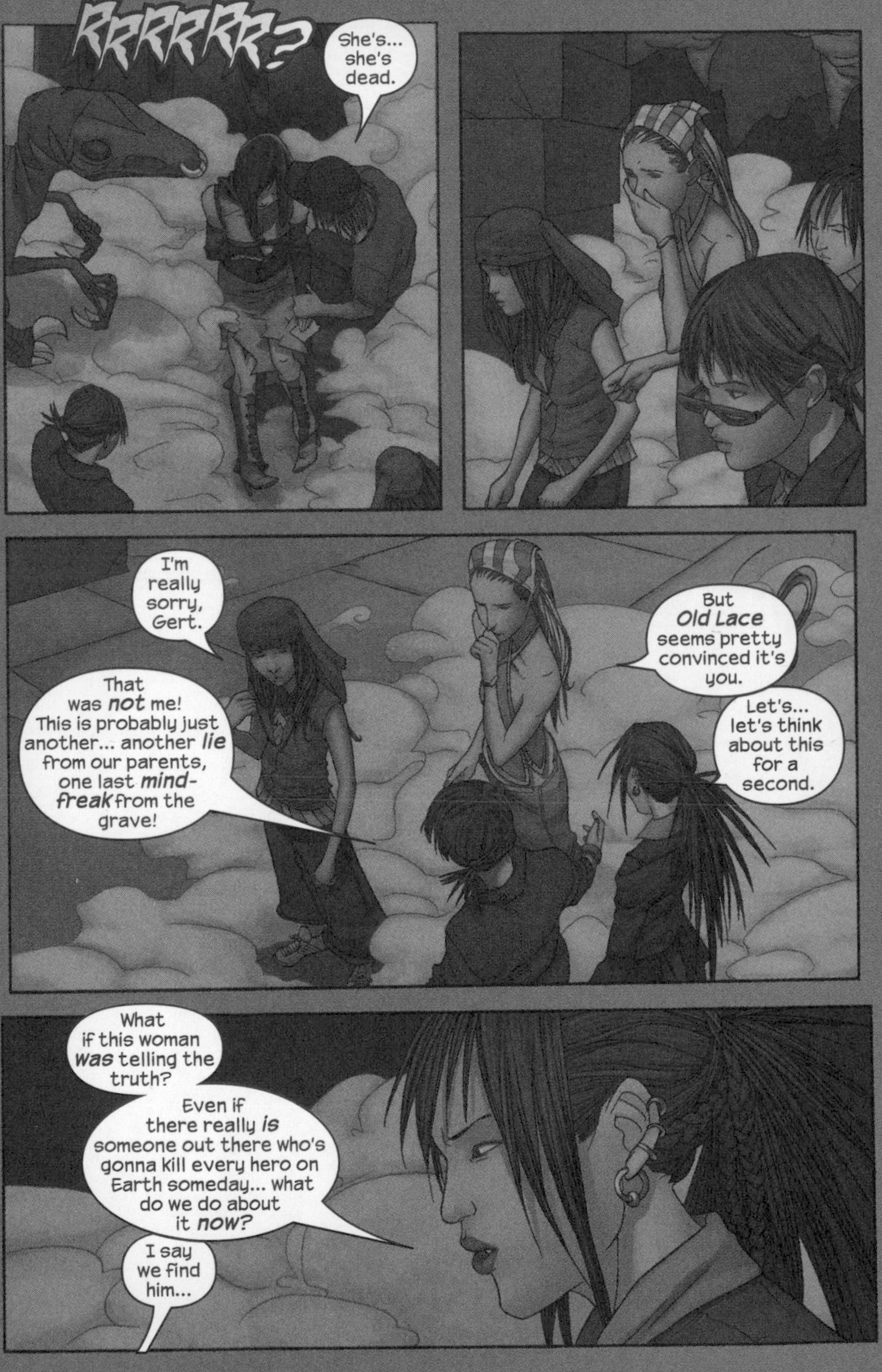
RRRRRR?
She's... she's dead.
I'm really sorry, Gert.
That was not me! This is probably just another... another lie from our parents, one last mind-freak from the grave!
But Old Lace seems pretty convinced it's you.
Let's... let's think about this for a second.
What if this woman was telling the truth?
Even if there really is someone out there who's gonna kill every hero on Earth someday... what do we do about it now?
I say we find him...

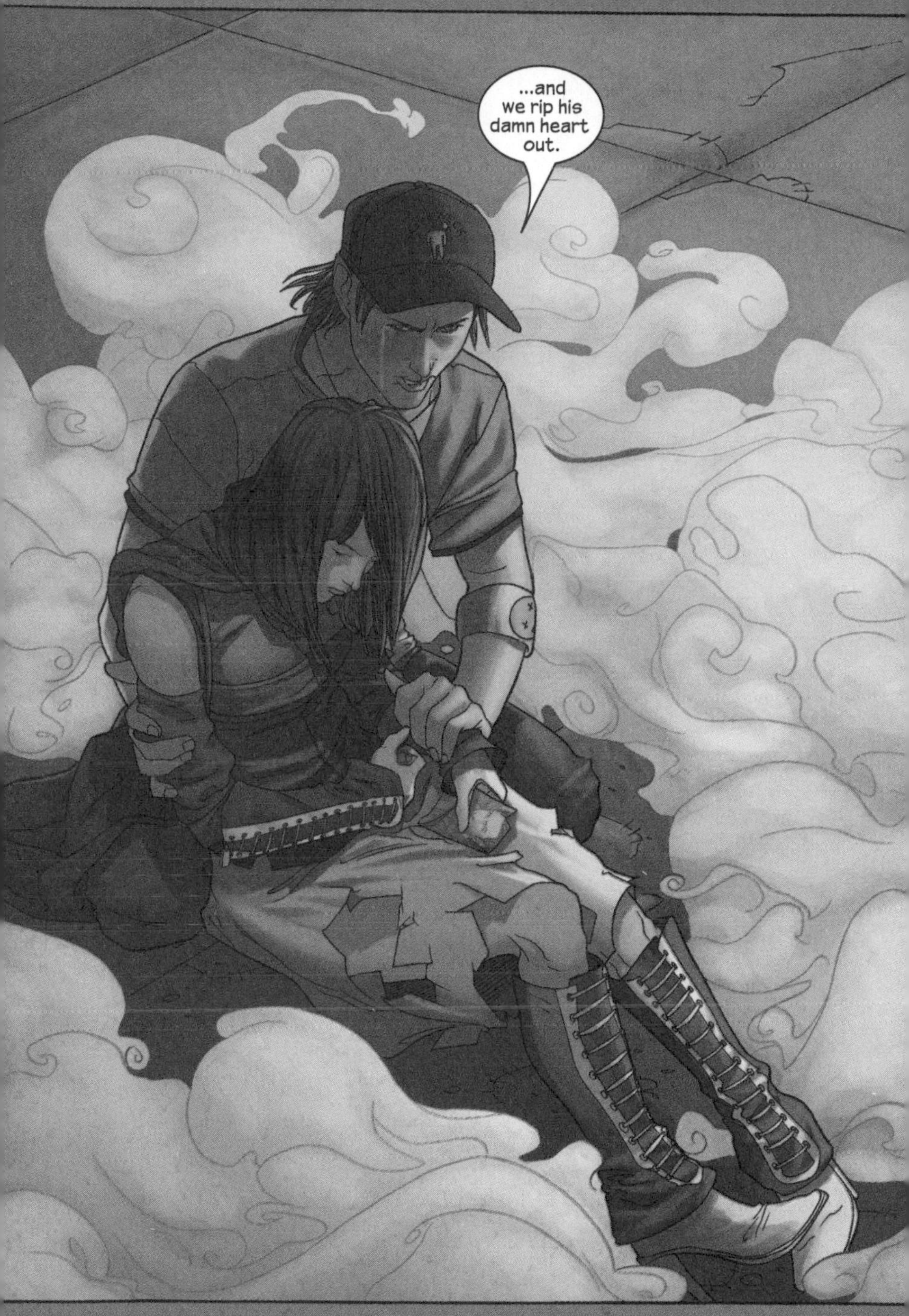
...and we rip his damn heart out.

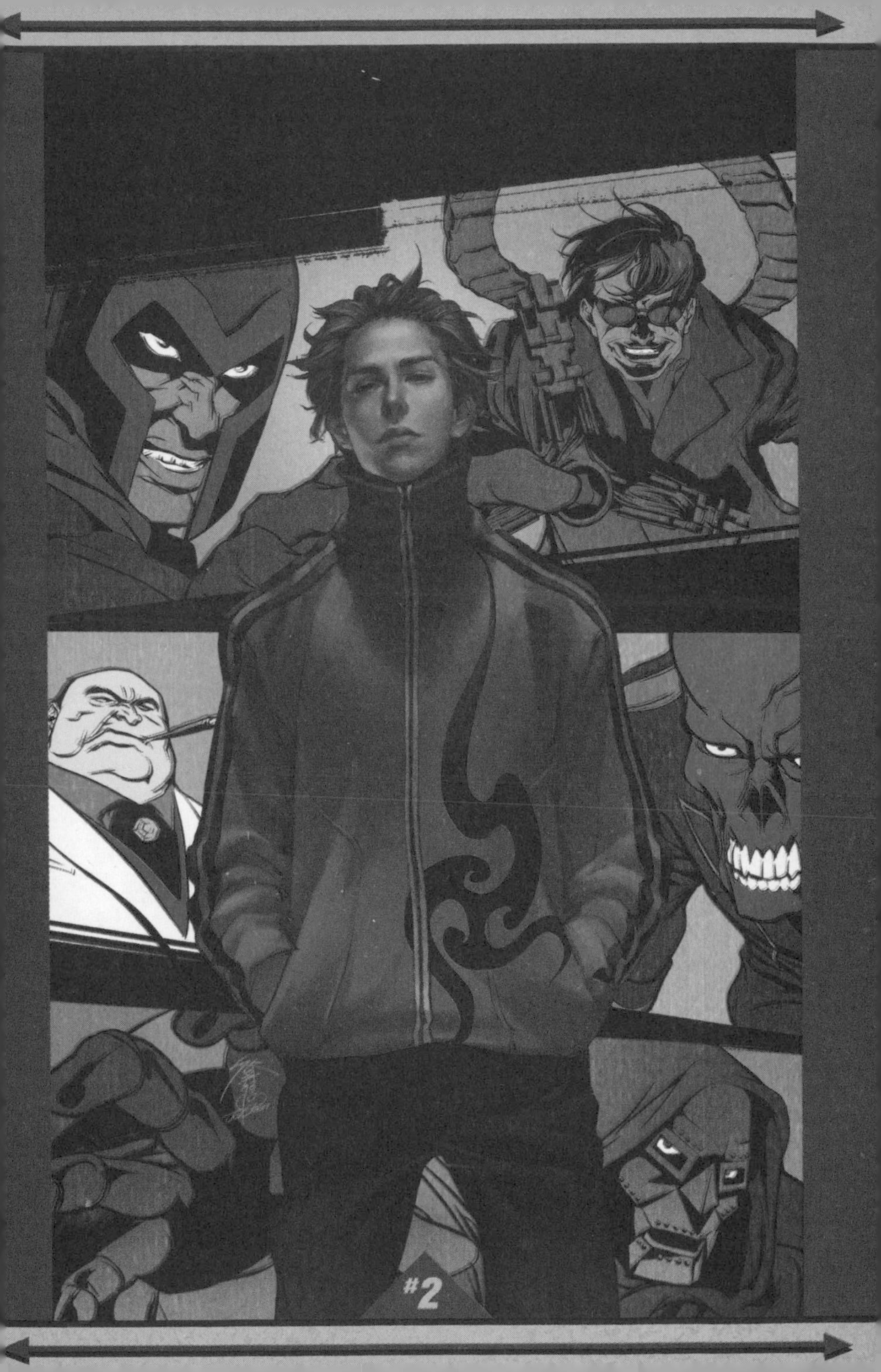
#2

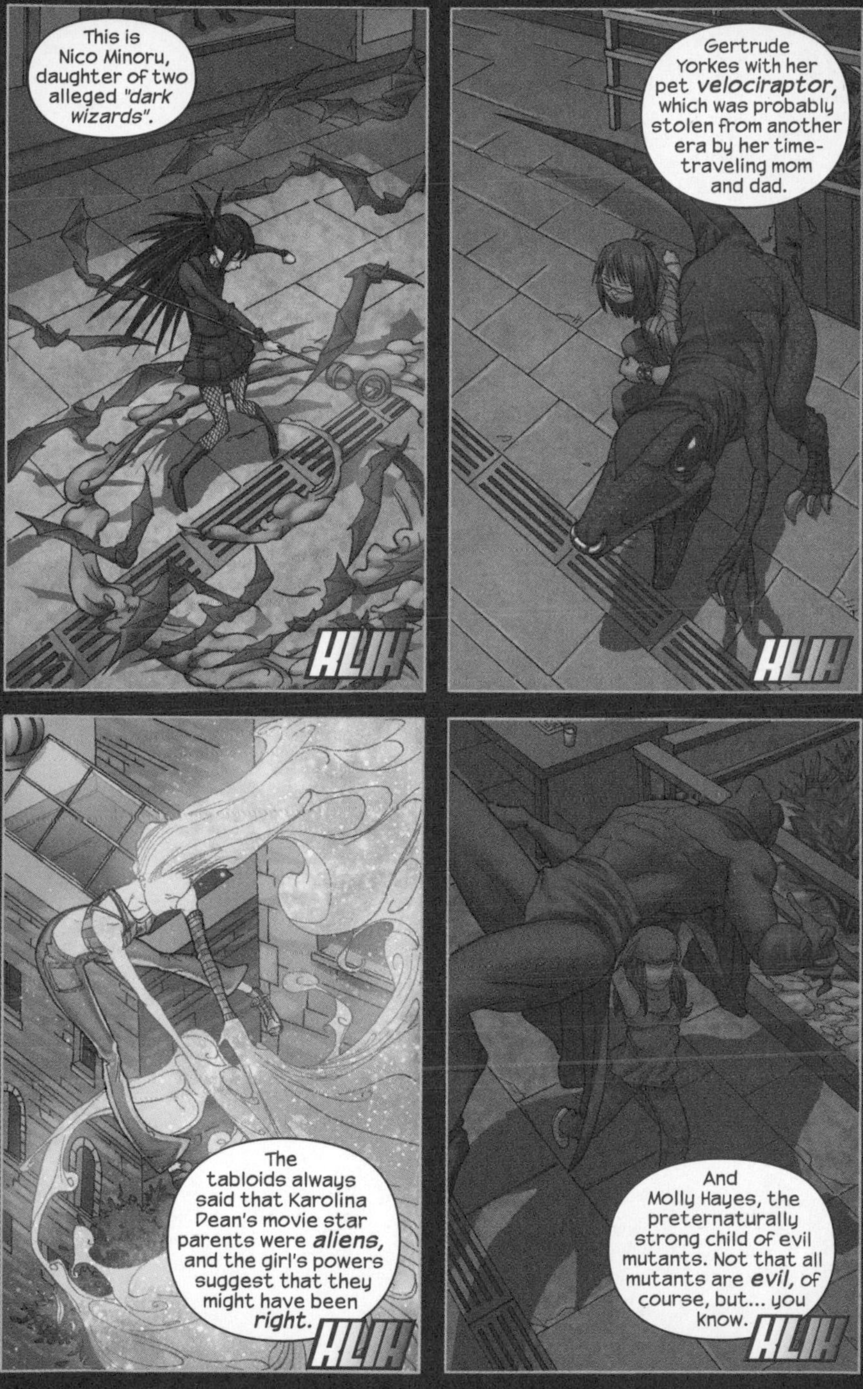

This is Nico Minoru, daughter of two alleged "dark wizards".
KLIK
Gertrude Yorkes with her pet velociraptor, which was probably stolen from another era by her time-traveling mom and dad.
KLIK
The tabloids always said that Karolina Dean's movie star parents were aliens, and the girl's powers suggest that they might have been right.
KLIK
And Molly Hayes, the preternaturally strong child of evil mutants. Not that all mutants are evil, of course, but... you know.
KLIK

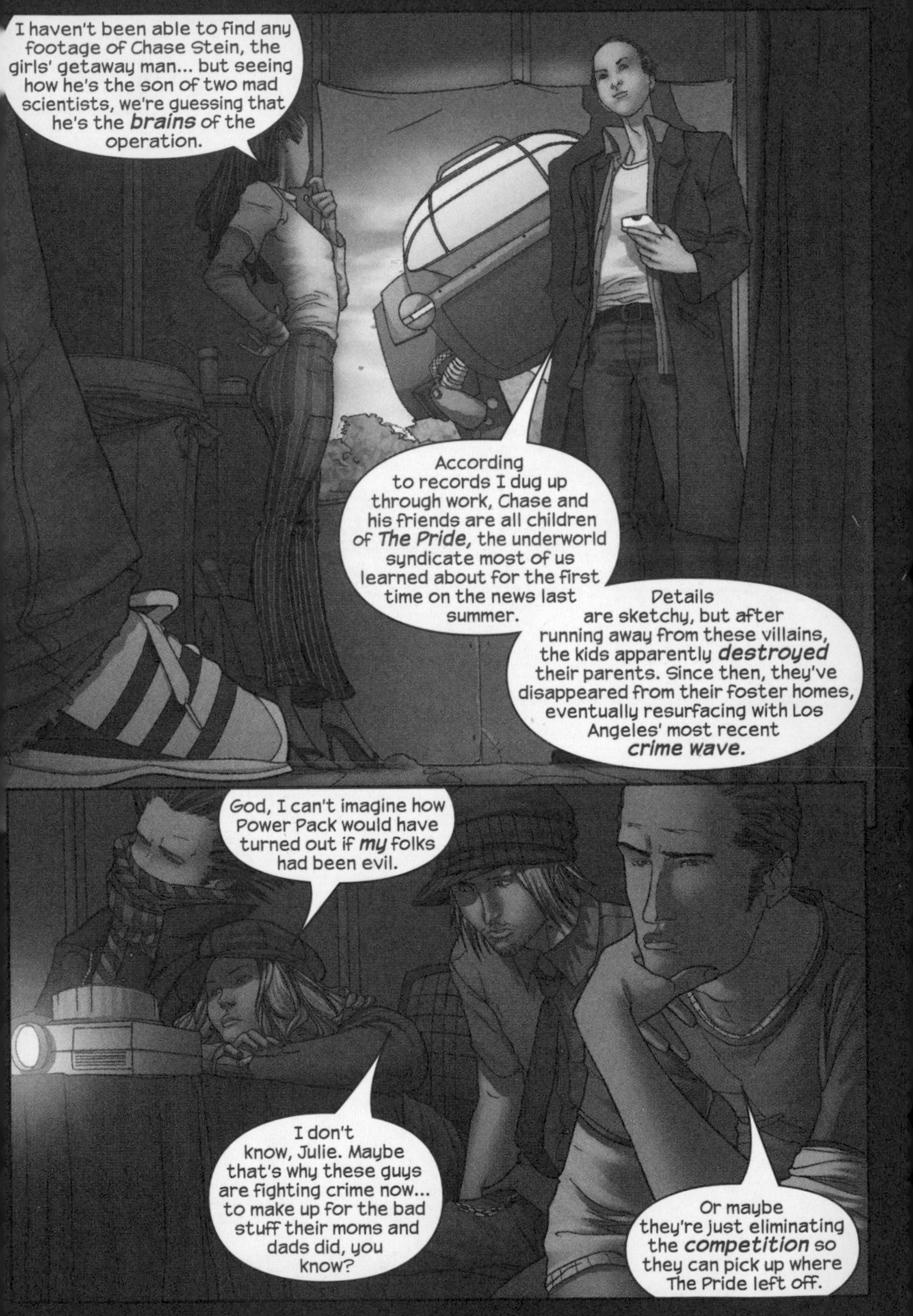
I haven't been able to find any footage of Chase Stein, the girls' getaway man... but seeing how he's the son of two mad scientists, we're guessing that he's the *brains* of the operation.
According to records I dug up through work, Chase and his friends are all children of *The Pride,* the underworld syndicate most of us learned about for the first time on the news last summer.
Details are sketchy, but after running away from these villains, the kids apparently *destroyed* their parents. Since then, they've disappeared from their foster homes, eventually resurfacing with Los Angeles' most recent *crime wave.*
God, I can't imagine how Power Pack would have turned out if *my* folks had been evil.
I don't know, Julie. Maybe that's why these guys are fighting crime now... to make up for the bad stuff their moms and dads did, you know?
Or maybe they're just eliminating the *competition* so they can pick up where The Pride left off.

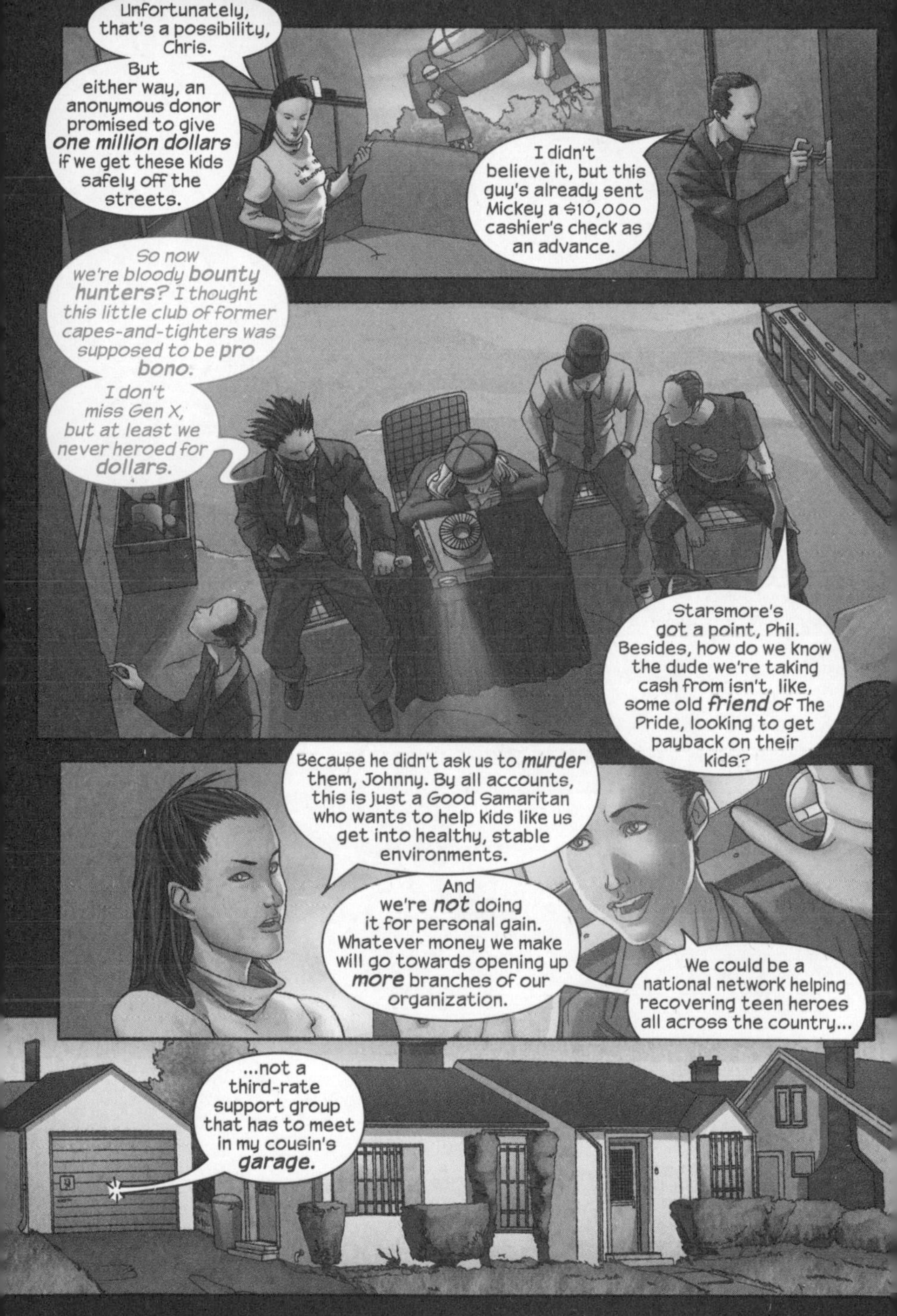
Unfortunately, that's a possibility, Chris.
But either way, an anonymous donor promised to give one million dollars if we get these kids safely off the streets.
I didn't believe it, but this guy's already sent Mickey a $10,000 cashier's check as an advance.
So now we're bloody bounty hunters? I thought this little club of former capes-and-tighters was supposed to be pro bono.
I don't miss Gen X, but at least we never heroed for dollars.
Starsmore's got a point, Phil. Besides, how do we know the dude we're taking cash from isn't, like, some old friend of The Pride, looking to get payback on their kids?
Because he didn't ask us to murder them, Johnny. By all accounts, this is just a Good Samaritan who wants to help kids like us get into healthy, stable environments.
And we're not doing it for personal gain. Whatever money we make will go towards opening up more branches of our organization.
We could be a national network helping recovering teen heroes all across the country...
...not a third-rate support group that has to meet in my cousin's garage.

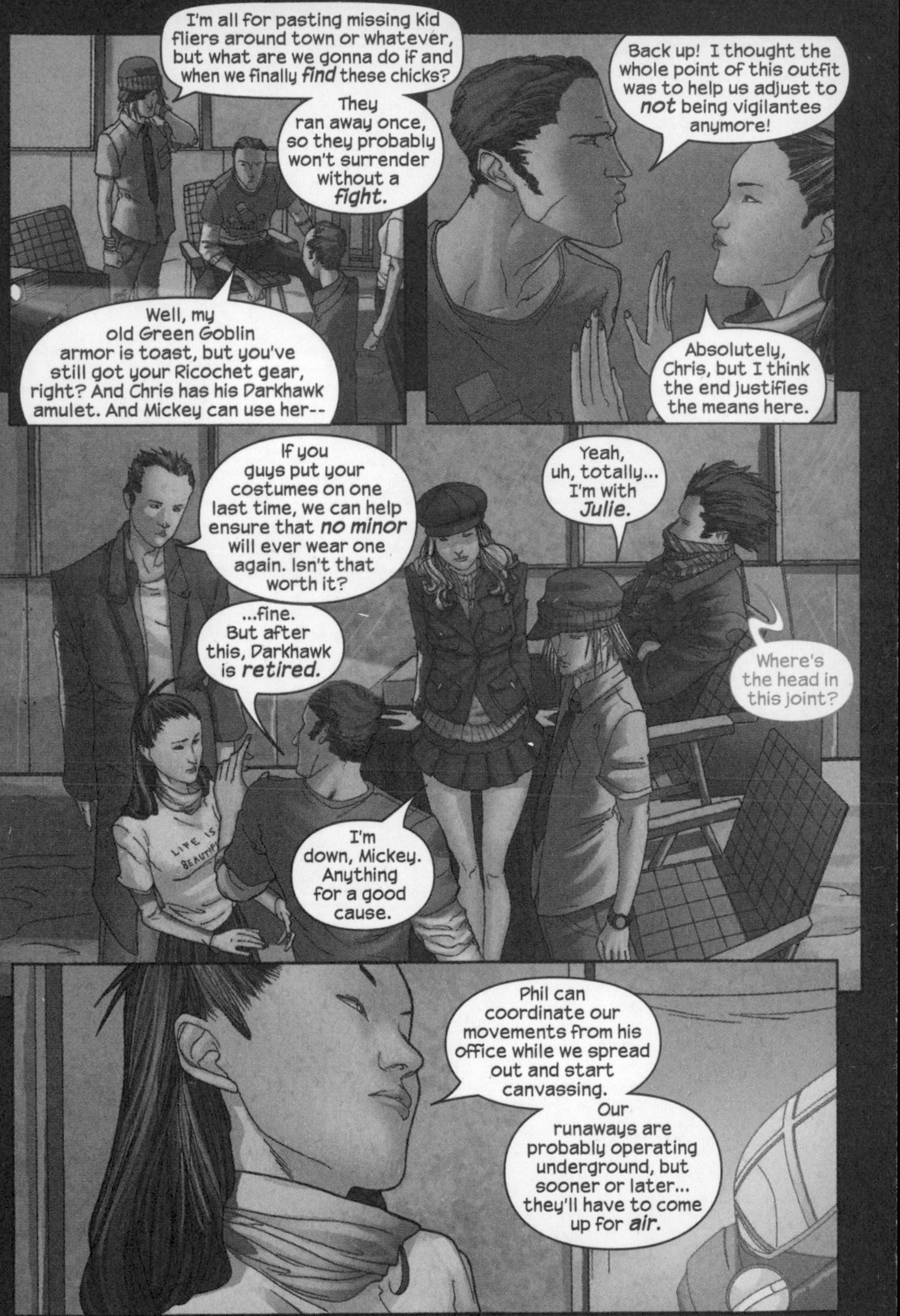

I'm all for pasting missing kid fliers around town or whatever, but what are we gonna do if and when we finally *find* these chicks?
They ran away once, so they probably won't surrender without a *fight.*
Well, my old Green Goblin armor is toast, but you've still got your Ricochet gear, right? And Chris has his Darkhawk amulet. And Mickey can use her--
Back up! I thought the whole point of this outfit was to help us adjust to *not* being vigilantes anymore!
Absolutely, Chris, but I think the end justifies the means here.
If you guys put your costumes on one last time, we can help ensure that *no minor* will ever wear one again. Isn't that worth it?
...fine. But after this, Darkhawk is *retired.*
Yeah, uh, totally... I'm with *Julie.*
Where's the head in this joint?
I'm down, Mickey. Anything for a good cause.
LIFE IS BEAUTIFUL
Phil can coordinate our movements from his office while we spread out and start canvassing.
Our runaways are probably operating underground, but sooner or later... they'll have to come up for *air.*

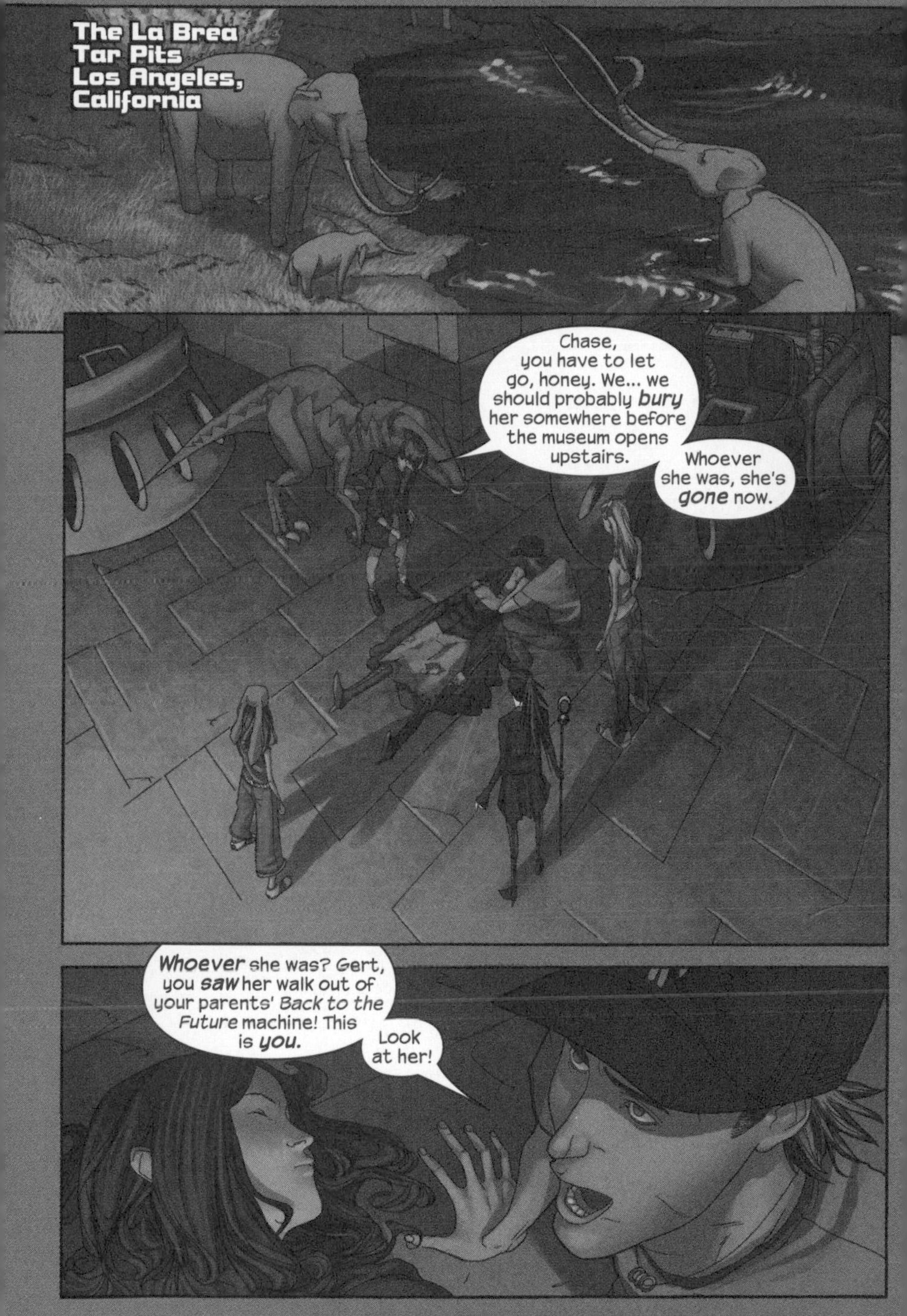
The La Brea Tar Pits Los Angeles, California
Chase, you have to let go, honey. We... we should probably *bury* her somewhere before the museum opens upstairs.
Whoever she was, she's *gone* now.
Whoever she was? Gert, you *saw* her walk out of your parents' *Back to the Future* machine! This is *you.*
Look at her!

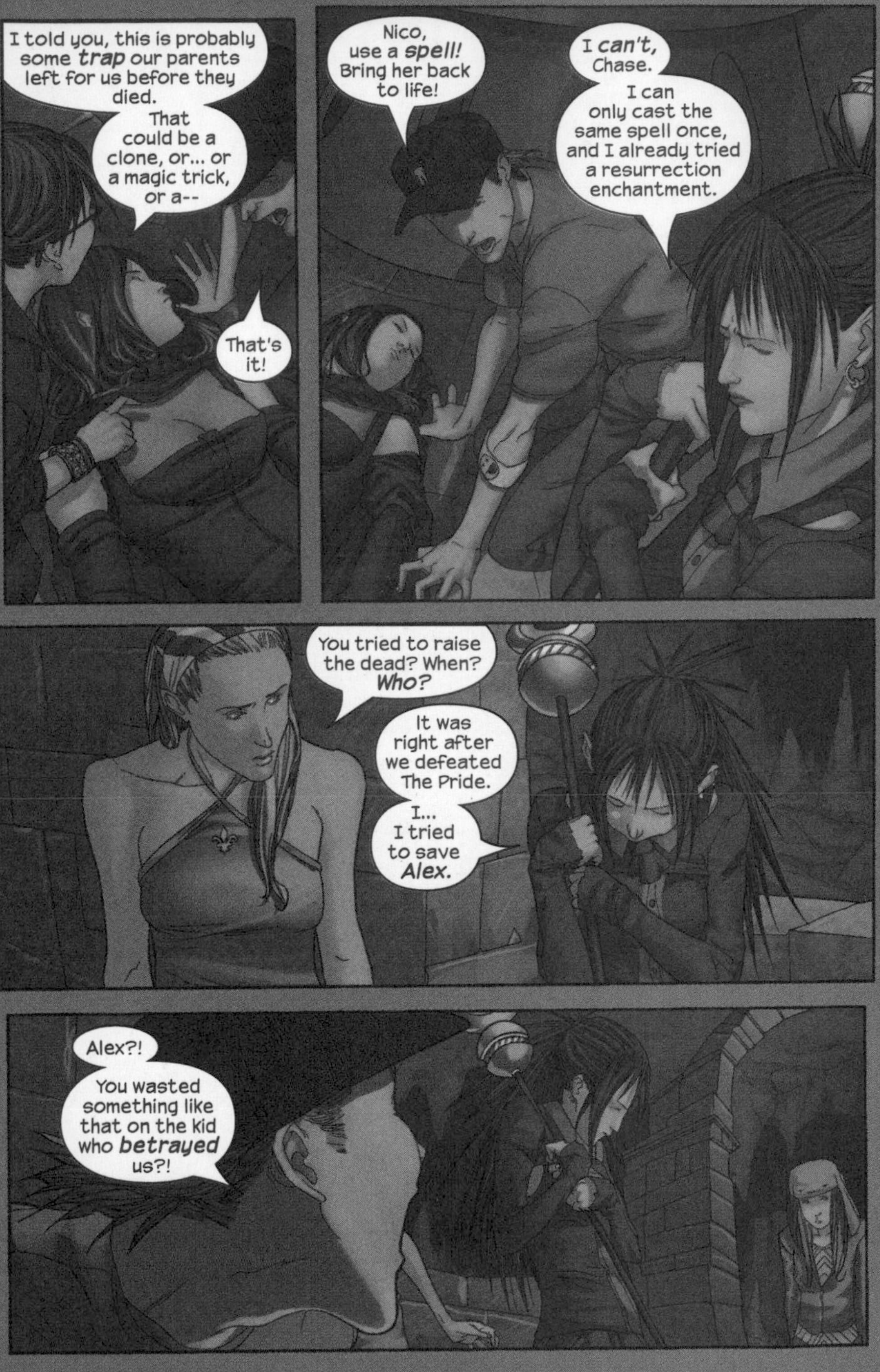
I told you, this is probably some trap our parents left for us before they died.
That could be a clone, or... or a magic trick, or a--
That's it!
Nico, use a spell! Bring her back to life!
I can't, Chase.
I can only cast the same spell once, and I already tried a resurrection enchantment.
You tried to raise the dead? When? Who?
It was right after we defeated The Pride.
I... I tried to save Alex.
Alex?!
You wasted something like that on the kid who betrayed us?!

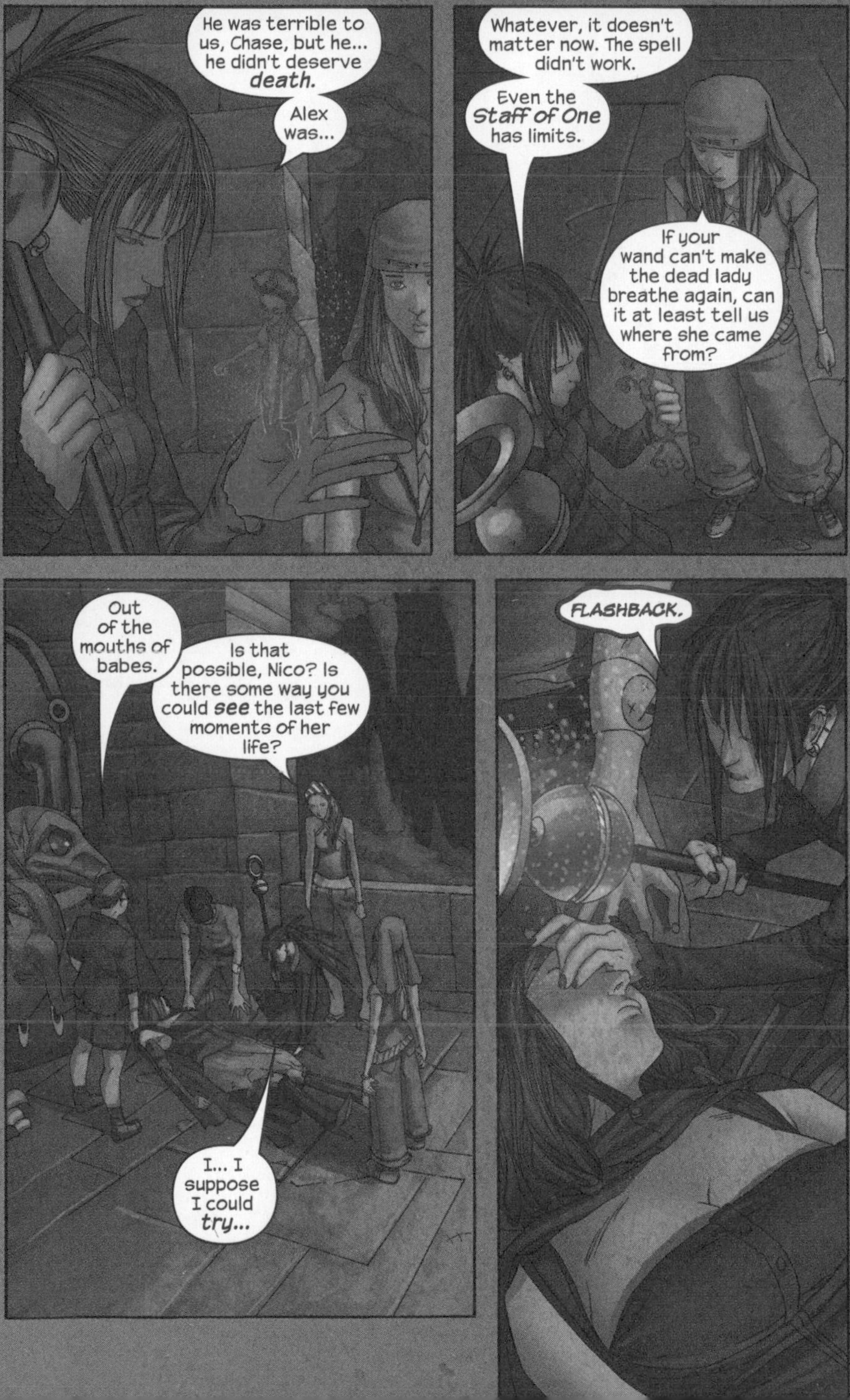
He was terrible to us, Chase, but he... he didn't deserve *death.*
Alex was...
Whatever, it doesn't matter now. The spell didn't work.
Even the *Staff of One* has limits.
If your wand can't make the dead lady breathe again, can it at least tell us where she came from?
Out of the mouths of babes.
Is that possible, Nico? Is there some way you could *see* the last few moments of her life?
I... I suppose I could *try...*
FLASHBACK.

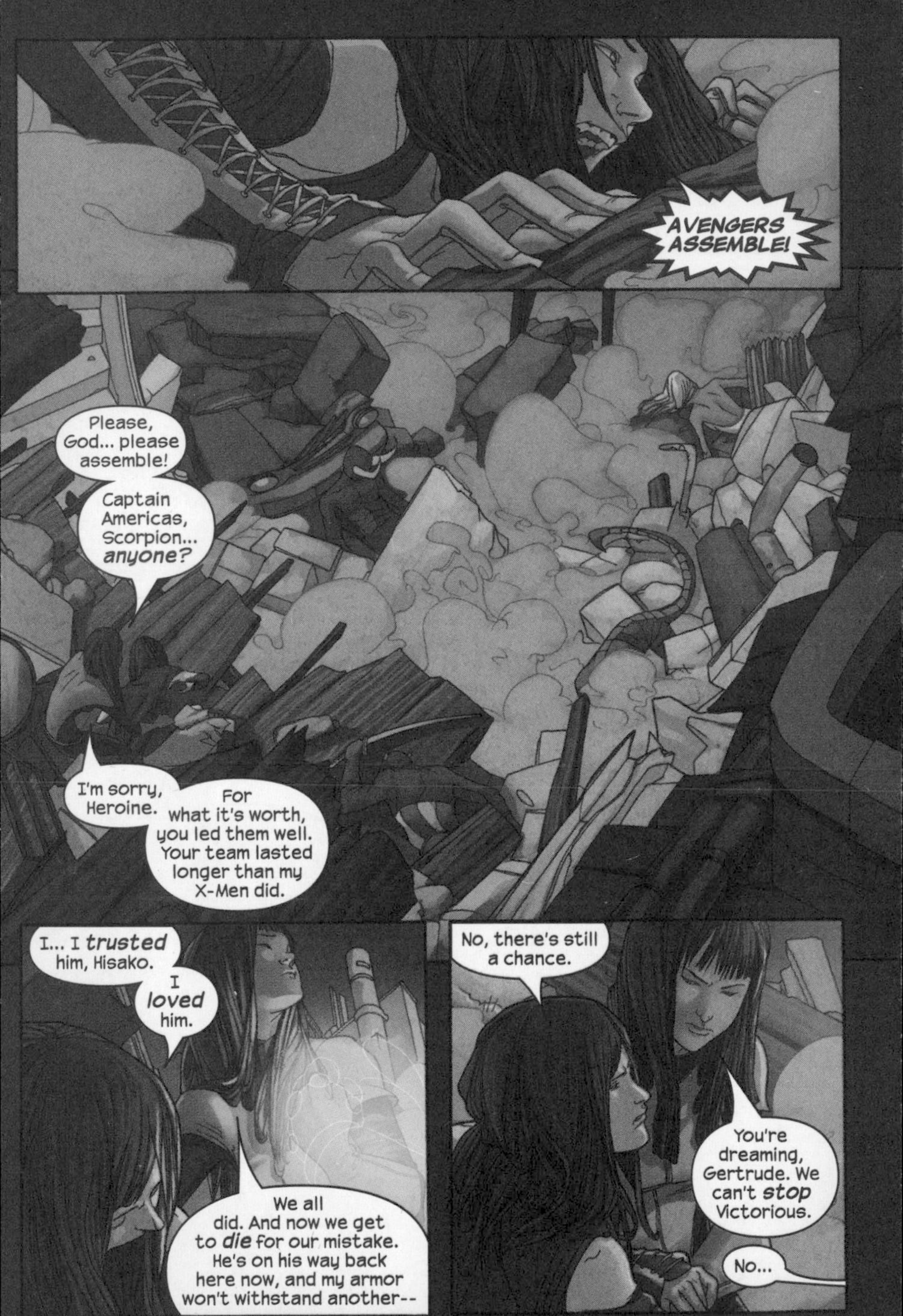
AVENGERS ASSEMBLE!
Please, God... please assemble!
Captain Americas, Scorpion... *anyone?*
I'm sorry, Heroine.
For what it's worth, you led them well. Your team lasted longer than my X-Men did.
I... I *trusted* him, Hisako.
I *loved* him.
We all did. And now we get to *die* for our mistake. He's on his way back here now, and my armor won't withstand another--
No, there's still a chance.
You're dreaming, Gertrude. We can't *stop* Victorious.
No...

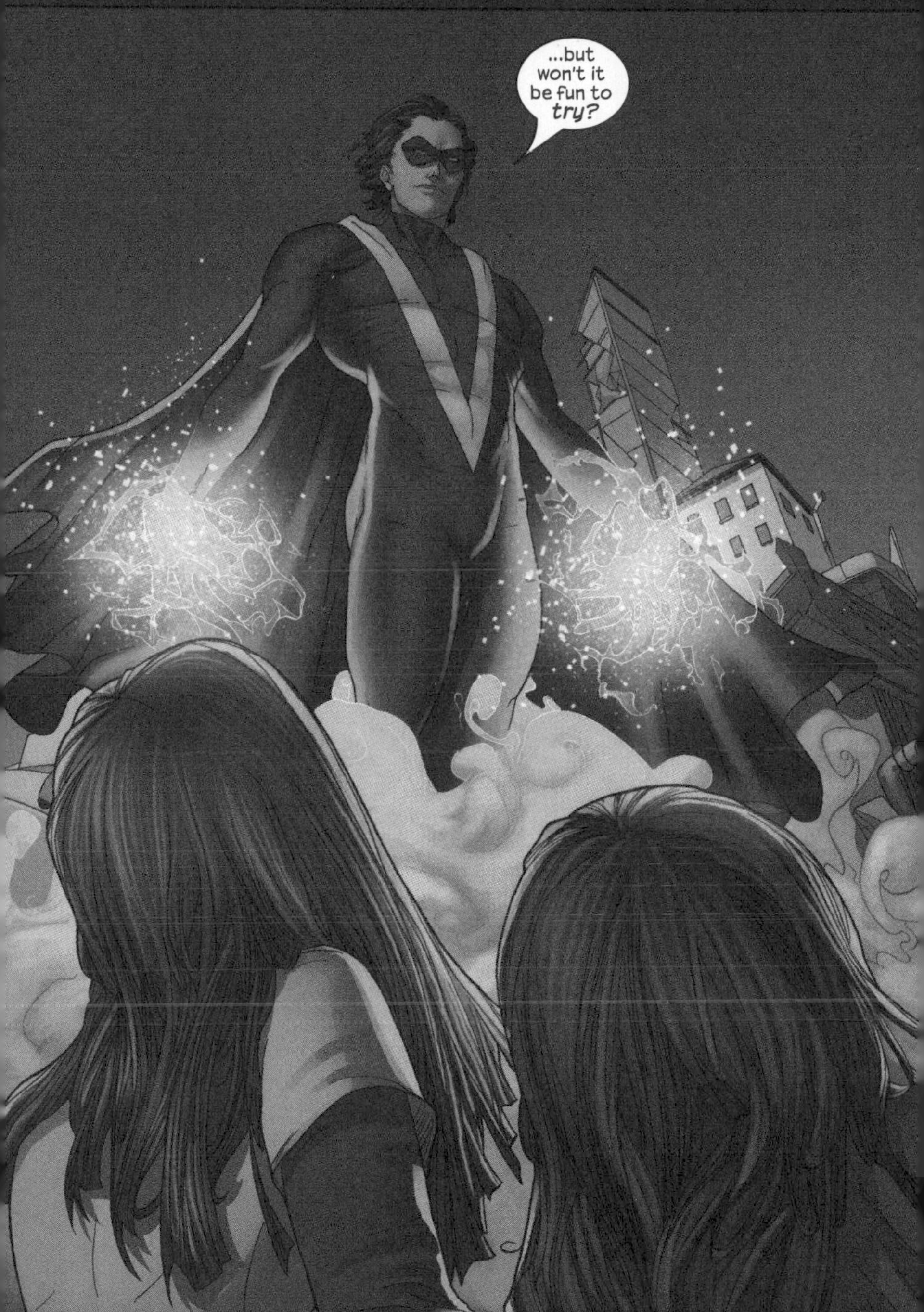
...but won't it be fun to *try?*

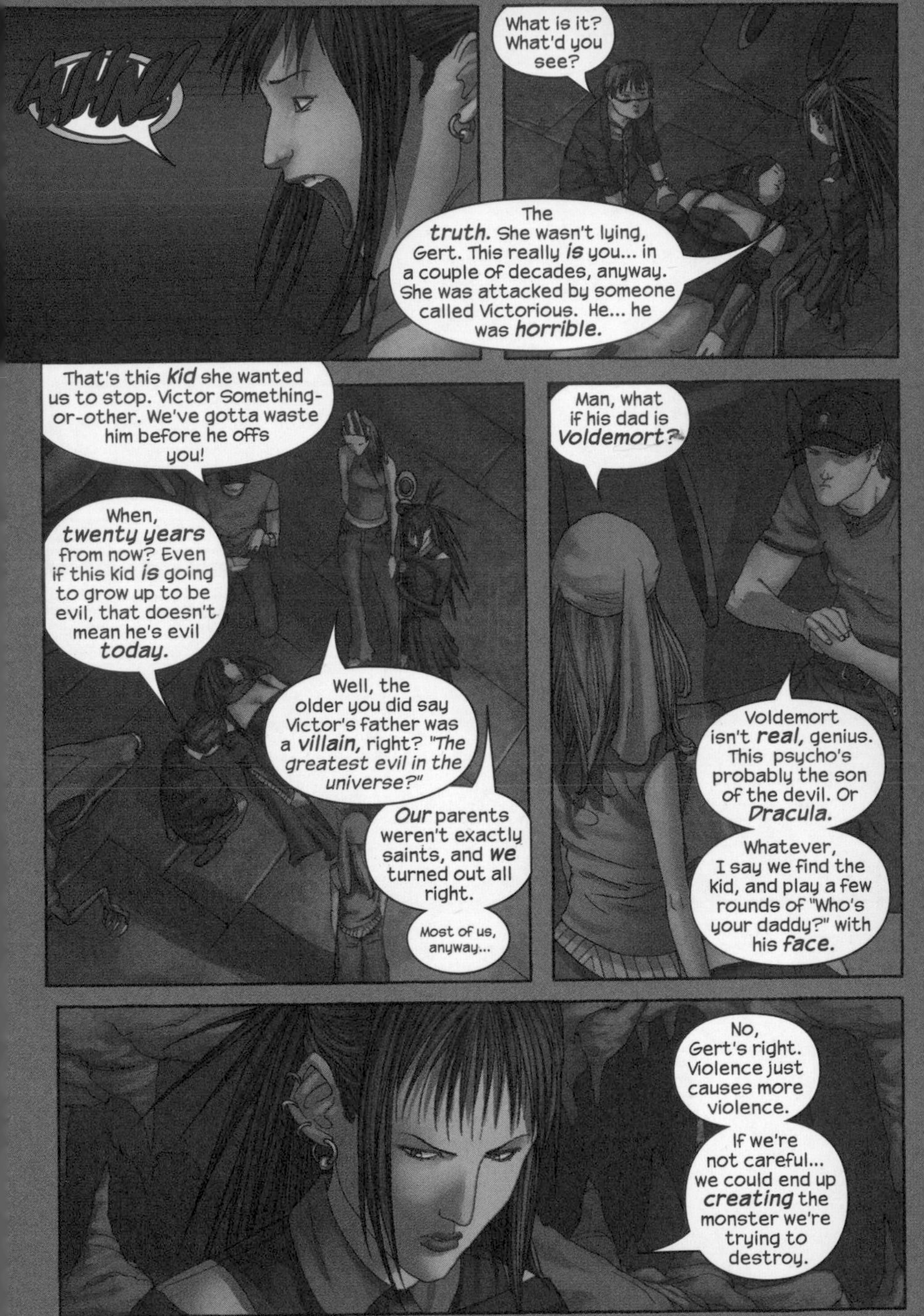

AAHH!
What is it? What'd you see?
The truth. She wasn't lying, Gert. This really is you... in a couple of decades, anyway. She was attacked by someone called Victorious. He... he was horrible.
That's this kid she wanted us to stop. Victor Something-or-other. We've gotta waste him before he offs you!
When, twenty years from now? Even if this kid is going to grow up to be evil, that doesn't mean he's evil today.
Well, the older you did say Victor's father was a villain, right? "The greatest evil in the universe?"
Our parents weren't exactly saints, and we turned out all right.
Most of us, anyway...
Man, what if his dad is Voldemort?
Voldemort isn't real, genius. This psycho's probably the son of the devil. Or Dracula.
Whatever, I say we find the kid, and play a few rounds of "Who's your daddy?" with his face.
No, Gert's right. Violence just causes more violence.
If we're not careful... we could end up creating the monster we're trying to destroy.

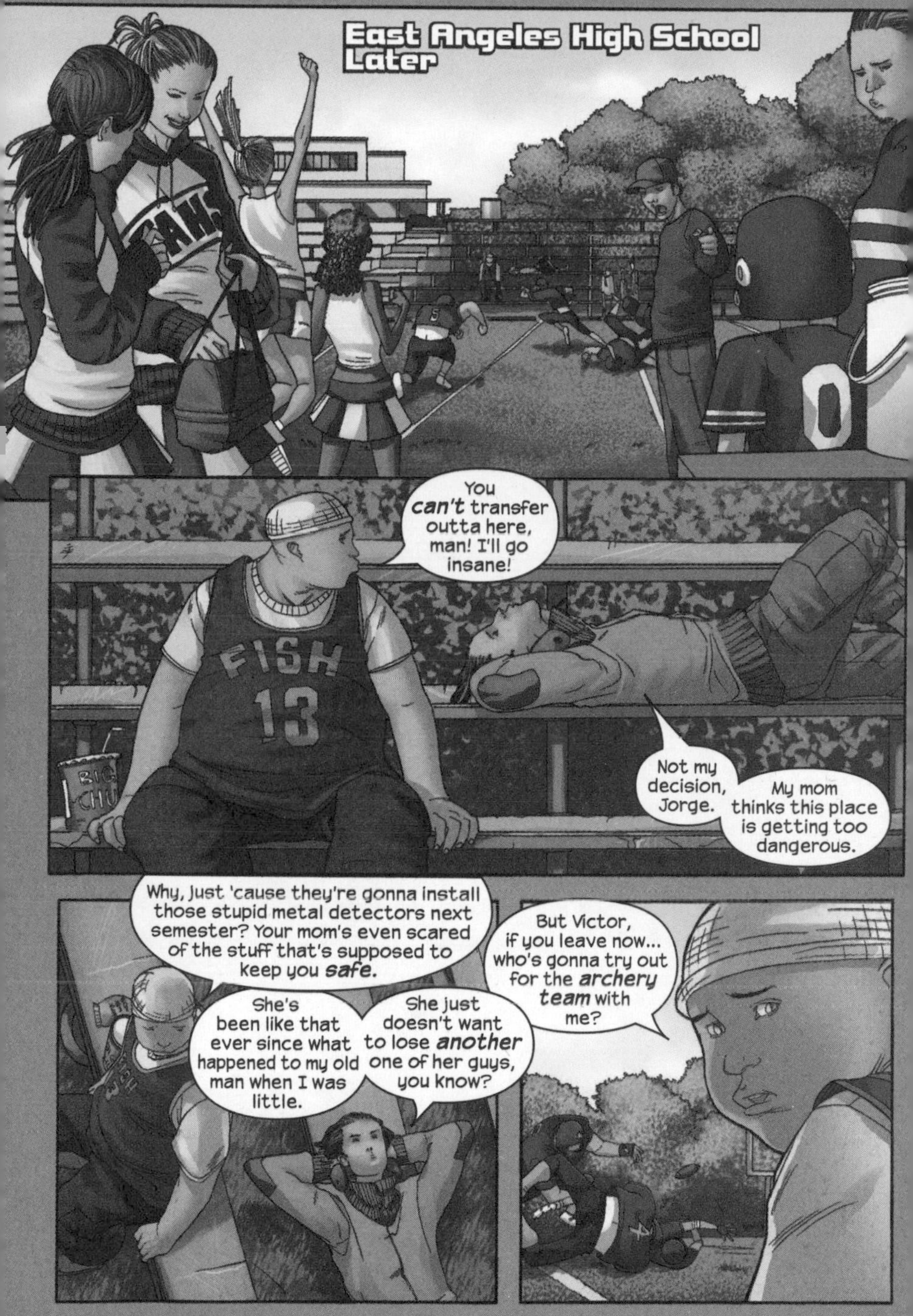
East Angeles High School
Later
You can't transfer outta here, man! I'll go insane!
FISH 13
Not my decision, Jorge.
My mom thinks this place is getting too dangerous.
Why, just 'cause they're gonna install those stupid metal detectors next semester? Your mom's even scared of the stuff that's supposed to keep you safe.
She's been like that ever since what happened to my old man when I was little.
She just doesn't want to lose another one of her guys, you know?
But Victor, if you leave now... who's gonna try out for the archery team with me?

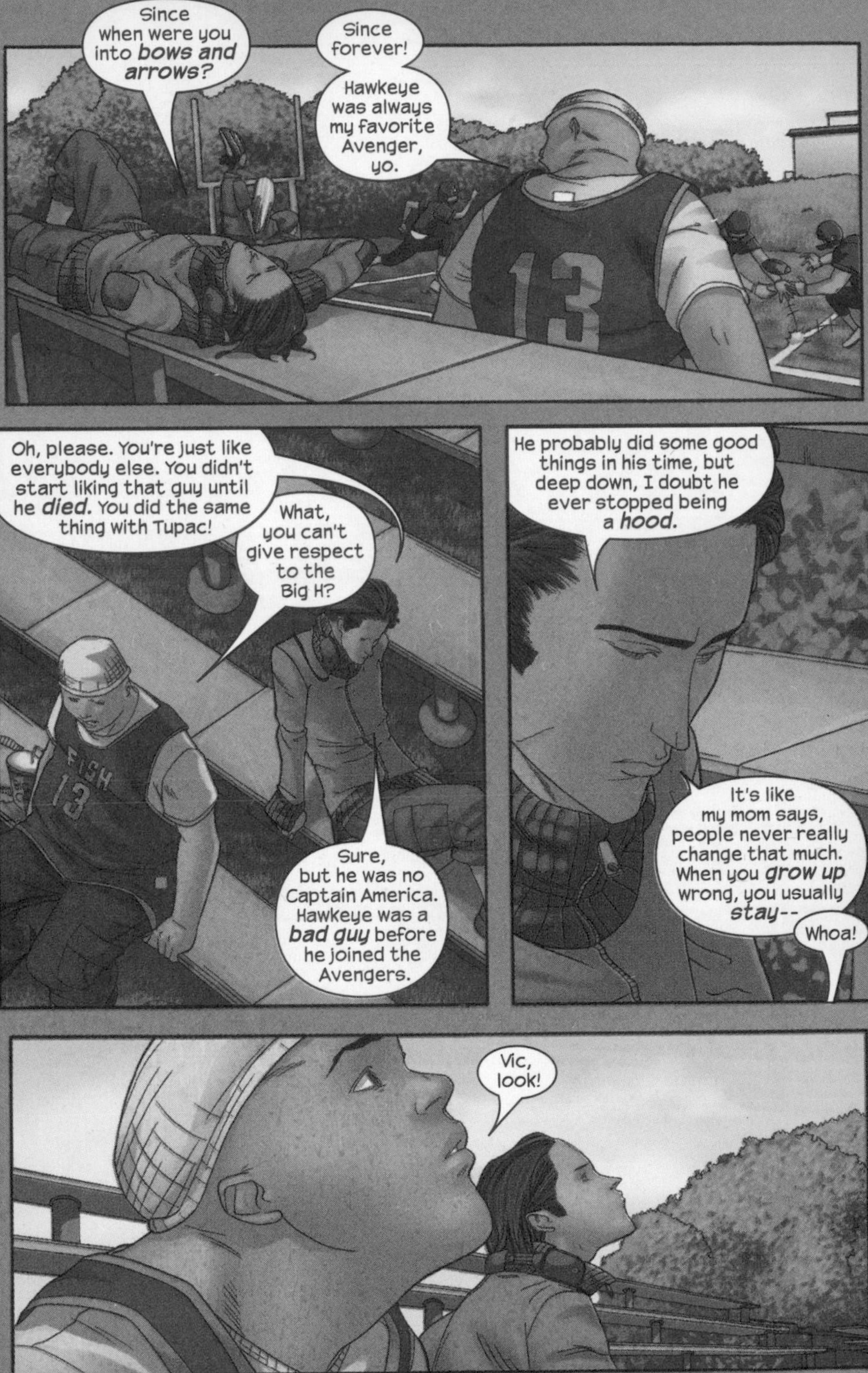
Since when were you into bows and arrows?
Since forever!
Hawkeye was always my favorite Avenger, yo.
Oh, please. You're just like everybody else. You didn't start liking that guy until he died. You did the same thing with Tupac!
What, you can't give respect to the Big H?
Sure, but he was no Captain America. Hawkeye was a bad guy before he joined the Avengers.
He probably did some good things in his time, but deep down, I doubt he ever stopped being a hood.
It's like my mom says, people never really change that much. When you grow up wrong, you usually stay--
Whoa!
Vic, look!

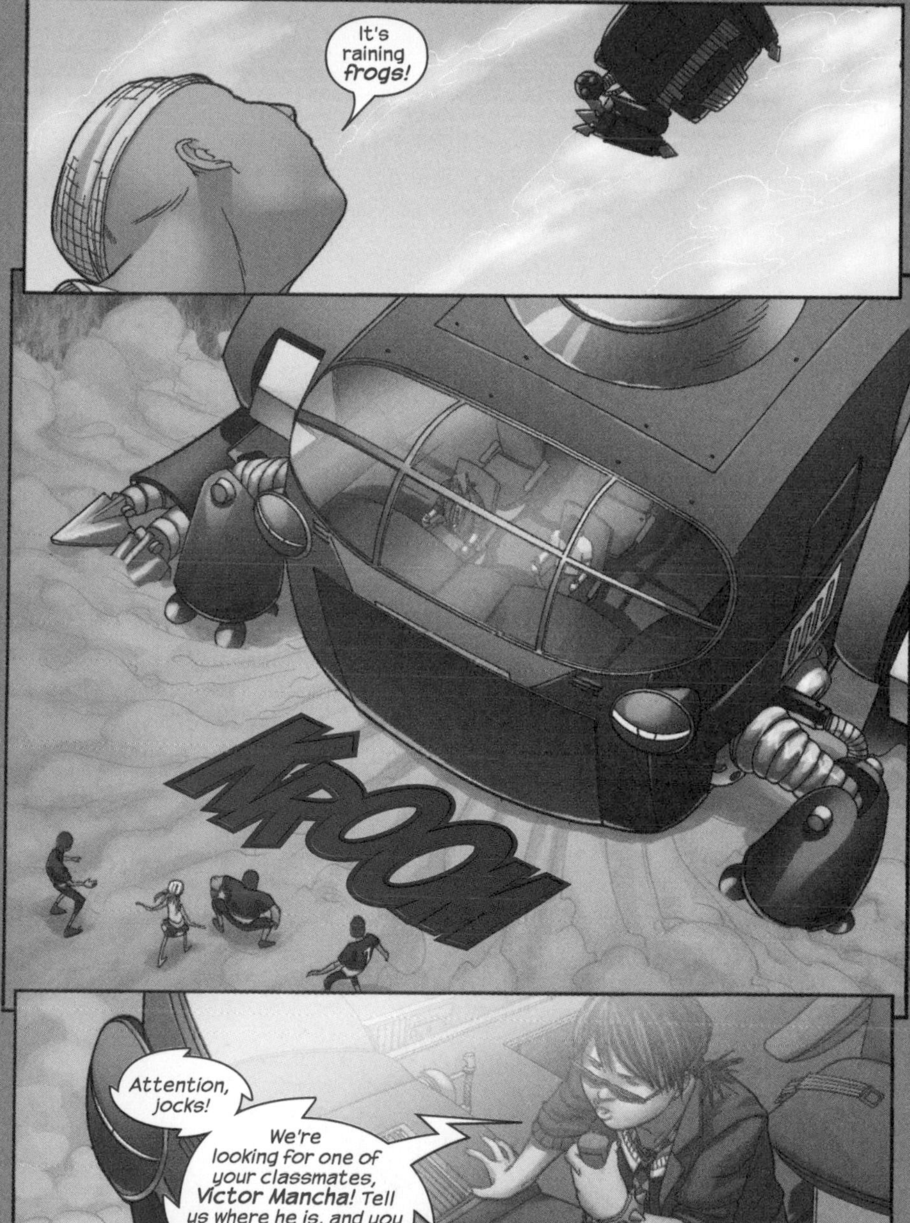
It's raining frogs!
KROOM
Attention, jocks!
We're looking for one of your classmates, Victor Mancha! Tell us where he is, and you can return to your meaningless ball chasing!

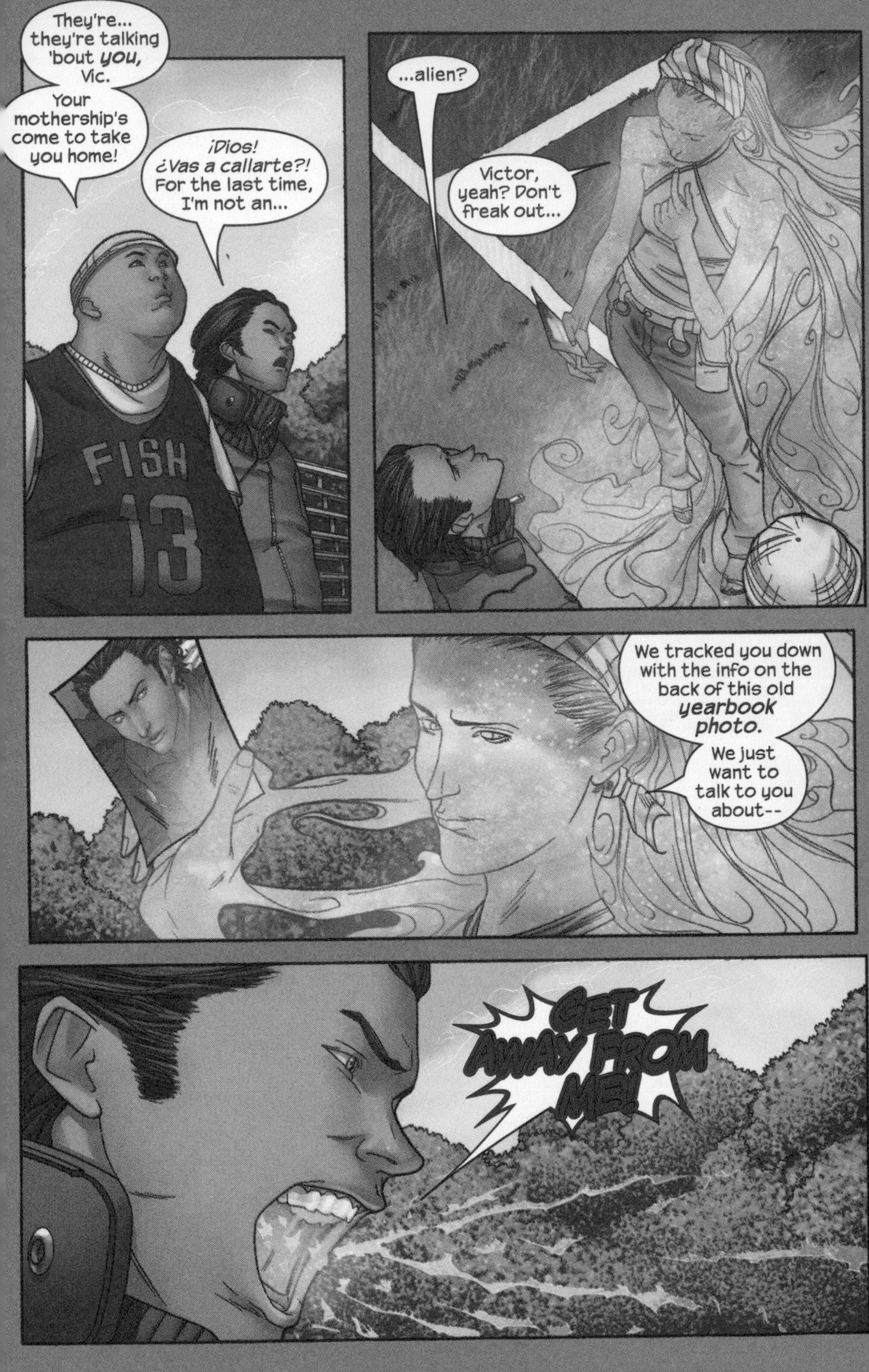
They're... they're talking 'bout *you,* Vic.
Your mothership's come to take you home!
¡Dios! ¿Vas a callarte?! For the last time, I'm not an...
...alien?
Victor, yeah? Don't freak out...
We tracked you down with the info on the back of this old **yearbook photo.**
We just want to talk to you about--
GET AWAY FROM ME!

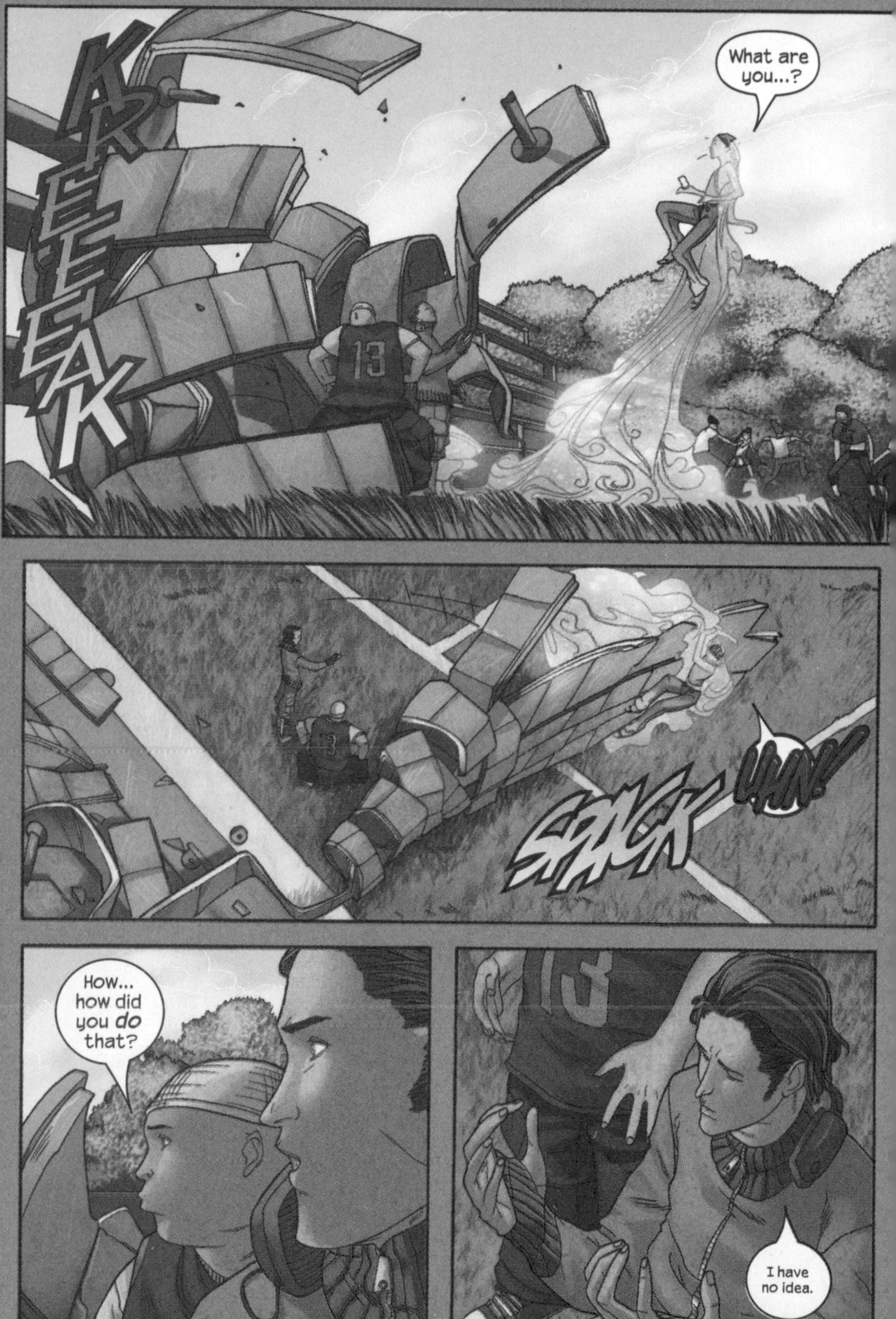
KRREEEAK
What are you...?
SPACK
UHN!
How... how did you *do* that?
I have no idea.

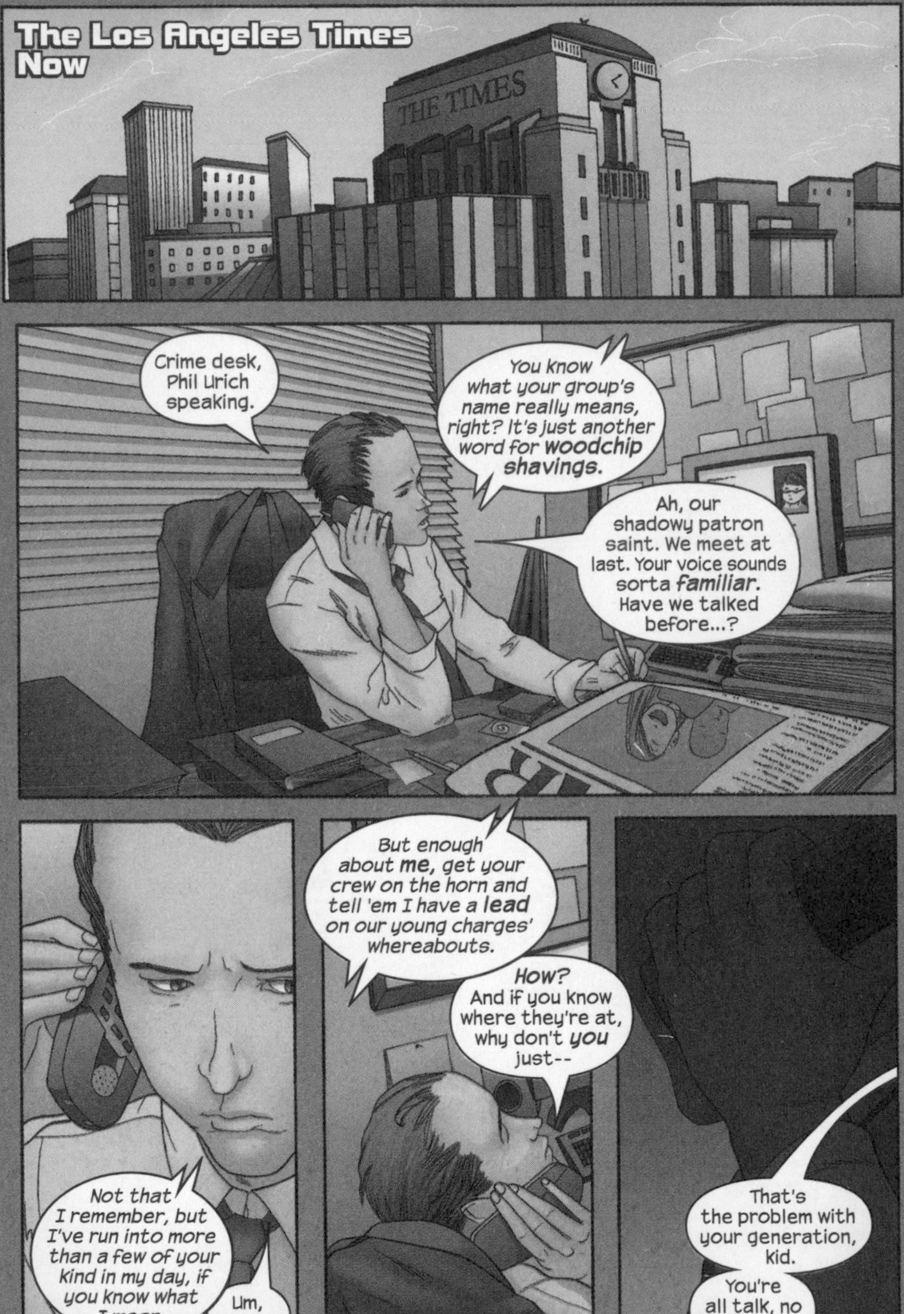
The Los Angeles Times
Now
THE TIMES
Crime desk, Phil Urich speaking.
You know what your group's name really means, right? It's just another word for woodchip shavings.
Ah, our shadowy patron saint. We meet at last. Your voice sounds sorta familiar. Have we talked before...?
Not that I remember, but I've run into more than a few of your kind in my day, if you know what I mean.
Um, no, I--
But enough about me, get your crew on the horn and tell 'em I have a lead on our young charges' whereabouts.
How? And if you know where they're at, why don't you just--
That's the problem with your generation, kid.
You're all talk, no action...

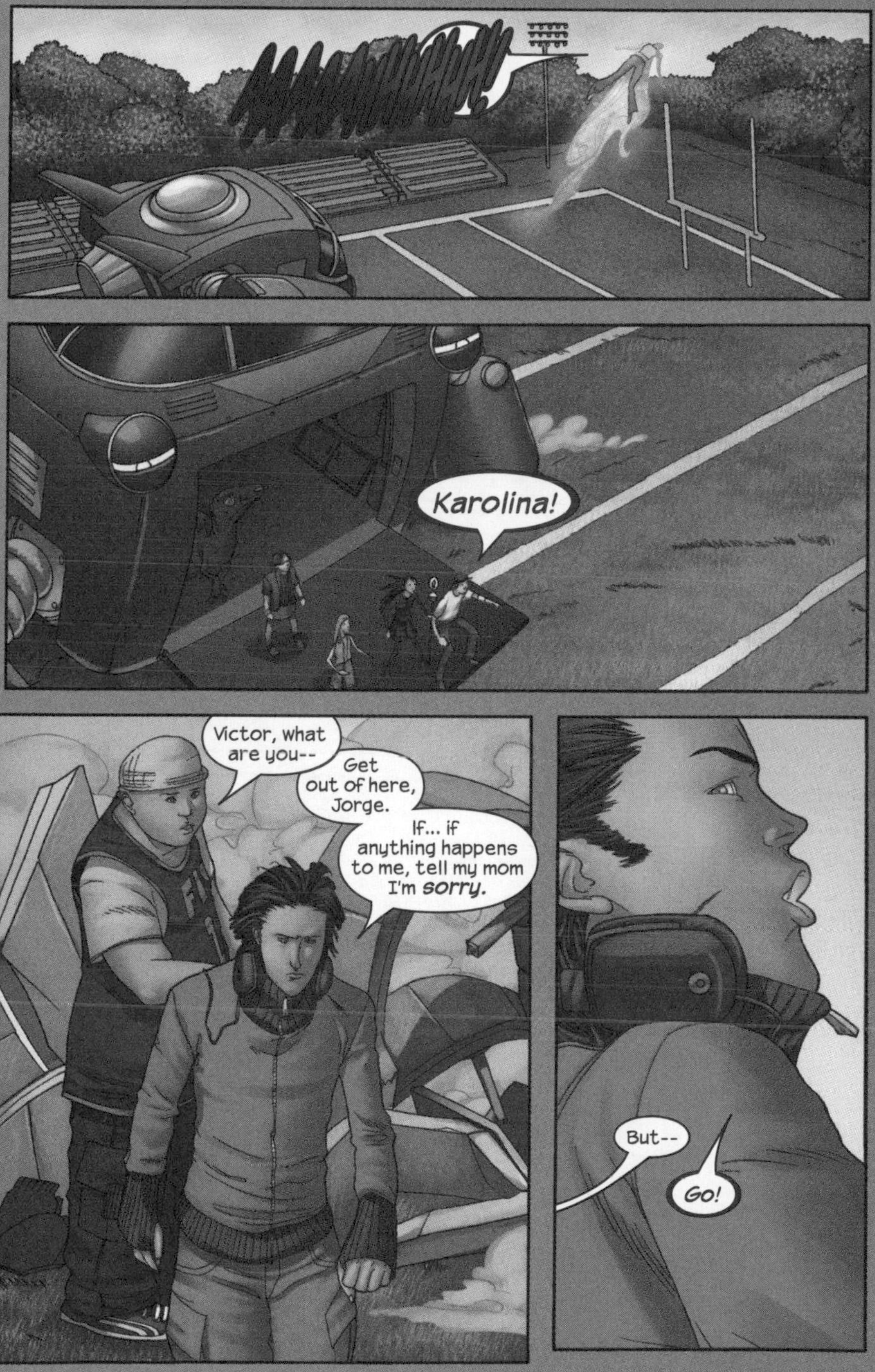
AAAAAAAHHHHH!!
Karolina!
Victor, what are you--
Get out of here, Jorge.
If... if anything happens to me, tell my mom I'm *sorry*.
But--
Go!

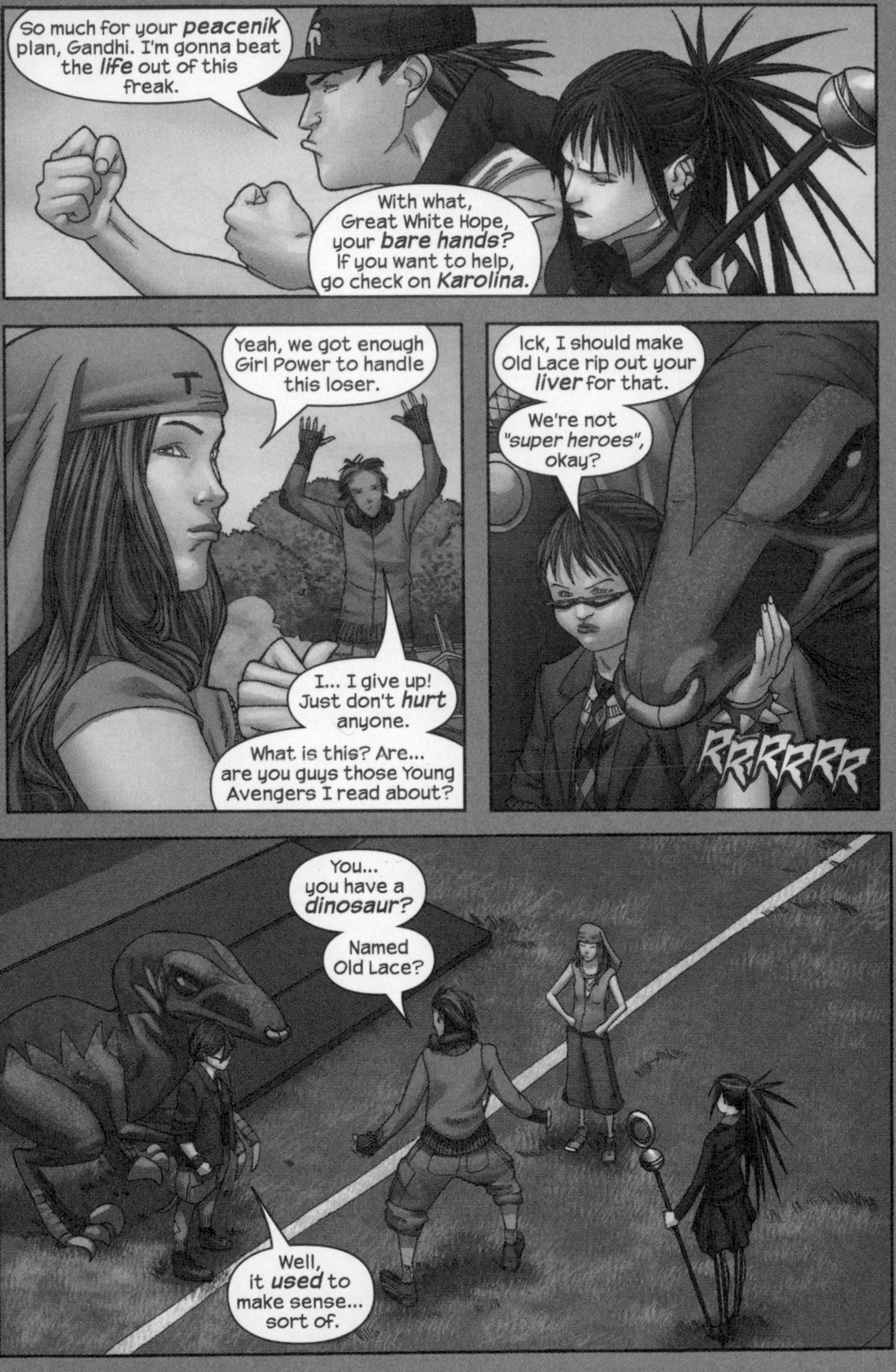
So much for your peacenik plan, Gandhi. I'm gonna beat the life out of this freak.
With what, Great White Hope, your bare hands? If you want to help, go check on Karolina.
Yeah, we got enough Girl Power to handle this loser.
I... I give up! Just don't hurt anyone.
What is this? Are... are you guys those Young Avengers I read about?
Ick, I should make Old Lace rip out your liver for that.
We're not "super heroes", okay?
RRRRRR
You... you have a dinosaur?
Named Old Lace?
Well, it used to make sense... sort of.

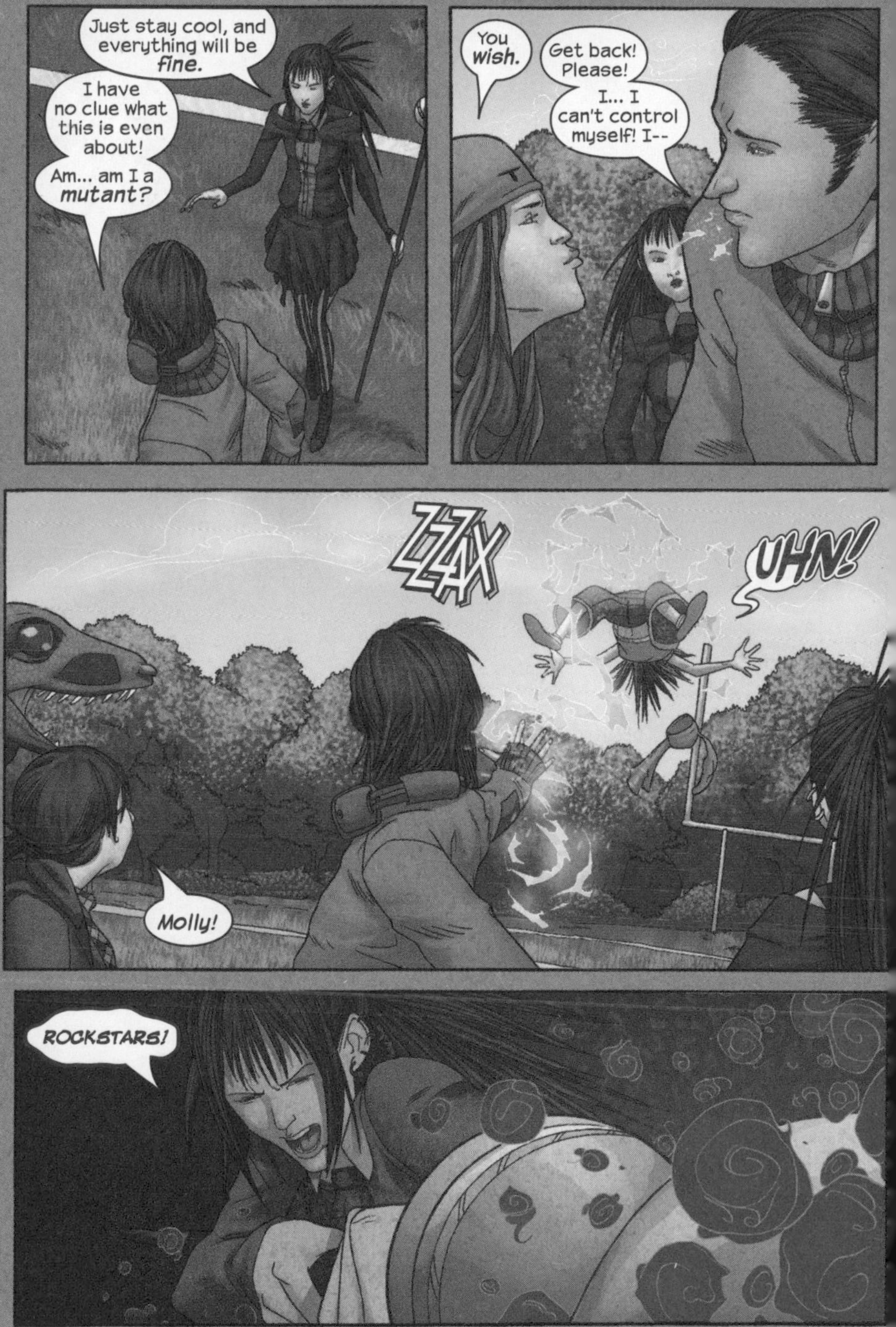
Just stay cool, and everything will be *fine.*
I have no clue what this is even about!
Am... am I a *mutant?*
You *wish.*
Get back! Please!
I... I can't control myself! I--
ZZZAX
UHN!
Molly!
ROCKSTARS!

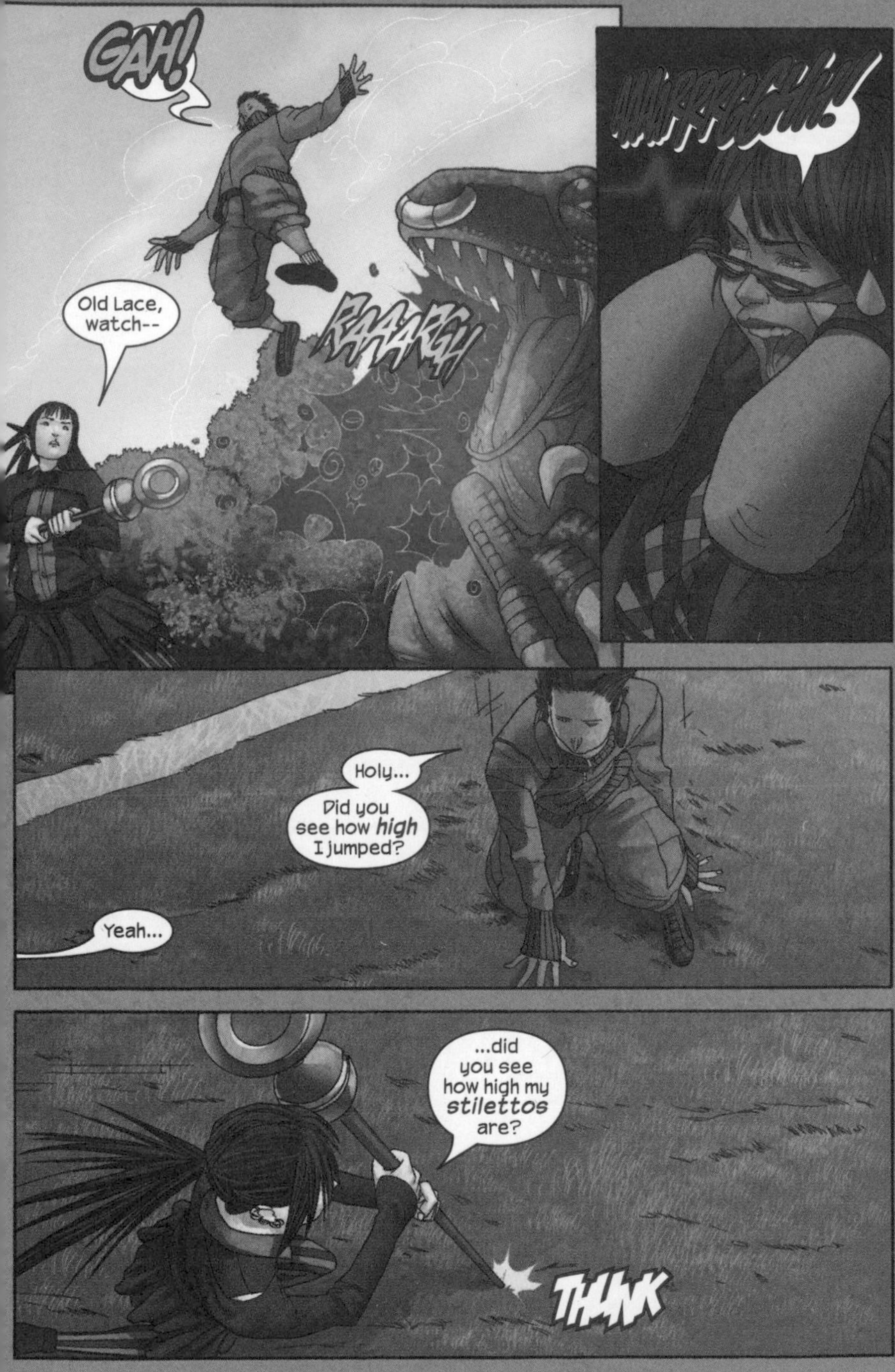
GAH!
Old Lace, watch--
RAAARGH
Holy...
Did you see how *high* I jumped?
Yeah...
...did you see how high my *stilettos* are?
THUNK

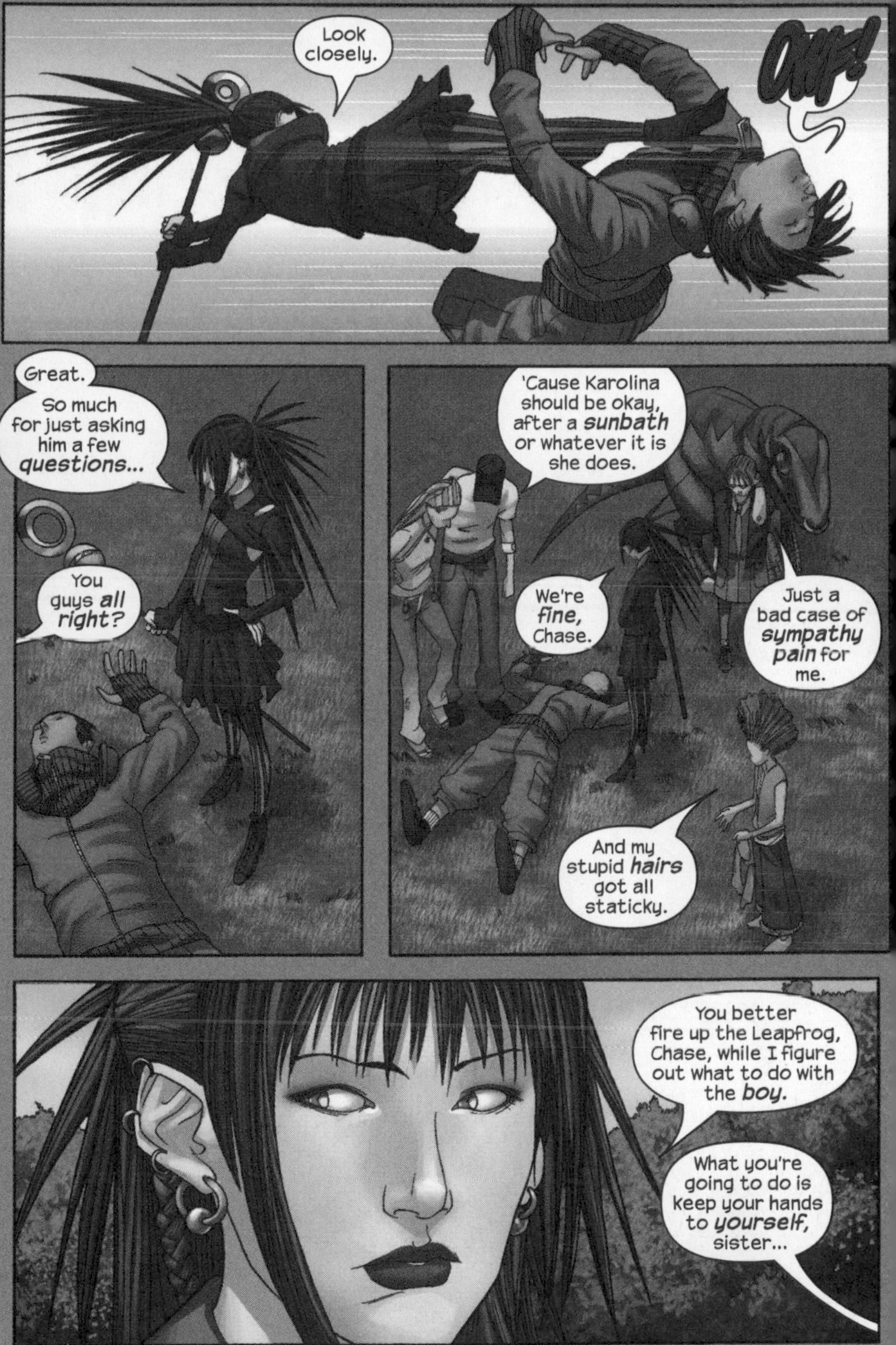

Look closely.
OOF!
Great.
So much for just asking him a few questions...
You guys all right?
'Cause Karolina should be okay, after a sunbath or whatever it is she does.
We're fine, Chase.
Just a bad case of sympathy pain for me.
And my stupid hairs got all staticky.
You better fire up the Leapfrog, Chase, while I figure out what to do with the boy.
What you're going to do is keep your hands to yourself, sister...

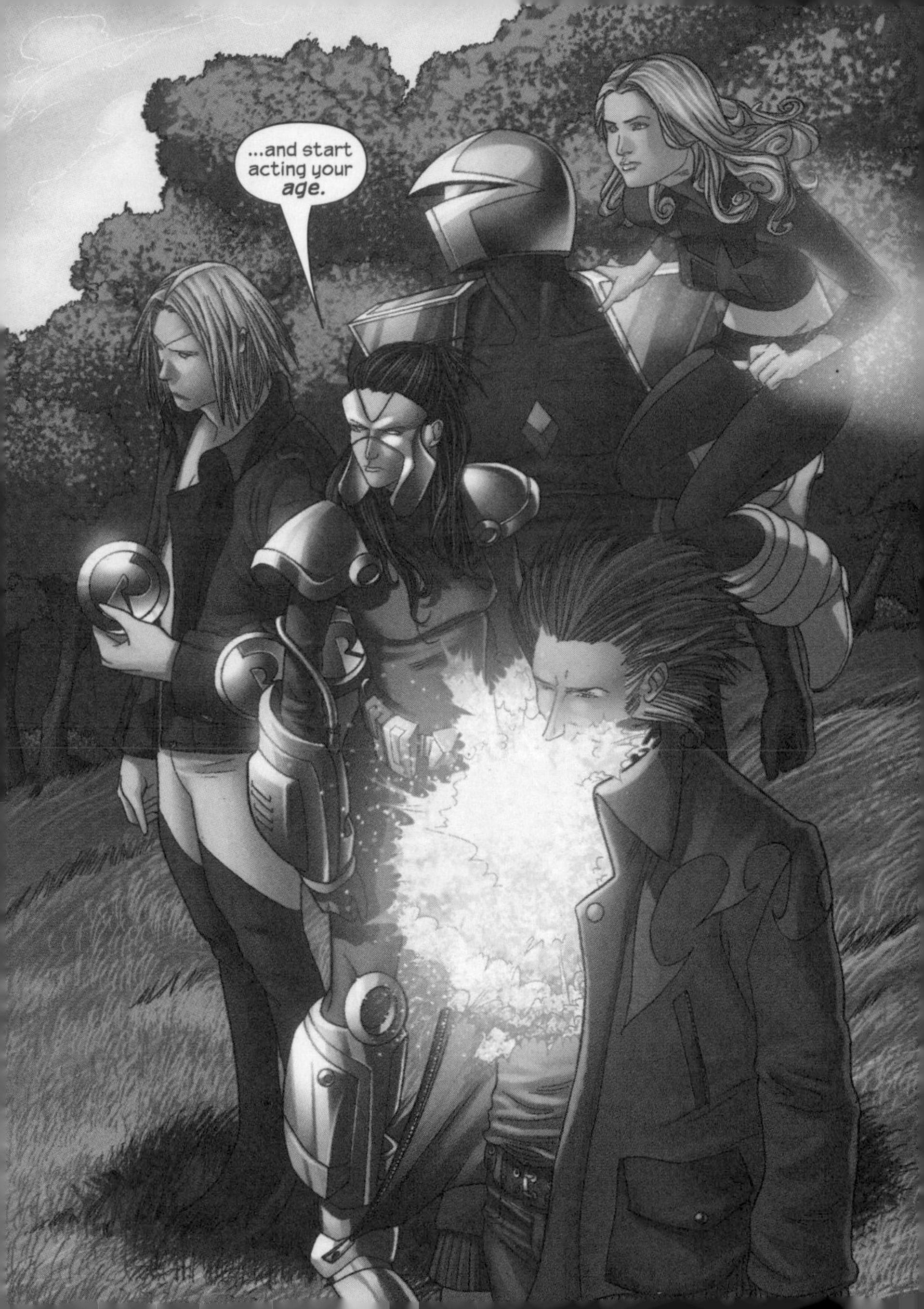
...and start acting your *age.*

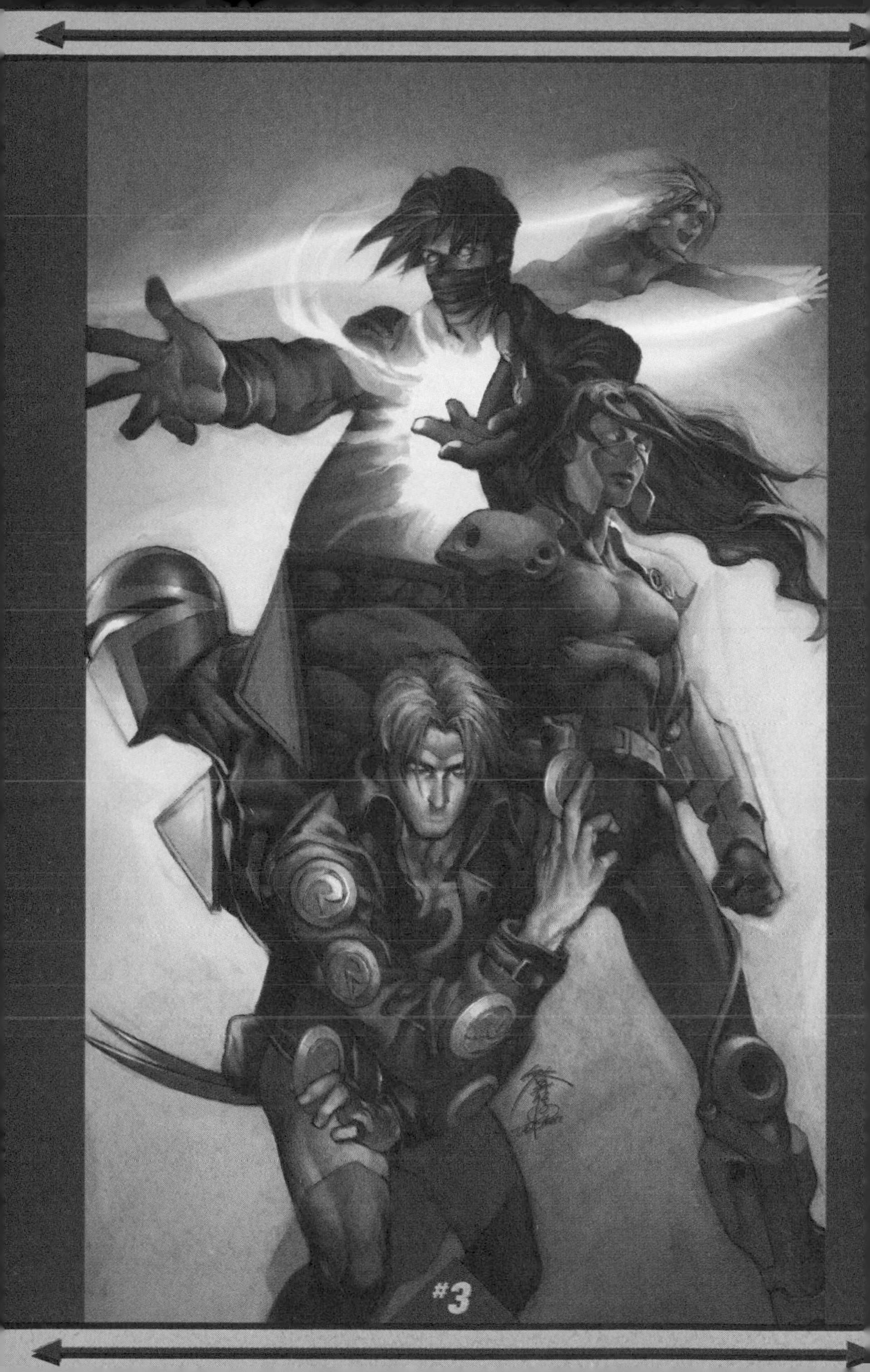
#3

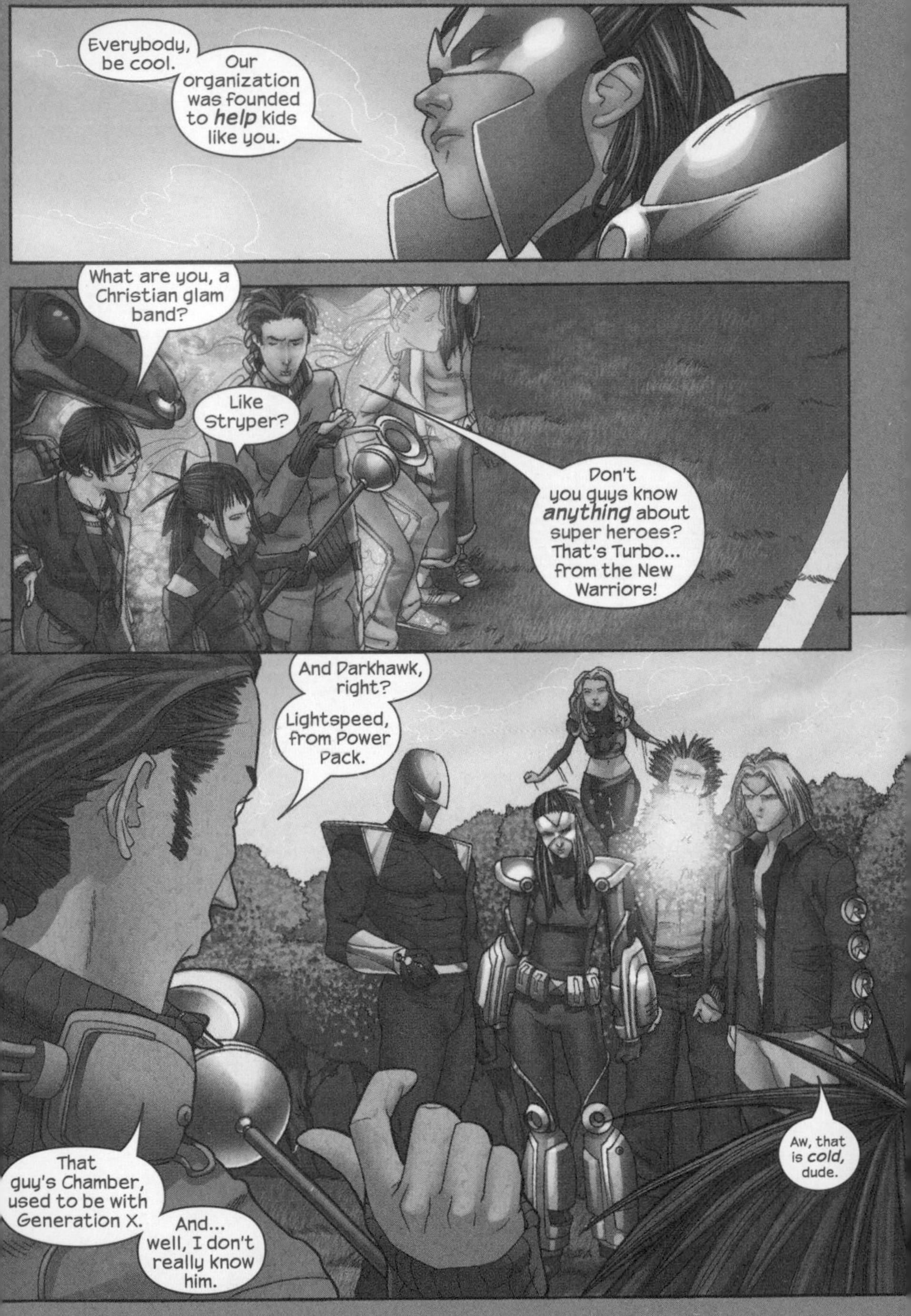

Everybody, be cool.
Our organization was founded to *help* kids like you.
What are you, a Christian glam band?
Like Stryper?
Don't you guys know *anything* about super heroes? That's Turbo... from the New Warriors!
And Darkhawk, right?
Lightspeed, from Power Pack.
That guy's Chamber, used to be with Generation X.
And... well, I don't really know him.
Aw, that is *cold,* dude.

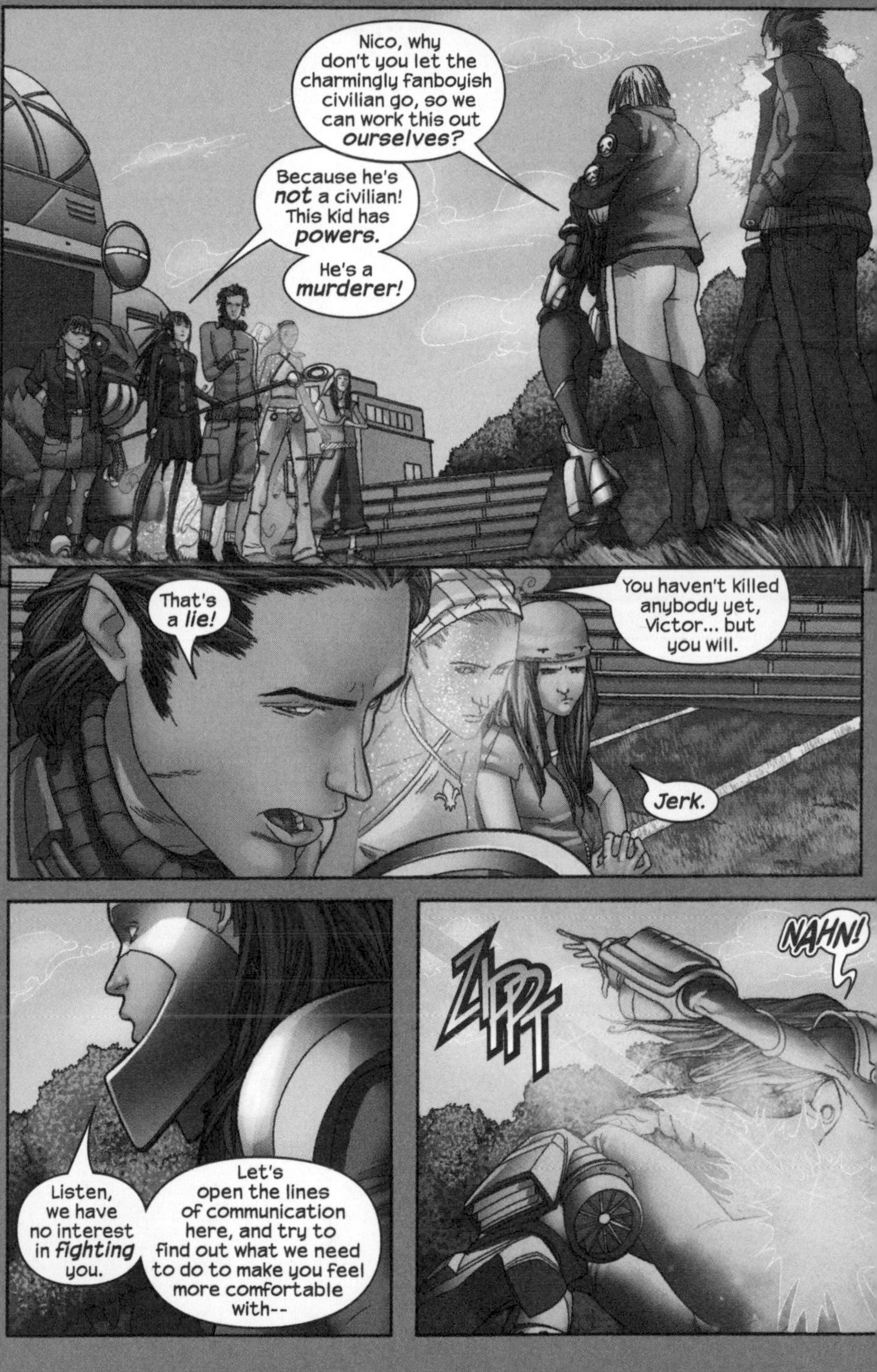
Nico, why don't you let the charmingly fanboyish civilian go, so we can work this out *ourselves?*
Because he's *not* a civilian! This kid has *powers.*
He's a *murderer!*
That's a *lie!*
You haven't killed anybody yet, Victor... but you will.
Jerk.
Listen, we have no interest in *fighting* you.
Let's open the lines of communication here, and try to find out what we need to do to make you feel more comfortable with--
ZAPPT
NAHN!

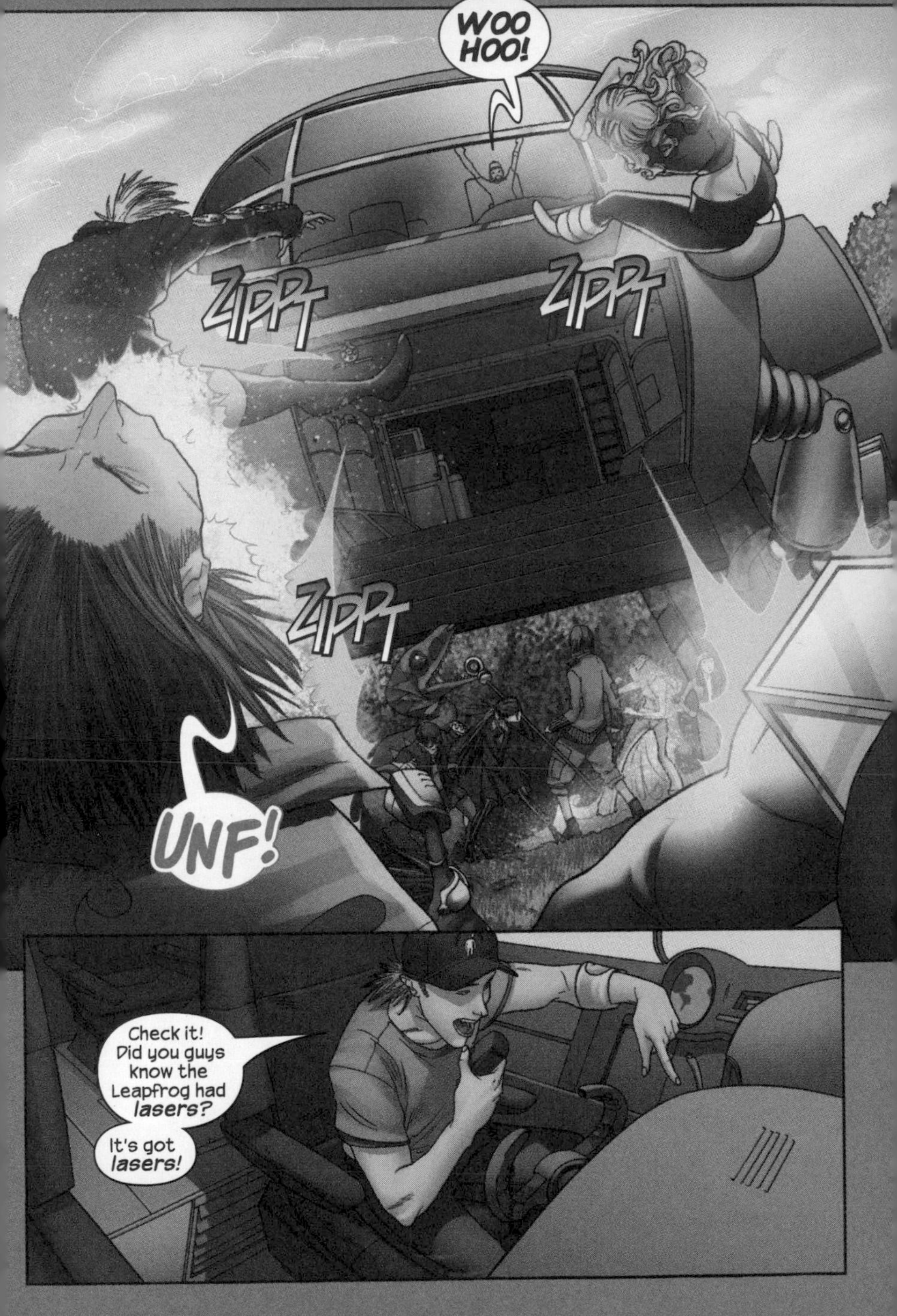
WOO HOO!
ZIPPT
ZIPPT
ZIPPT
UNF!
Check it! Did you guys know the Leapfrog had lasers?
It's got lasers!

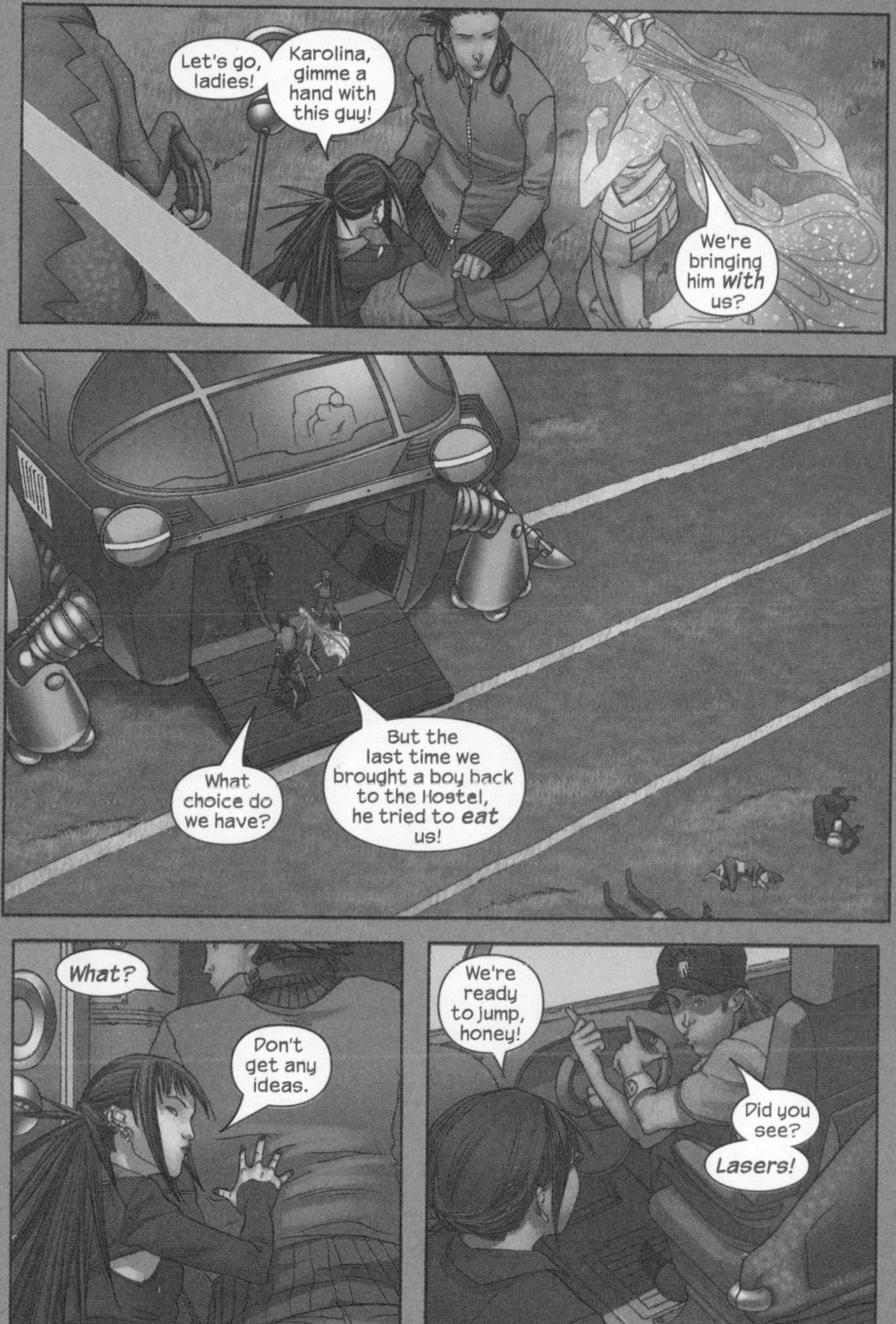
Let's go, ladies!
Karolina, gimme a hand with this guy!
We're bringing him *with* us?
What choice do we have?
But the last time we brought a boy back to the Hostel, he tried to *eat* us!
What?
Don't get any ideas.
We're ready to jump, honey!
Did you see?
Lasers!

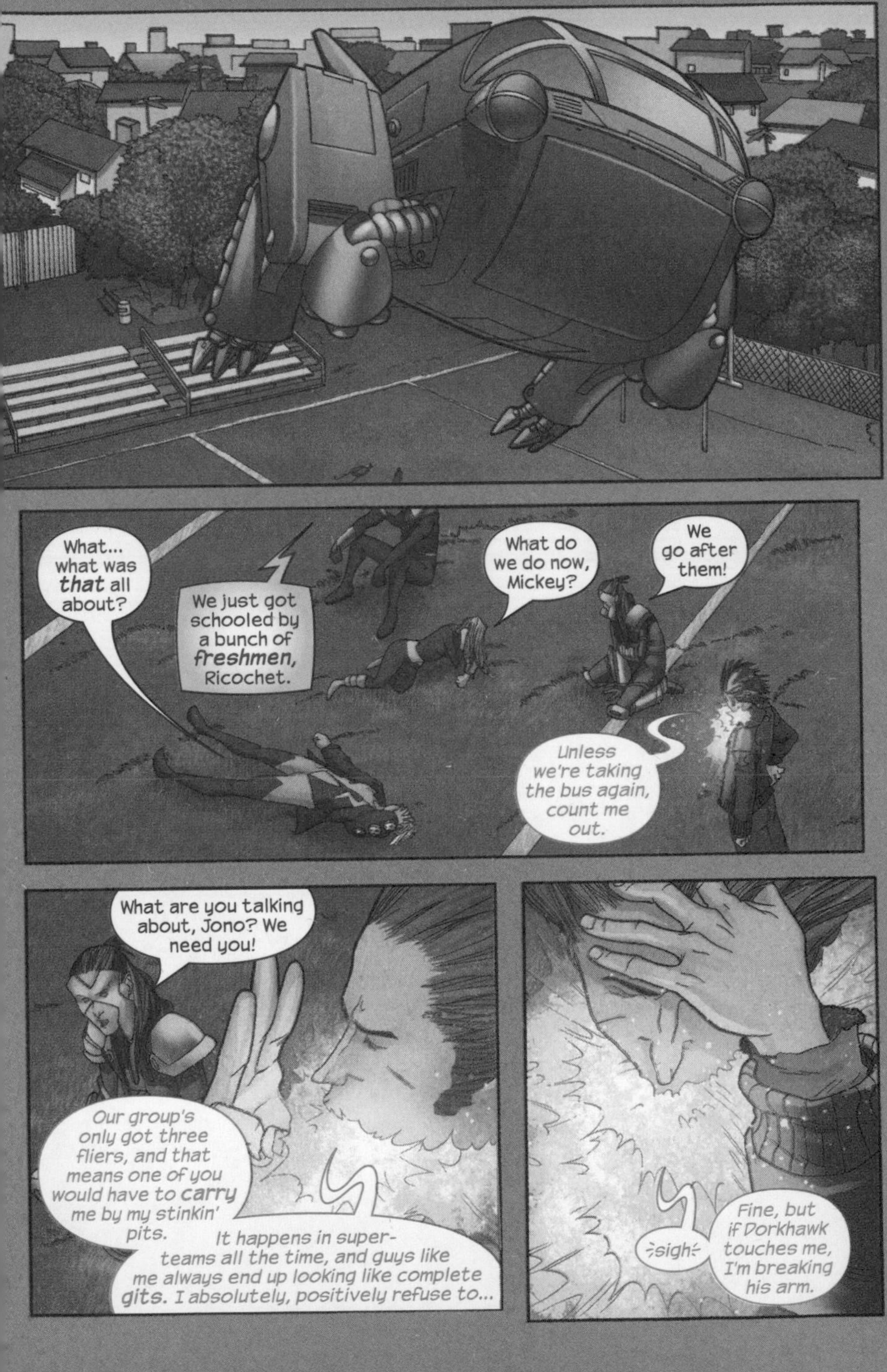

What... what was that all about?
We just got schooled by a bunch of freshmen, Ricochet.
What do we do now, Mickey?
We go after them!
Unless we're taking the bus again, count me out.
What are you talking about, Jono? We need you!
Our group's only got three fliers, and that means one of you would have to carry me by my stinkin' pits.
It happens in super-teams all the time, and guys like me always end up looking like complete gits. I absolutely, positively refuse to...
sigh
Fine, but if Dorkhawk touches me, I'm breaking his arm.

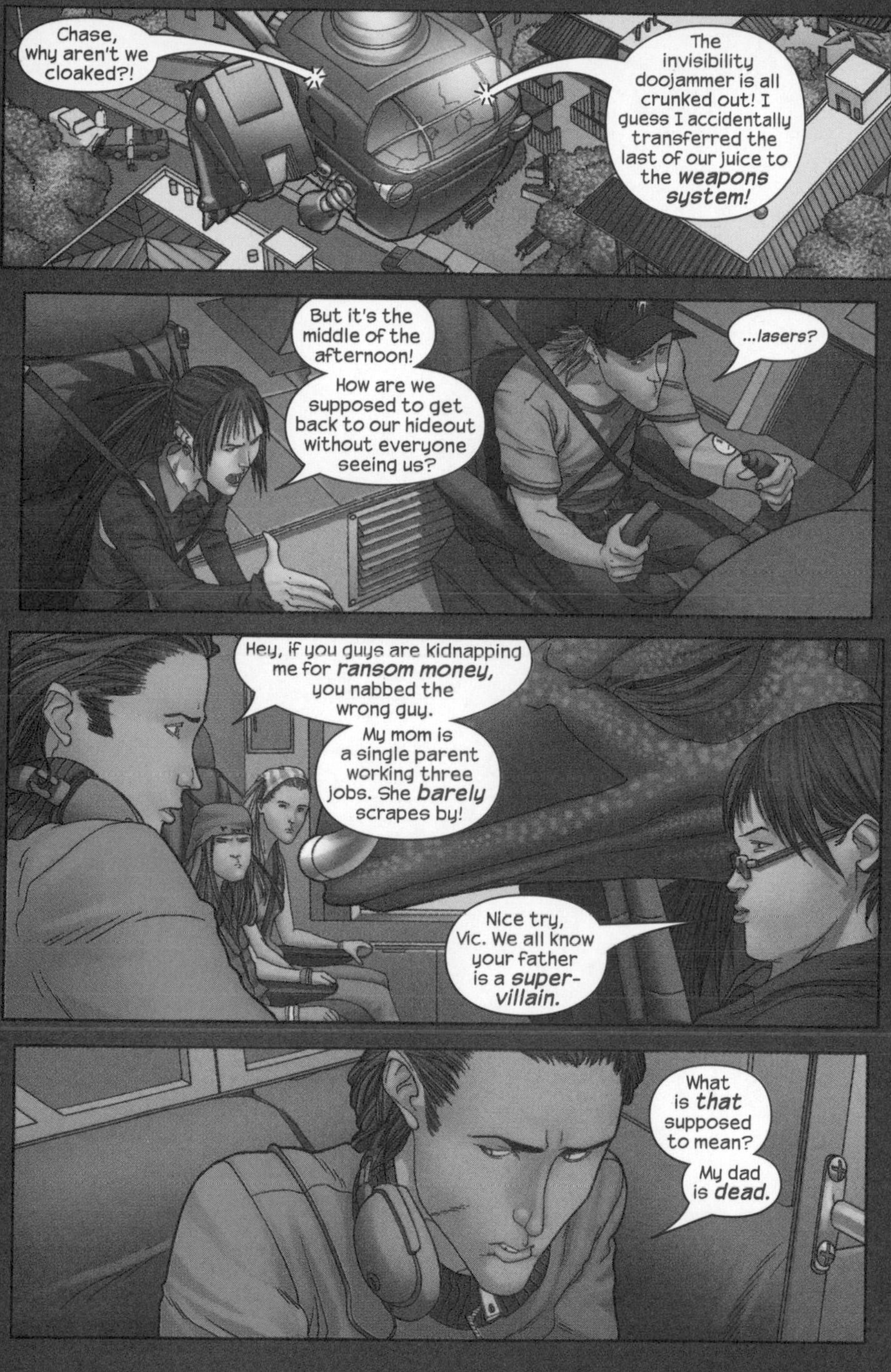
Chase, why aren't we cloaked?!
The invisibility doojammer is all crunked out! I guess I accidentally transferred the last of our juice to the weapons system!
But it's the middle of the afternoon!
How are we supposed to get back to our hideout without everyone seeing us?
...lasers?
Hey, if you guys are kidnapping me for ransom money, you nabbed the wrong guy.
My mom is a single parent working three jobs. She barely scrapes by!
Nice try, Vic. We all know your father is a super-villain.
What is that supposed to mean?
My dad is dead.

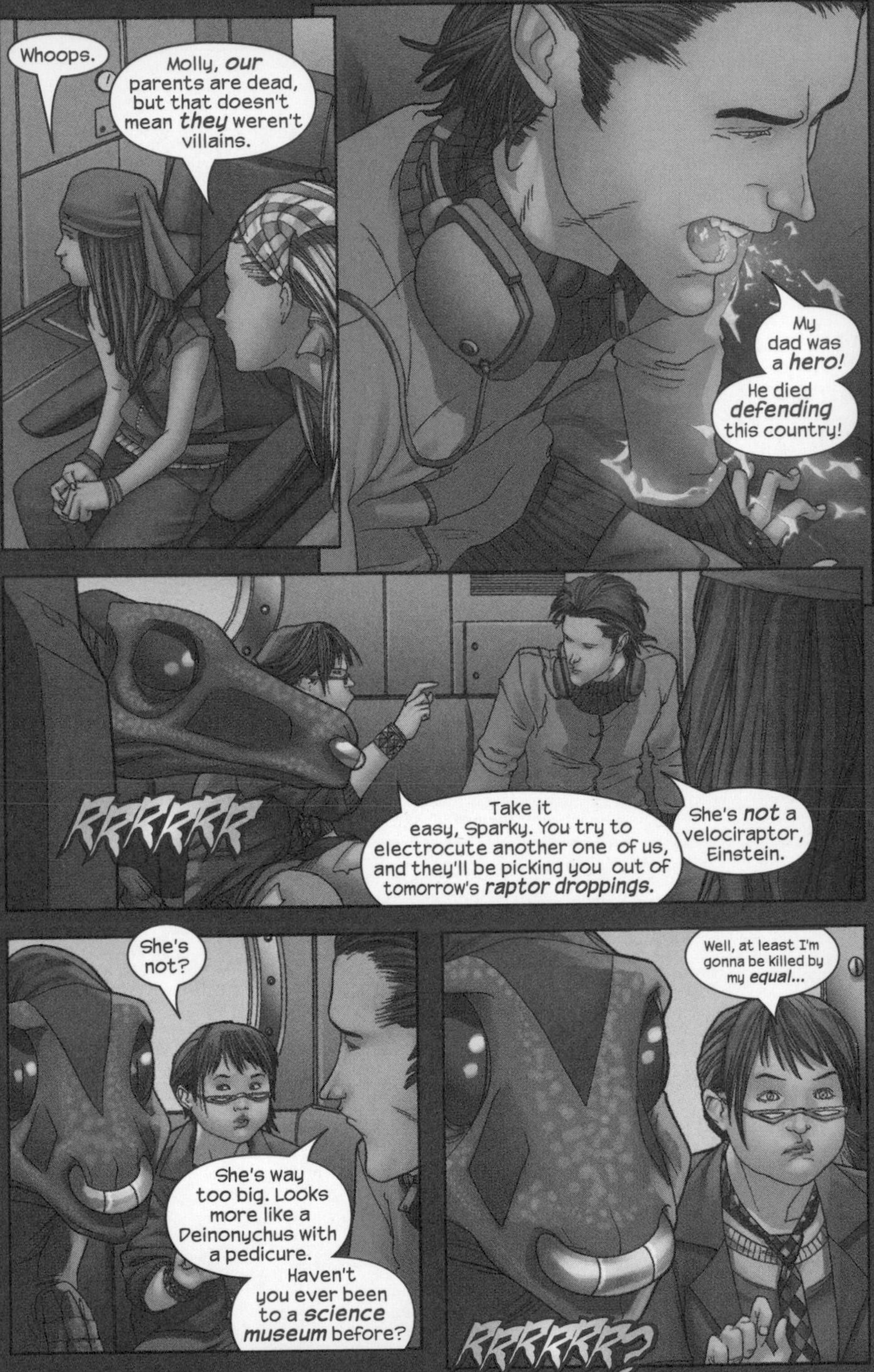

Whoops.
Molly, *our* parents are dead, but that doesn't mean *they* weren't villains.
My dad was a *hero!*
He died *defending* this country!
RRRRRR
Take it easy, Sparky. You try to electrocute another one of us, and they'll be picking you out of tomorrow's *raptor droppings.*
She's *not* a velociraptor, Einstein.
She's not?
She's way too big. Looks more like a Deinonychus with a pedicure.
Haven't you ever been to a *science museum* before?
Well, at least I'm gonna be killed by my *equal...*
RRRRRR?

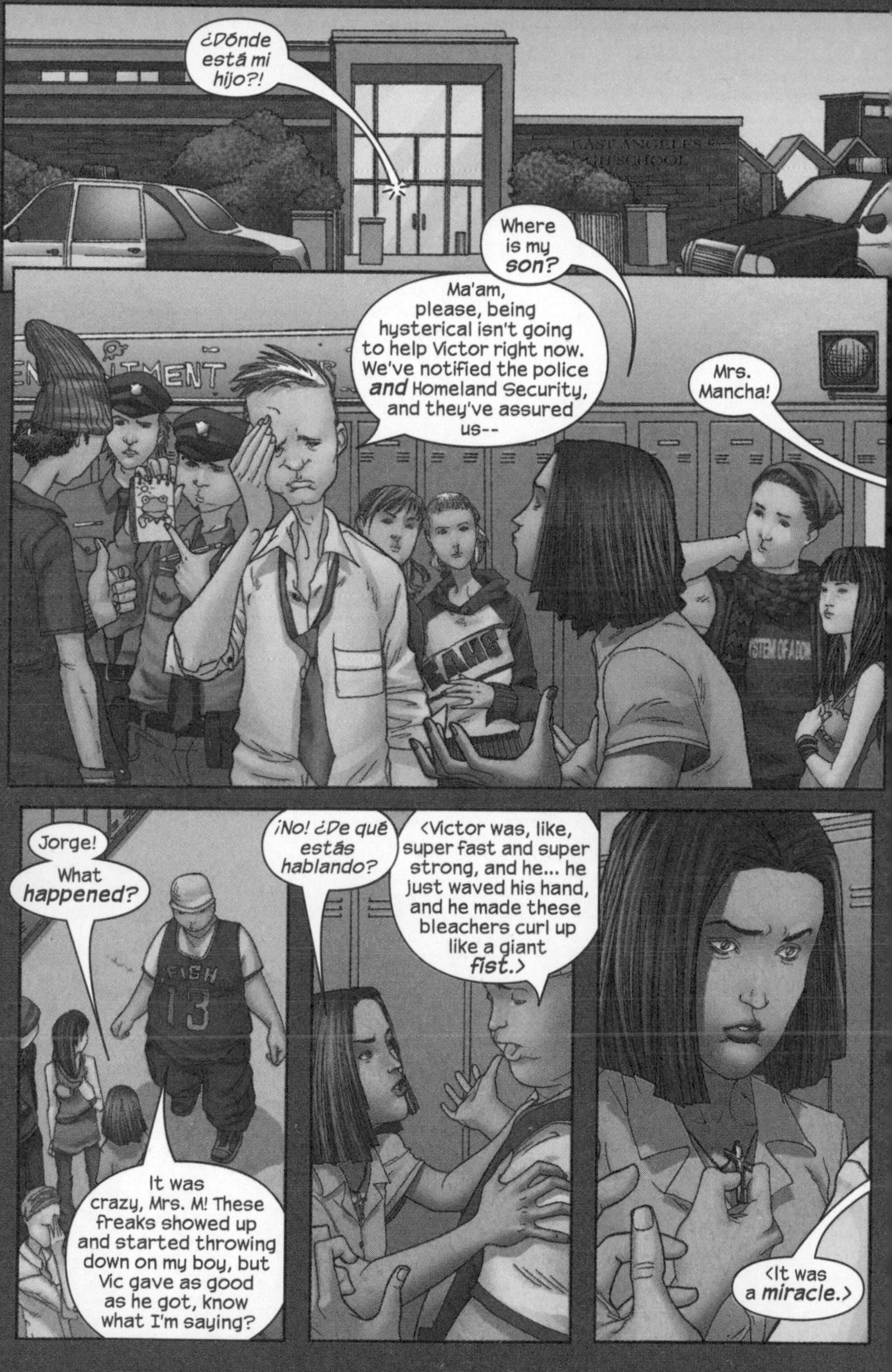
¿Dõnde está mi hijo?!
Where is my son?
Ma'am, please, being hysterical isn't going to help Victor right now. We've notified the police and Homeland Security, and they've assured us--
Mrs. Mancha!
Jorge! What happened?
It was crazy, Mrs. M! These freaks showed up and started throwing down on my boy, but Vic gave as good as he got, know what I'm saying?
¡No! ¿De qué estás hablando?
<Victor was, like, super fast and super strong, and he... he just waved his hand, and he made these bleachers curl up like a giant fist.>
<It was a miracle.>

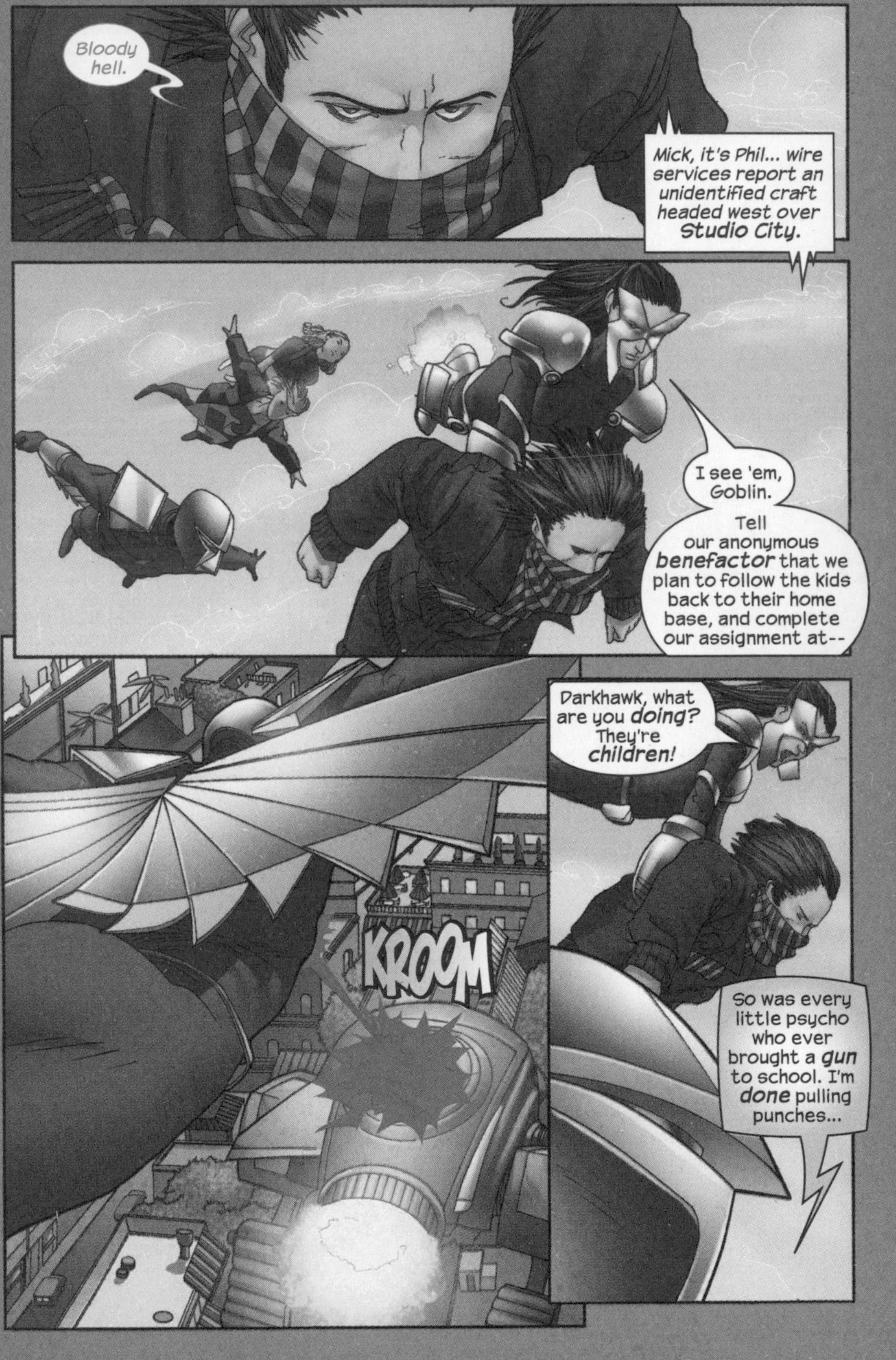

Bloody hell.
Mick, it's Phil... wire services report an unidentified craft headed west over Studio City.
I see 'em, Goblin.
Tell our anonymous benefactor that we plan to follow the kids back to their home base, and complete our assignment at--
Darkhawk, what are you doing? They're children!
KROOM
So was every little psycho who ever brought a gun to school. I'm done pulling punches...

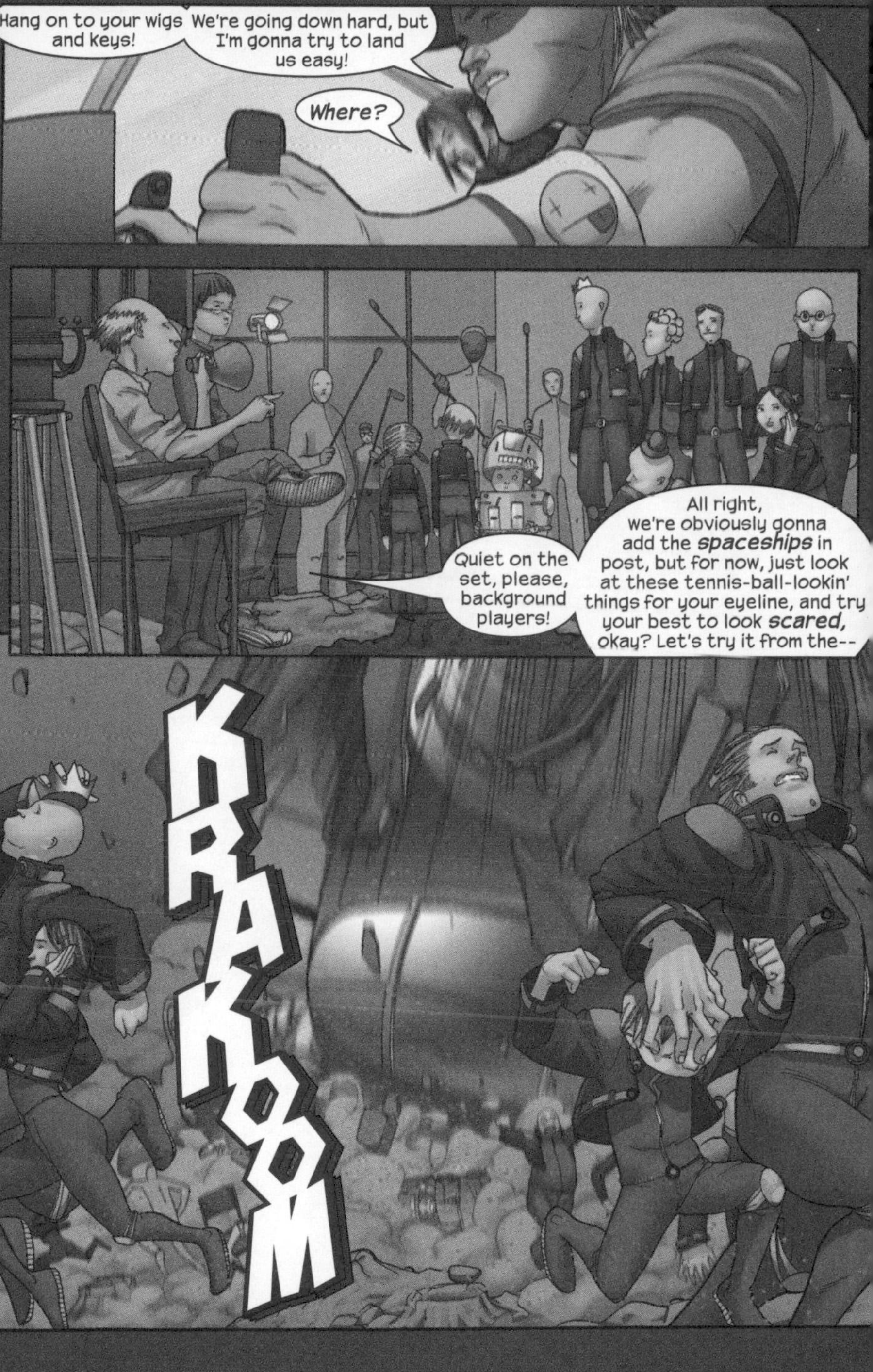
Hang on to your wigs and keys!
We're going down hard, but I'm gonna try to land us easy!
Where?
Quiet on the set, please, background players!
All right, we're obviously gonna add the spaceships in post, but for now, just look at these tennis-ball-lookin' things for your eyeline, and try your best to look scared, okay? Let's try it from the--
KRAKOOM

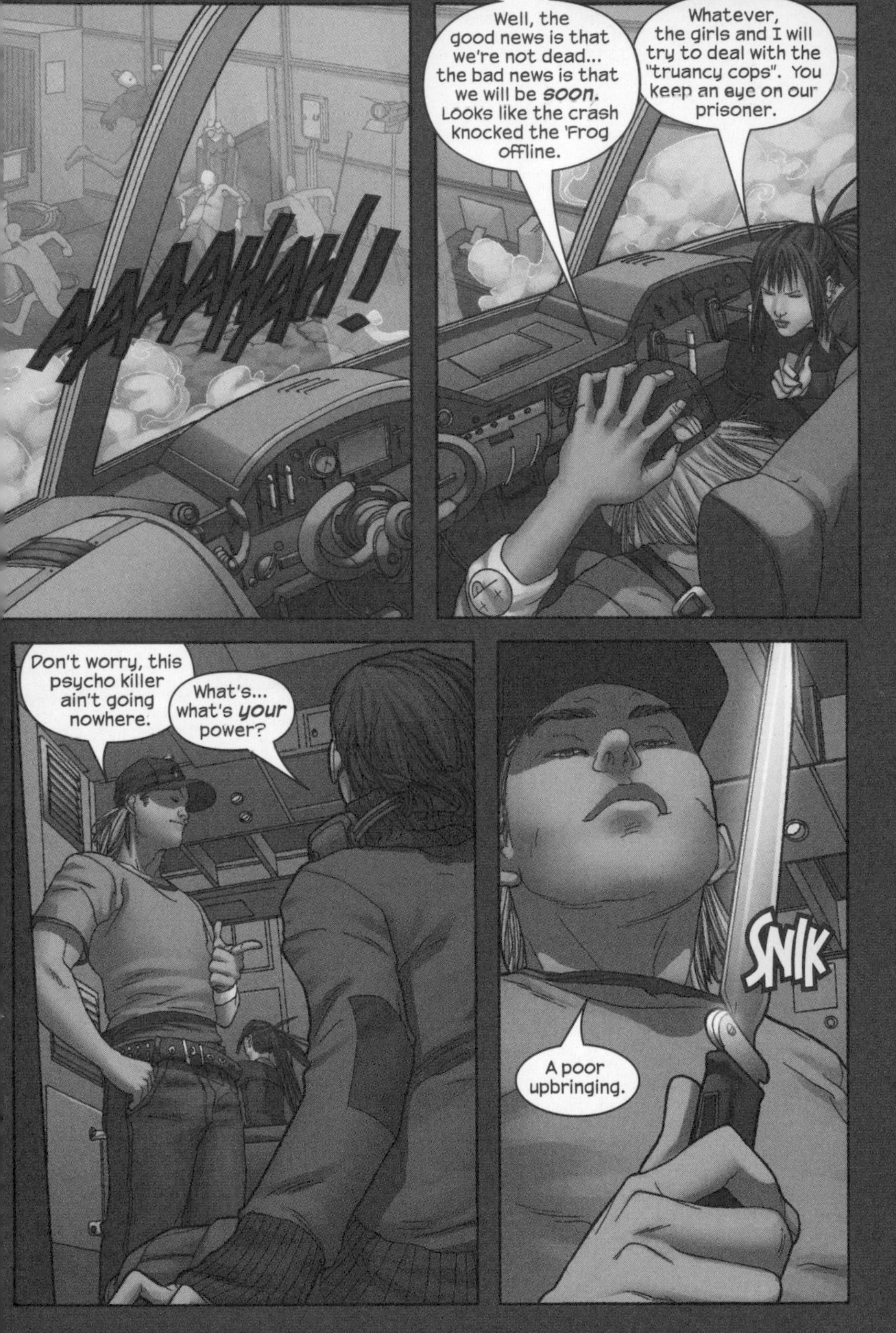
AAAAHAAH!!
...ouch.
Well, the good news is that we're not dead... the bad news is that we will be *soon.* Looks like the crash knocked the 'Frog offline.
Whatever, the girls and I will try to deal with the "truancy cops". You keep an eye on our prisoner.
Don't worry, this psycho killer ain't going nowhere.
What's... what's *your* power?
SNIK
A poor upbringing.

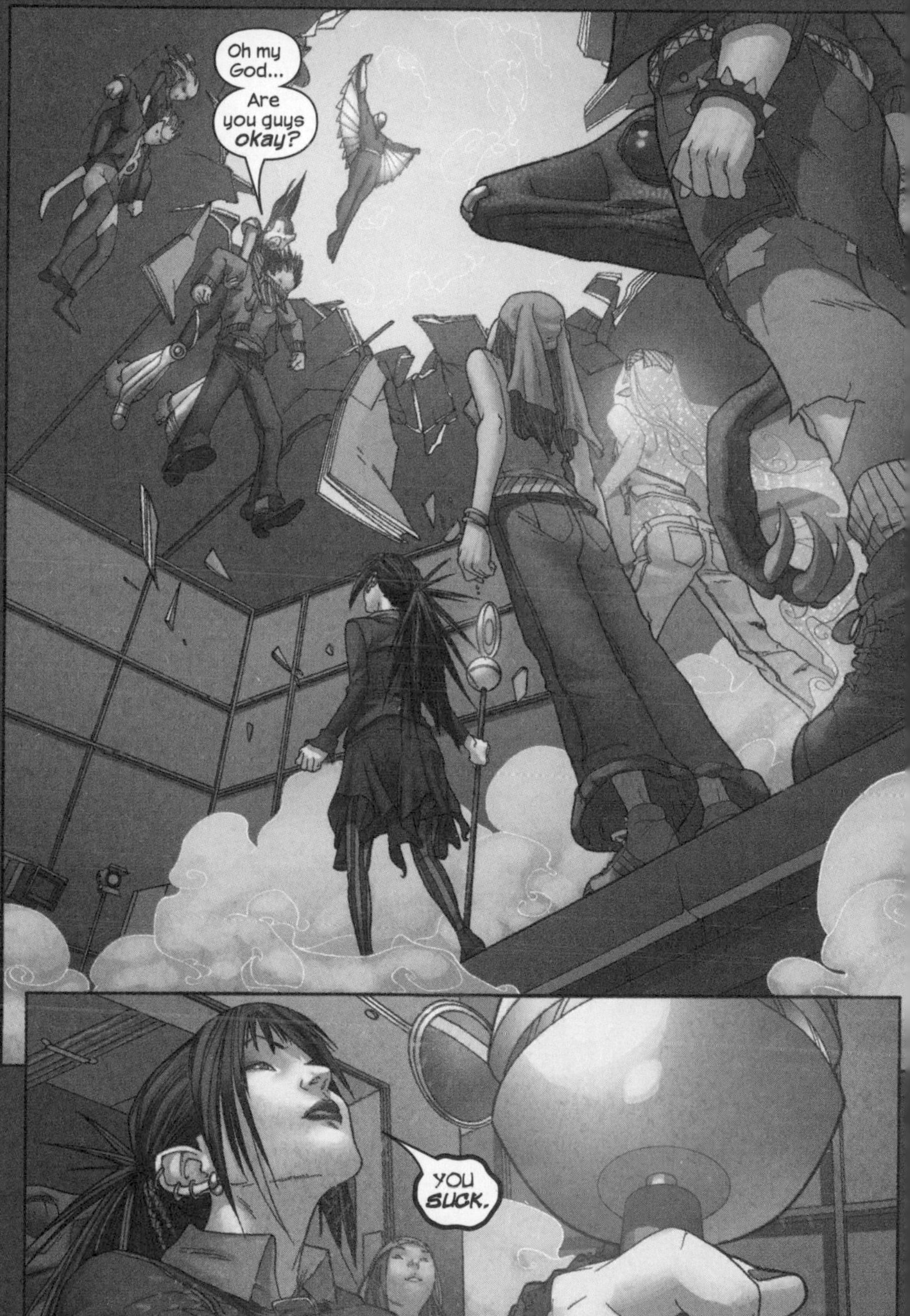
Oh my God...
Are you guys okay?
YOU SUCK.

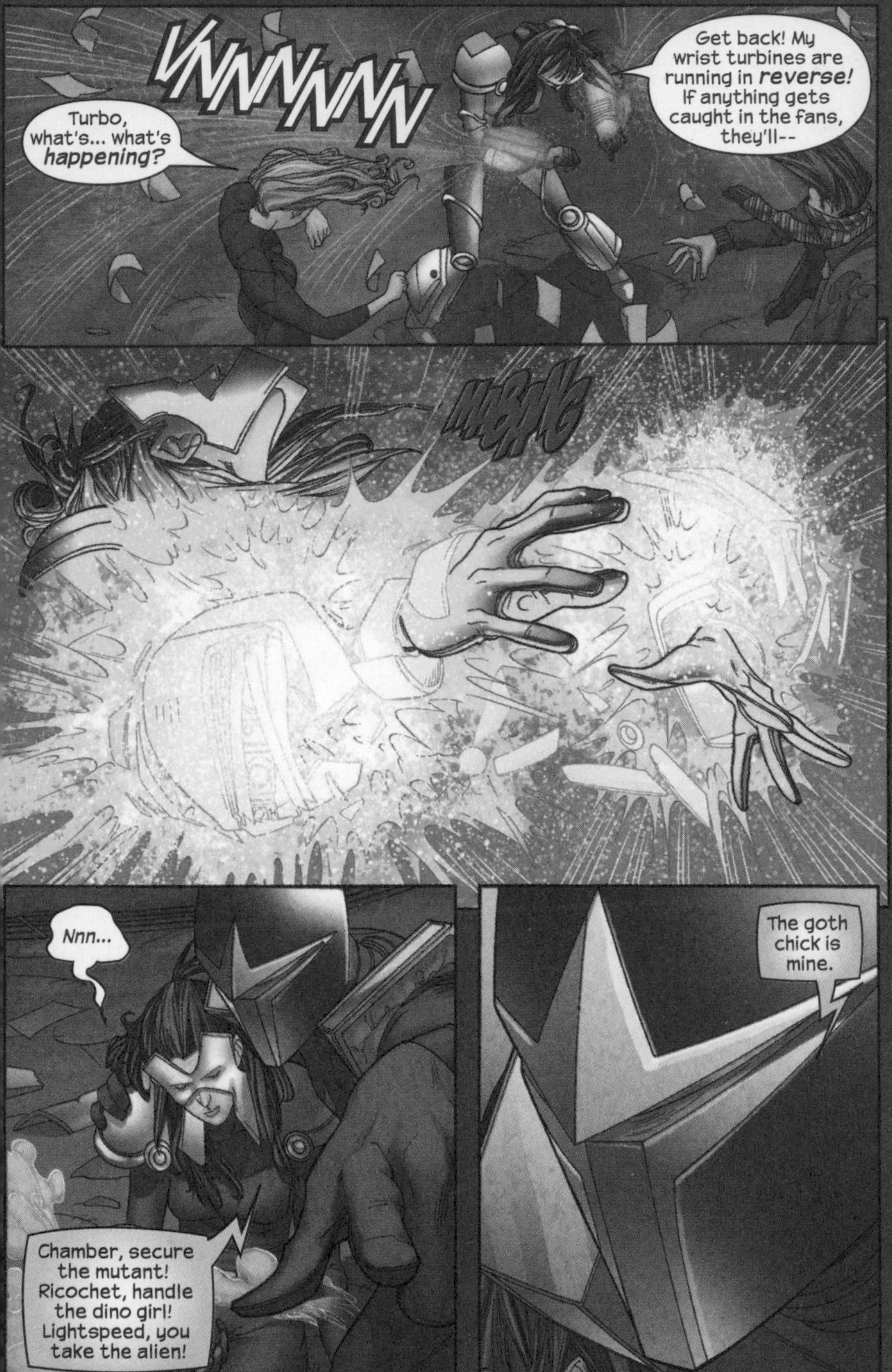

VNNNNNN
Turbo, what's... what's *happening?*
Get back! My wrist turbines are running in ***reverse!*** If anything gets caught in the fans, they'll--
Nnn...
Chamber, secure the mutant! Ricochet, handle the dino girl! Lightspeed, you take the alien!
The goth chick is mine.

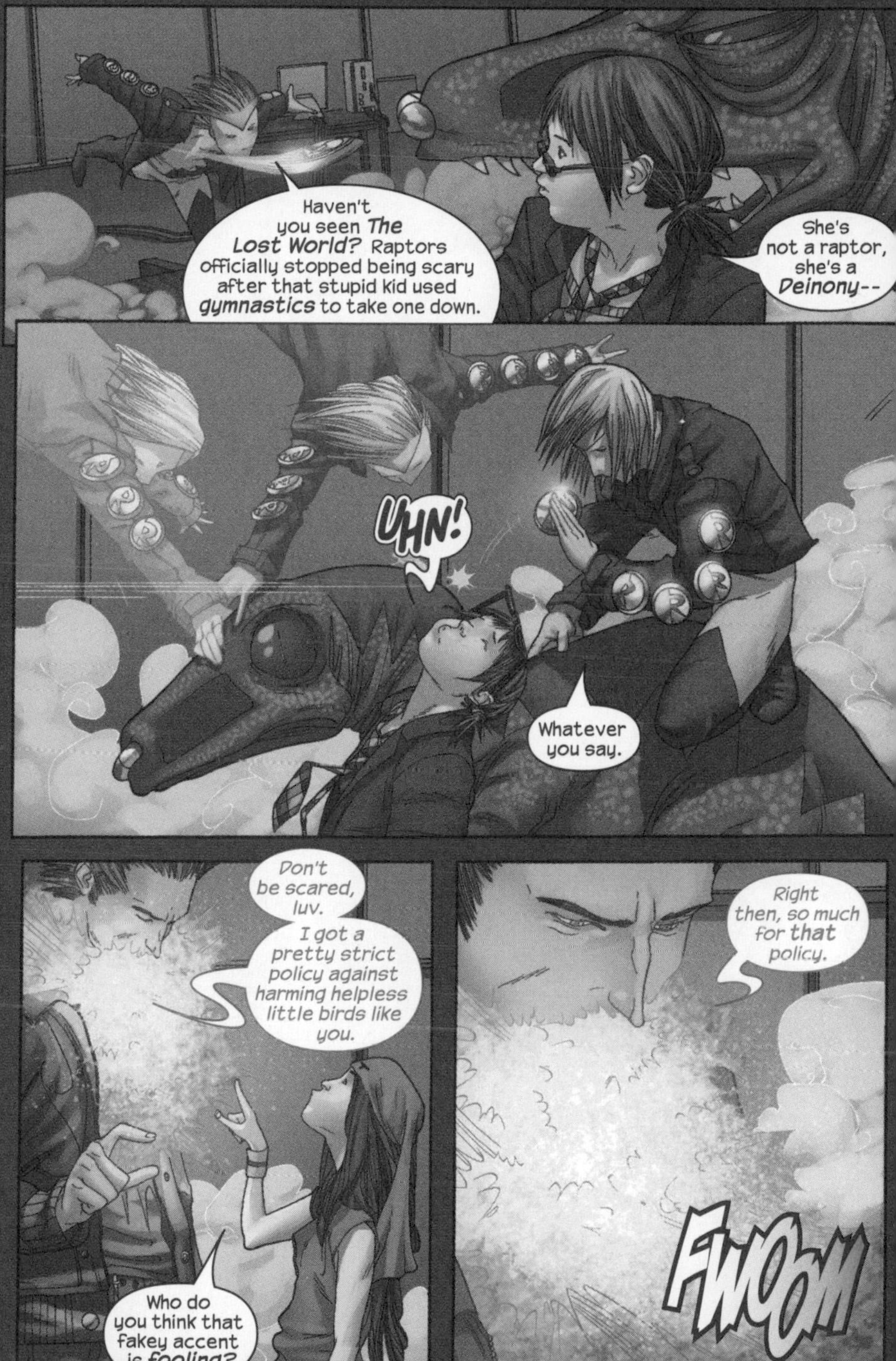
Haven't you seen The Lost World? Raptors officially stopped being scary after that stupid kid used gymnastics to take one down.
She's not a raptor, she's a Deinony--
UHN!
Whatever you say.
Don't be scared, luv.
I got a pretty strict policy against harming helpless little birds like you.
Who do you think that fakey accent is fooling?
Right then, so much for that policy.
FWOOM

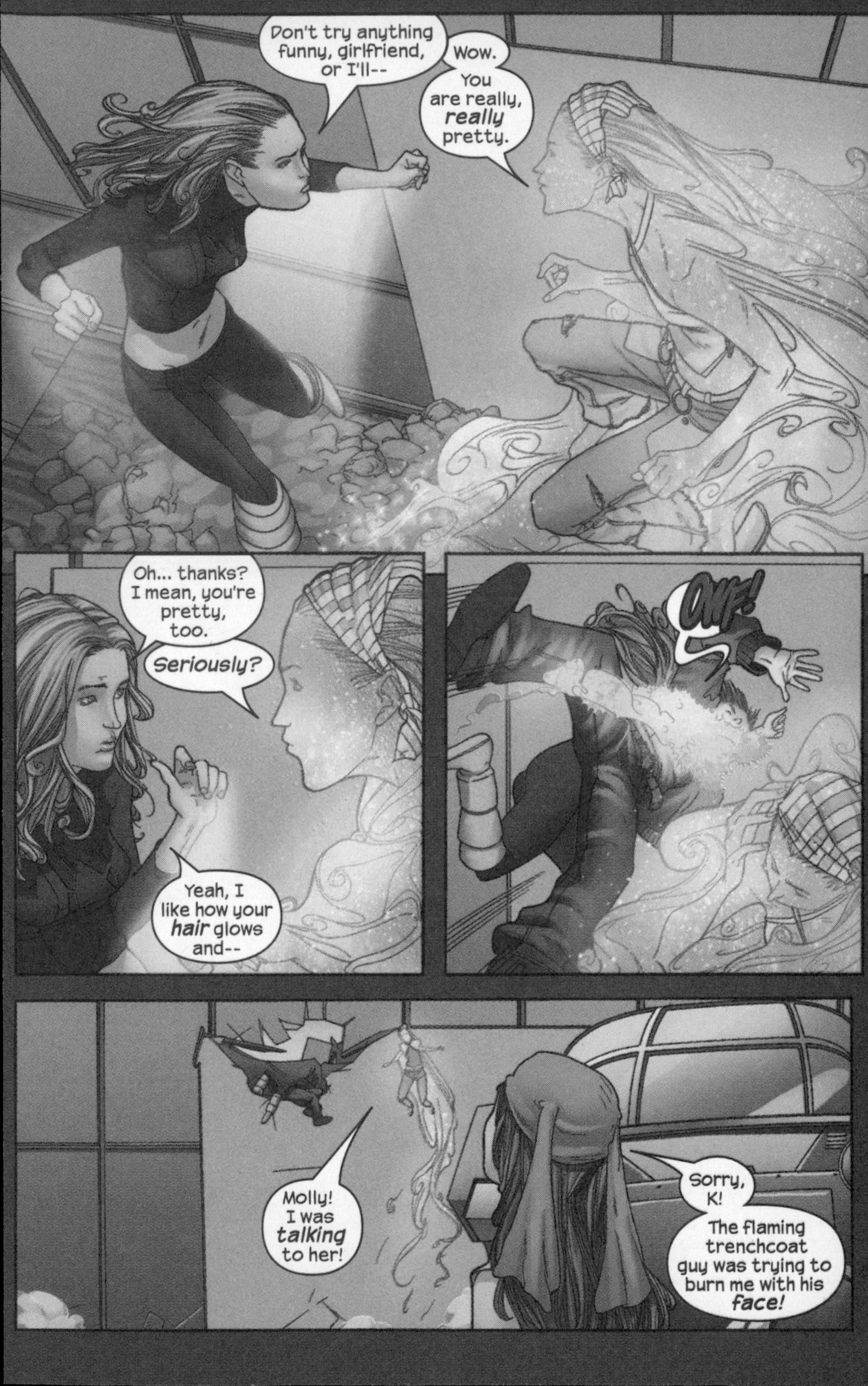
Don't try anything funny, girlfriend, or I'll--
Wow.
You are really, *really* pretty.
Oh... thanks? I mean, you're pretty, too.
Seriously?
Yeah, I like how your *hair* glows and--
OWF!
Molly! I was *talking* to her!
Sorry, K!
The flaming trenchcoat guy was trying to burn me with his *face!*

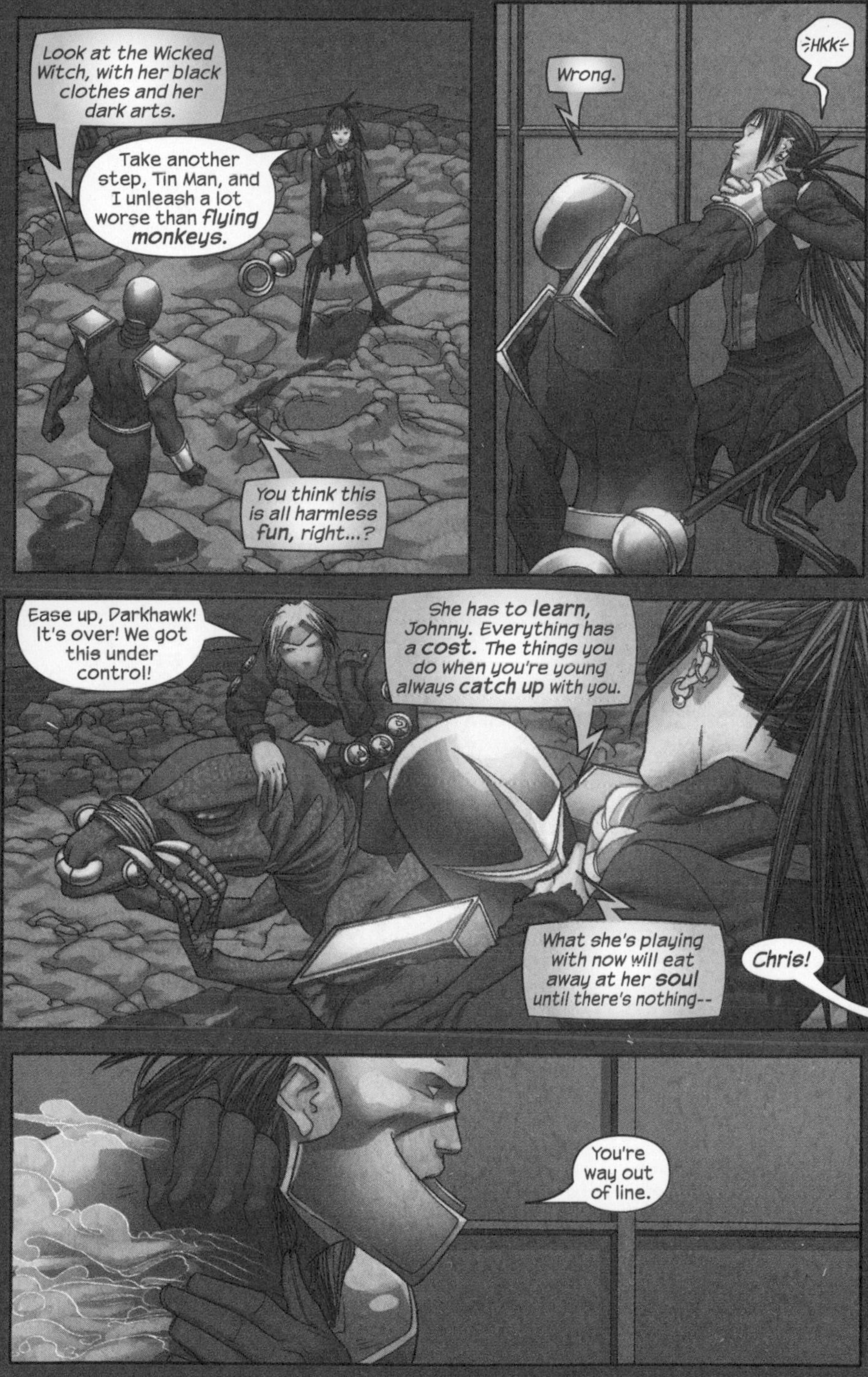
Look at the Wicked Witch, with her black clothes and her dark arts.
Take another step, Tin Man, and I unleash a lot worse than flying monkeys.
You think this is all harmless fun, right...?
Wrong.
HKK
Ease up, Darkhawk! It's over! We got this under control!
She has to learn, Johnny. Everything has a cost. The things you do when you're young always catch up with you.
What she's playing with now will eat away at her soul until there's nothing--
Chris!
You're way out of line.

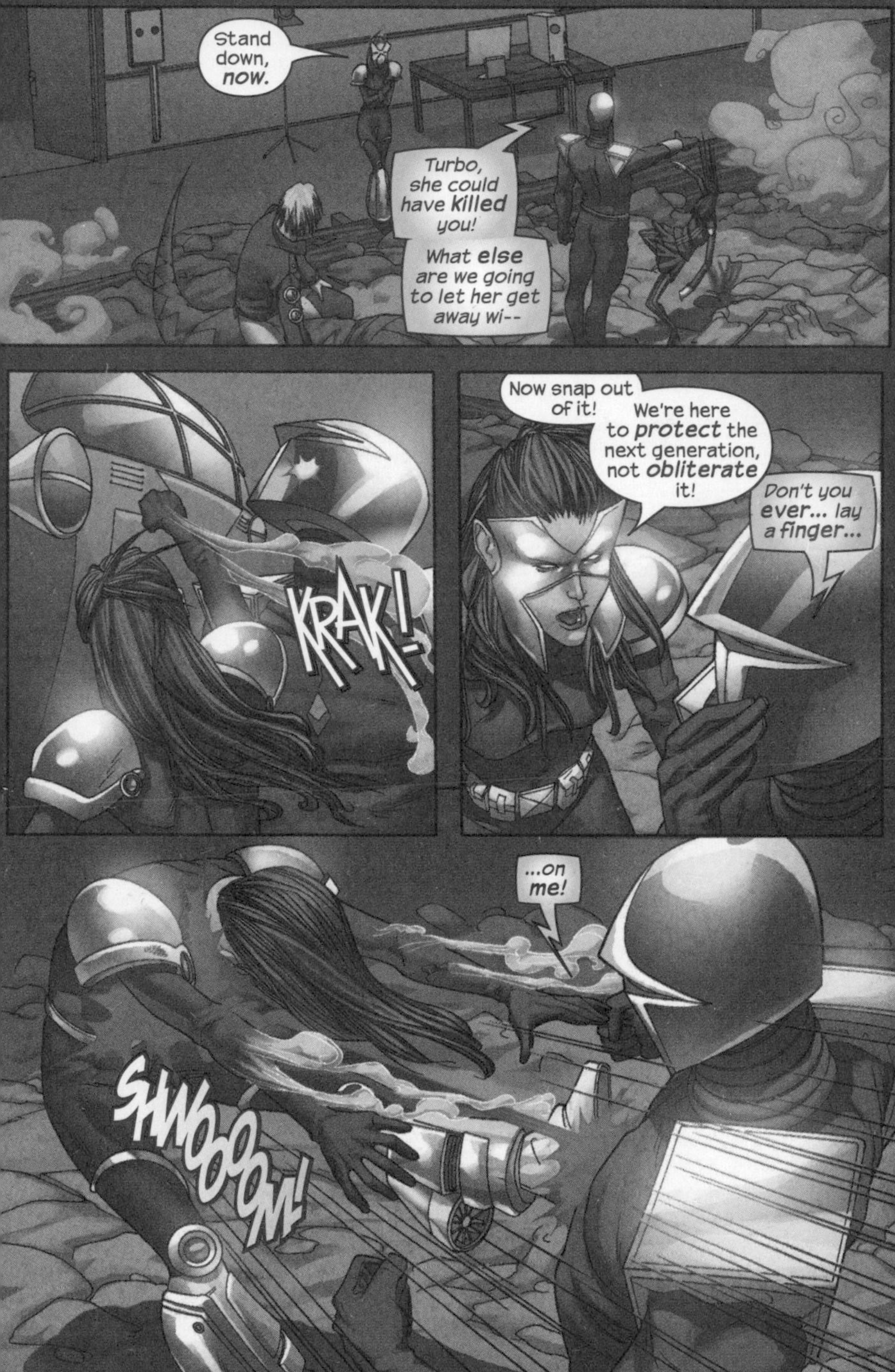

Stand down, now.
Turbo, she could have killed you!
What else are we going to let her get away wi--
KRAK!
Now snap out of it!
We're here to protect the next generation, not obliterate it!
Don't you ever... lay a finger...
...on me!
SHWOOOM!

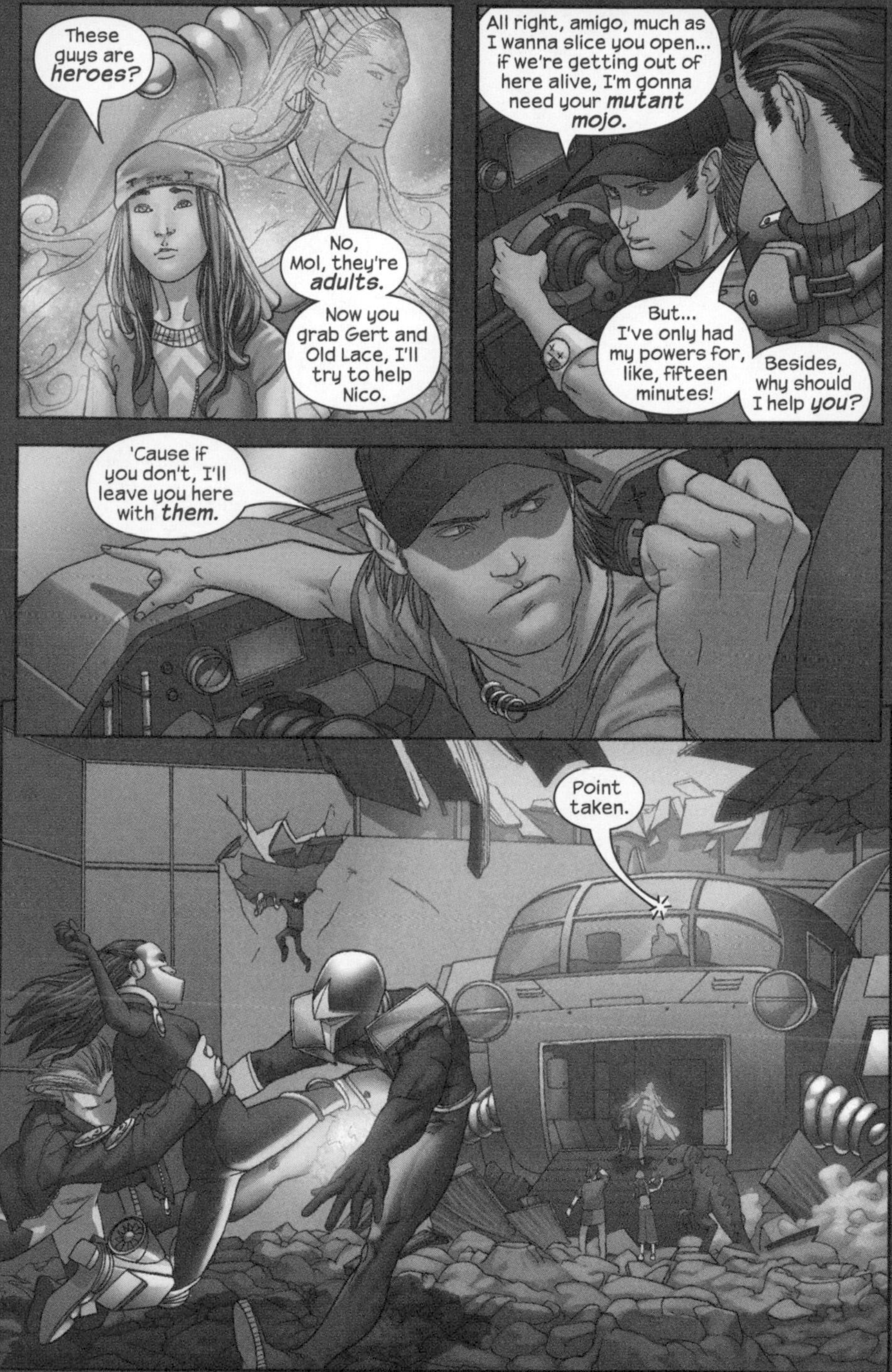
These guys are heroes?
No, Mol, they're adults.
Now you grab Gert and Old Lace, I'll try to help Nico.
All right, amigo, much as I wanna slice you open... if we're getting out of here alive, I'm gonna need your mutant mojo.
But... I've only had my powers for, like, fifteen minutes!
Besides, why should I help you?
'Cause if you don't, I'll leave you here with them.
Point taken.

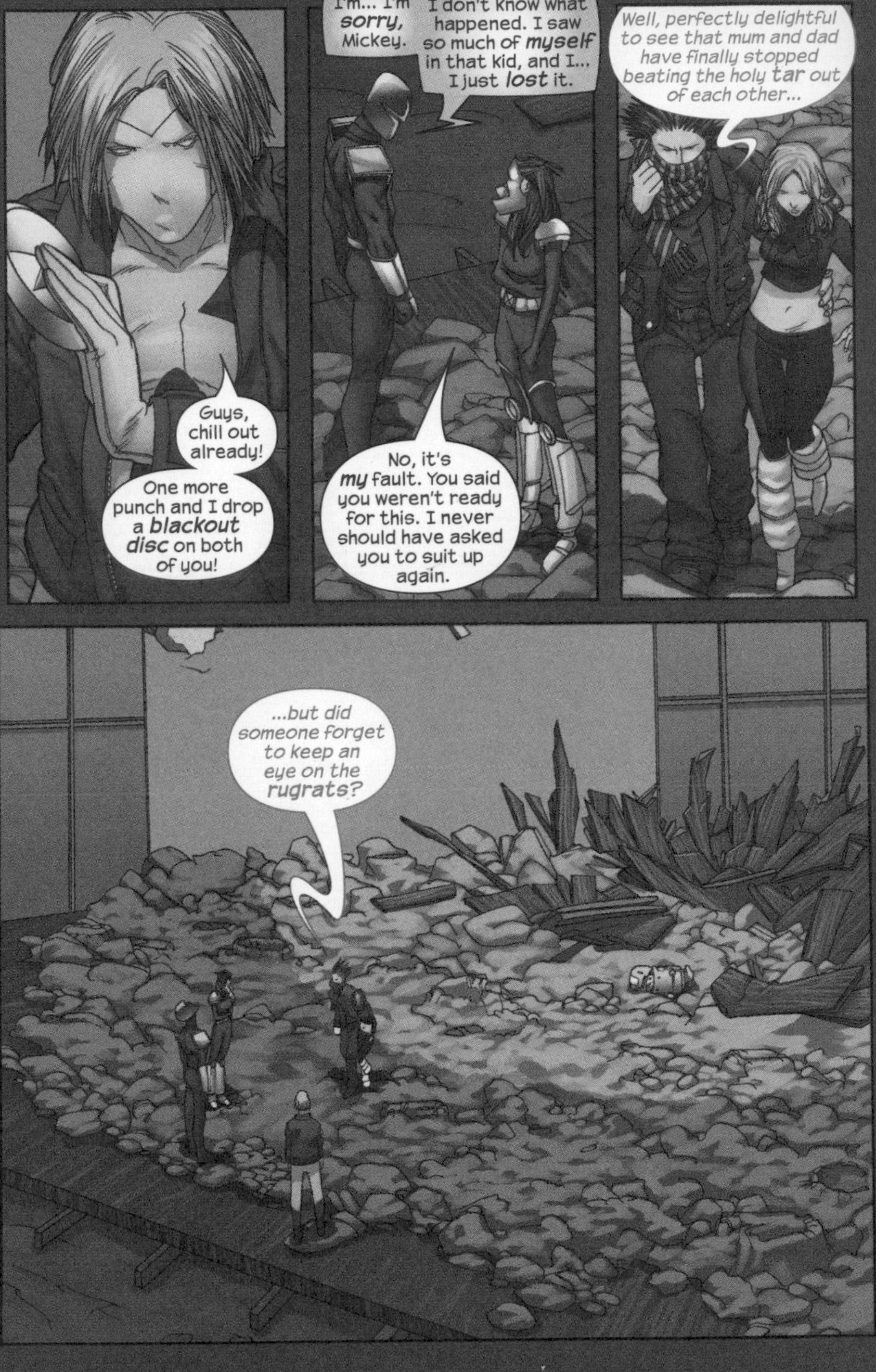
Guys, chill out already!
One more punch and I drop a blackout disc on both of you!
I'm... I'm sorry, Mickey.
I don't know what happened. I saw so much of myself in that kid, and I... I just lost it.
No, it's my fault. You said you weren't ready for this. I never should have asked you to suit up again.
Well, perfectly delightful to see that mum and dad have finally stopped beating the holy tar out of each other...
...but did someone forget to keep an eye on the rugrats?

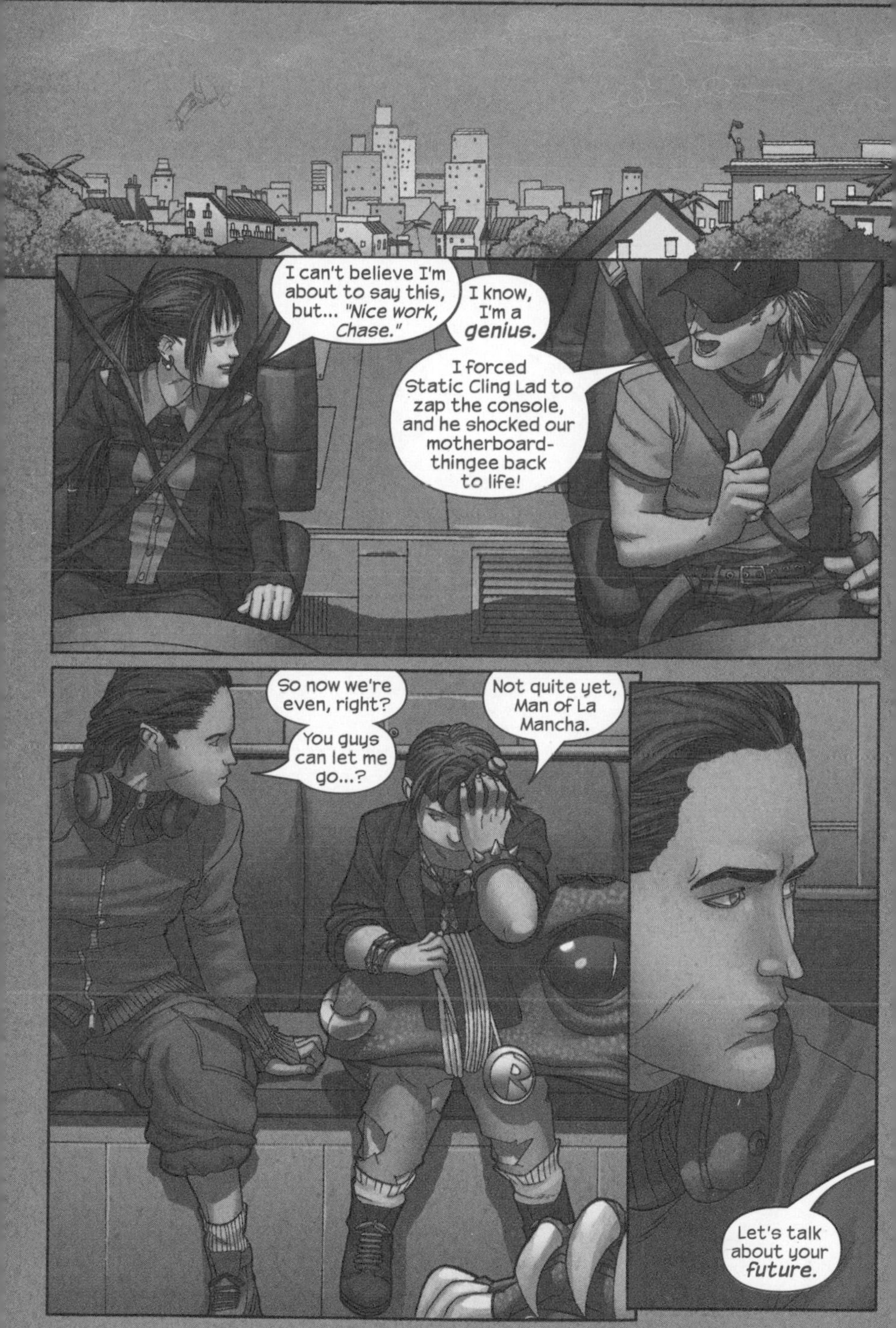
I can't believe I'm about to say this, but... "Nice work, Chase."
I know, I'm a genius.
I forced Static Cling Lad to zap the console, and he shocked our motherboard-thingee back to life!
So now we're even, right?
You guys can let me go...?
Not quite yet, Man of La Mancha.
Let's talk about your future.

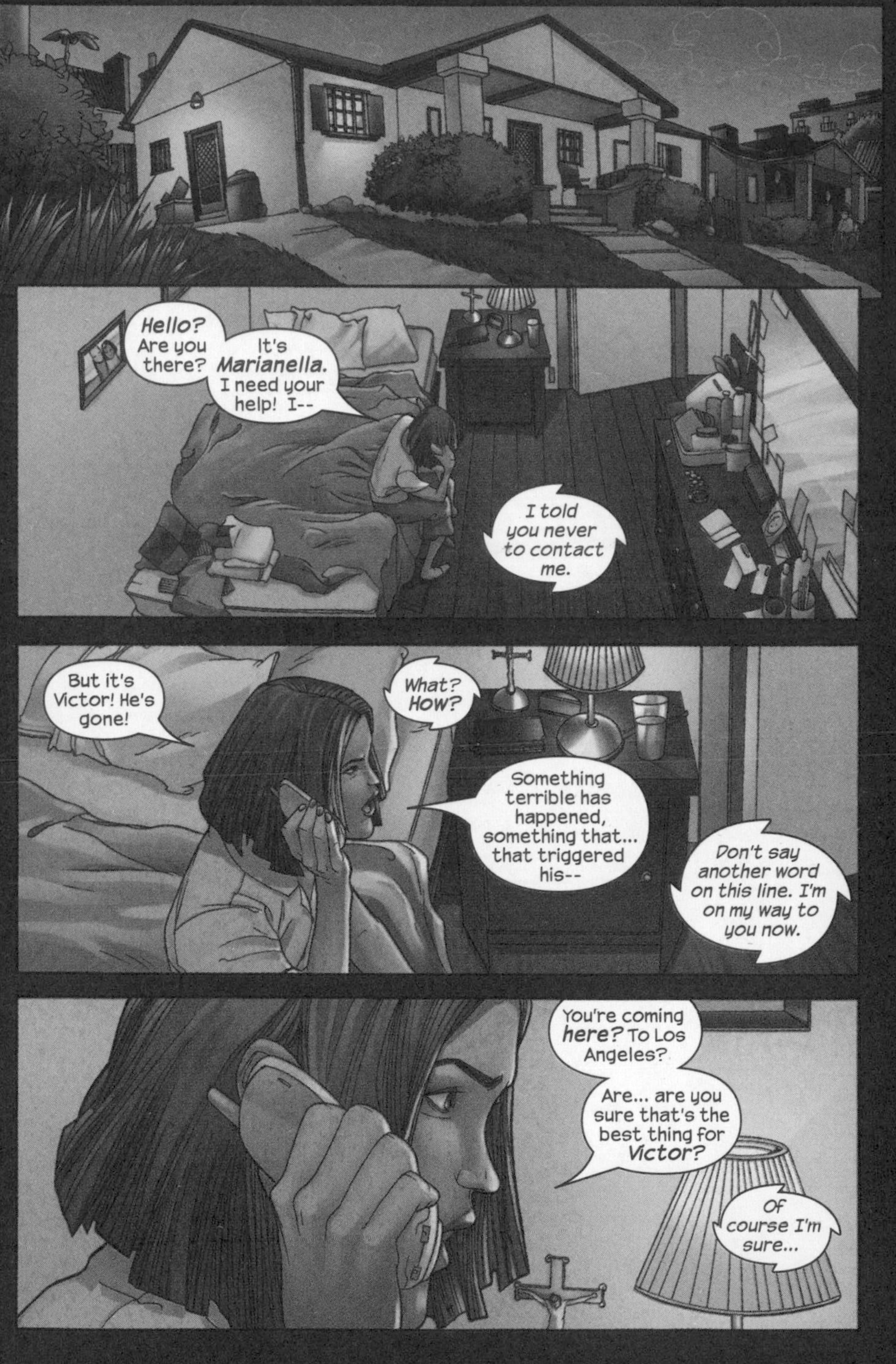
Hello? Are you there?
It's Marianella. I need your help! I--
I told you never to contact me.
But it's Victor! He's gone!
What? How?
Something terrible has happened, something that... that triggered his--
Don't say another word on this line. I'm on my way to you now.
You're coming here? To Los Angeles?
Are... are you sure that's the best thing for Victor?
Of course I'm sure...

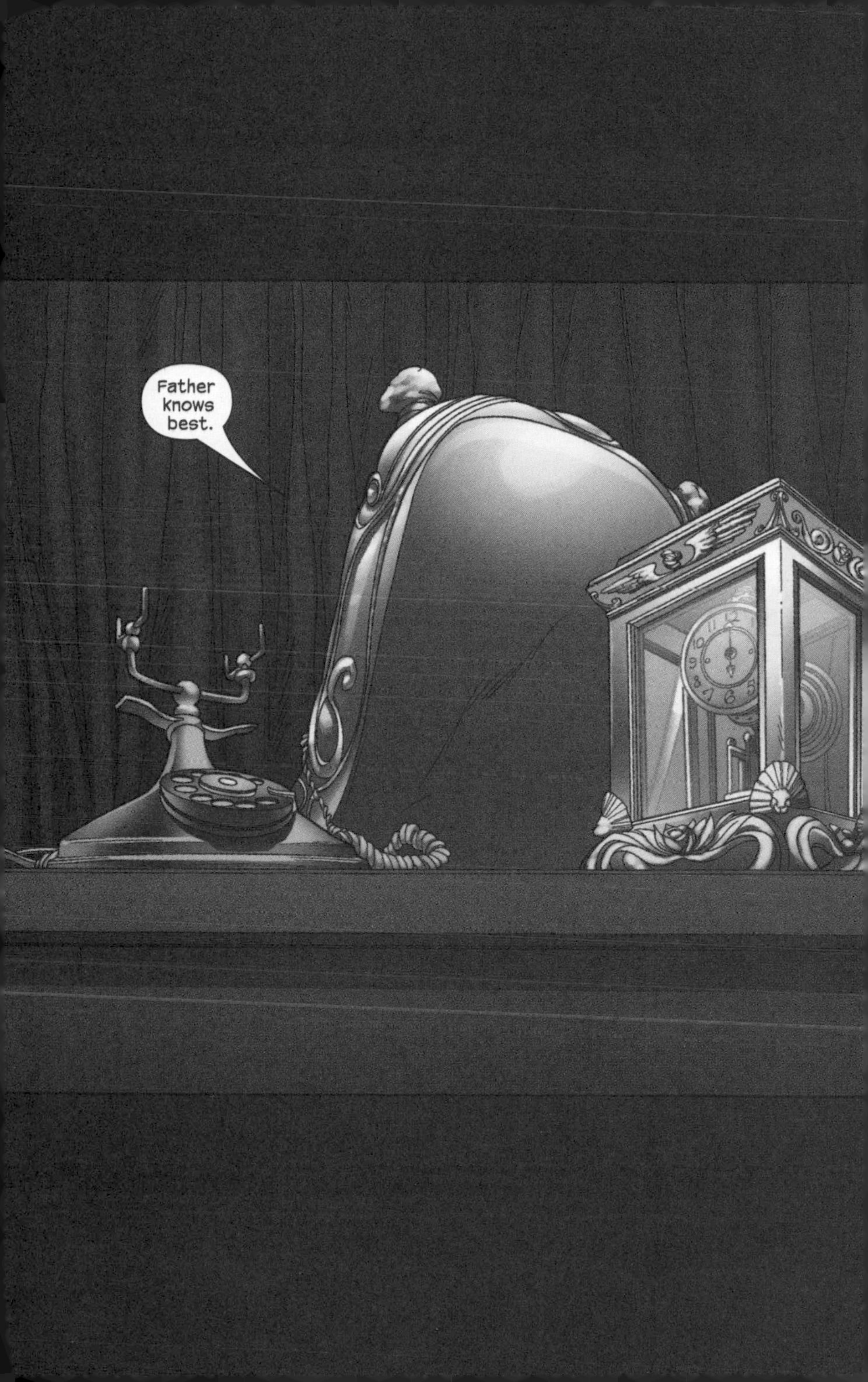
Father knows best.

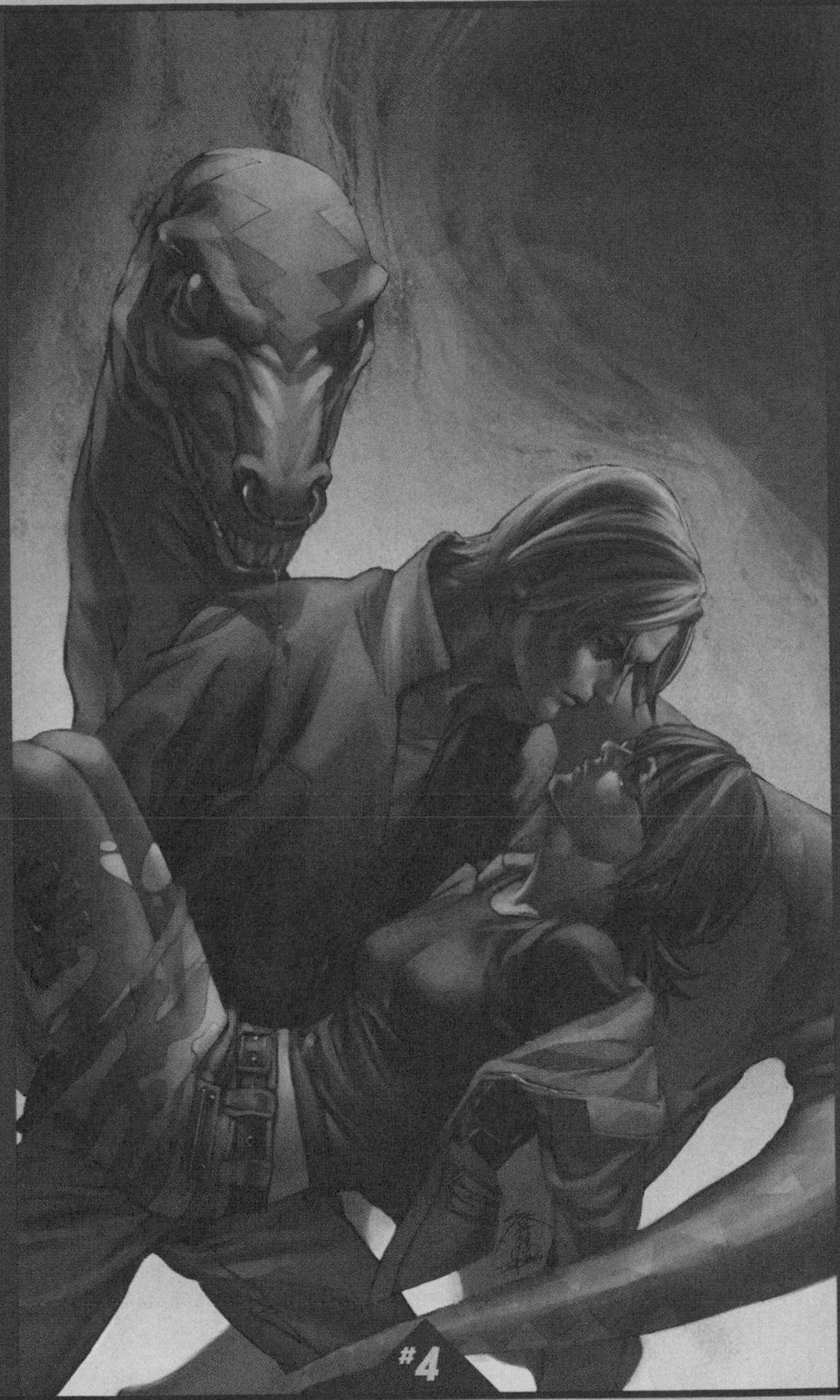
#4

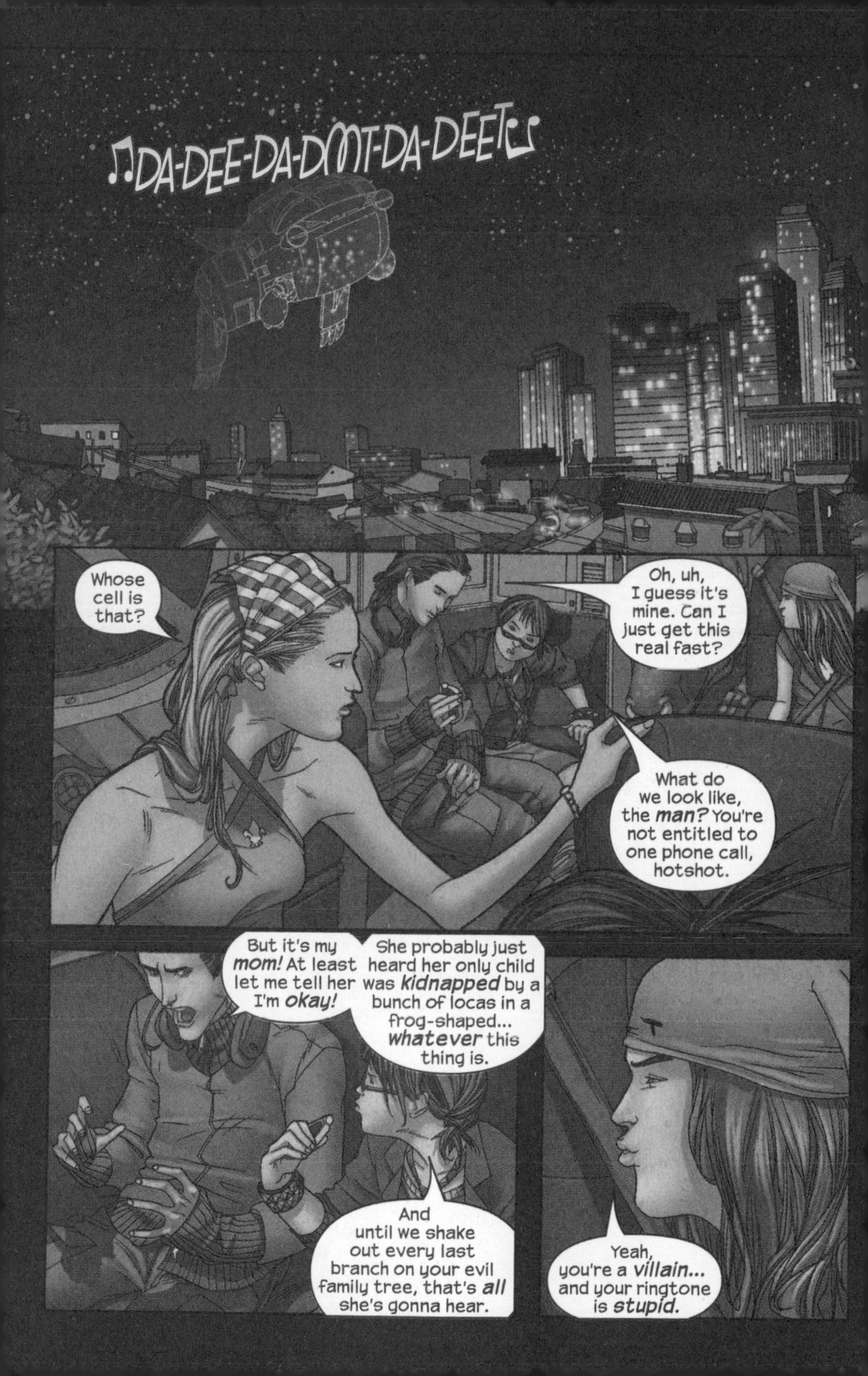
DA-DEE-DA-DMT-DA-DEET
Whose cell is that?
Oh, uh, I guess it's mine. Can I just get this real fast?
What do we look like, the *man?* You're not entitled to one phone call, hotshot.
But it's my *mom!* At least let me tell her I'm *okay!*
She probably just heard her only child was *kidnapped* by a bunch of locas in a frog-shaped... *whatever* this thing is.
And until we shake out every last branch on your evil family tree, that's *all* she's gonna hear.
Yeah, you're a *villain...* and your ringtone is *stupid.*

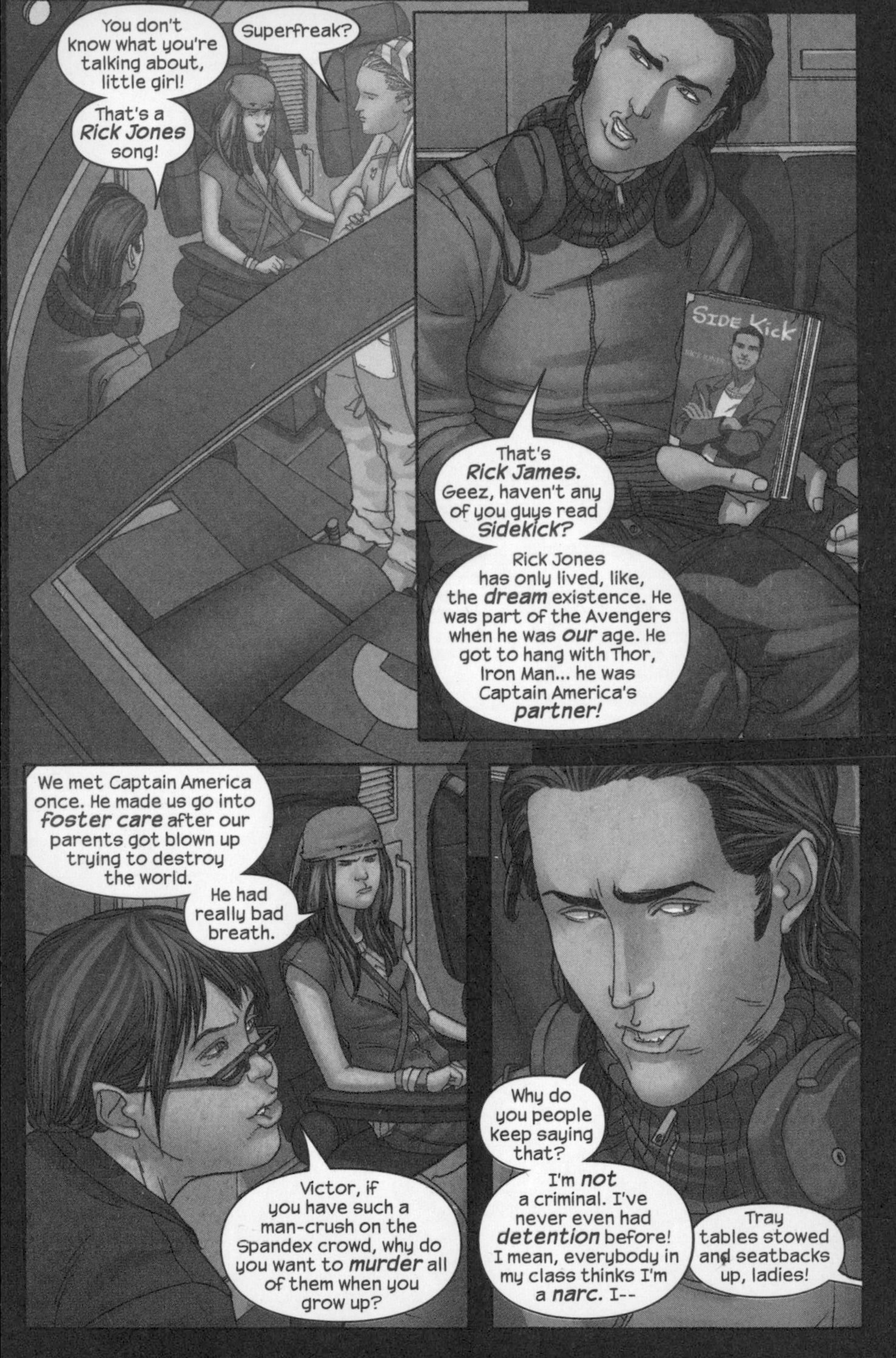

You don't know what you're talking about, little girl!
Superfreak?
That's a Rick Jones song!
SIDE KICK
That's Rick James. Geez, haven't any of you guys read Sidekick?
Rick Jones has only lived, like, the dream existence. He was part of the Avengers when he was our age. He got to hang with Thor, Iron Man... he was Captain America's partner!
We met Captain America once. He made us go into foster care after our parents got blown up trying to destroy the world.
He had really bad breath.
Victor, if you have such a man-crush on the Spandex crowd, why do you want to murder all of them when you grow up?
Why do you people keep saying that?
I'm not a criminal. I've never even had detention before! I mean, everybody in my class thinks I'm a narc. I--
Tray tables stowed and seatbacks up, ladies!

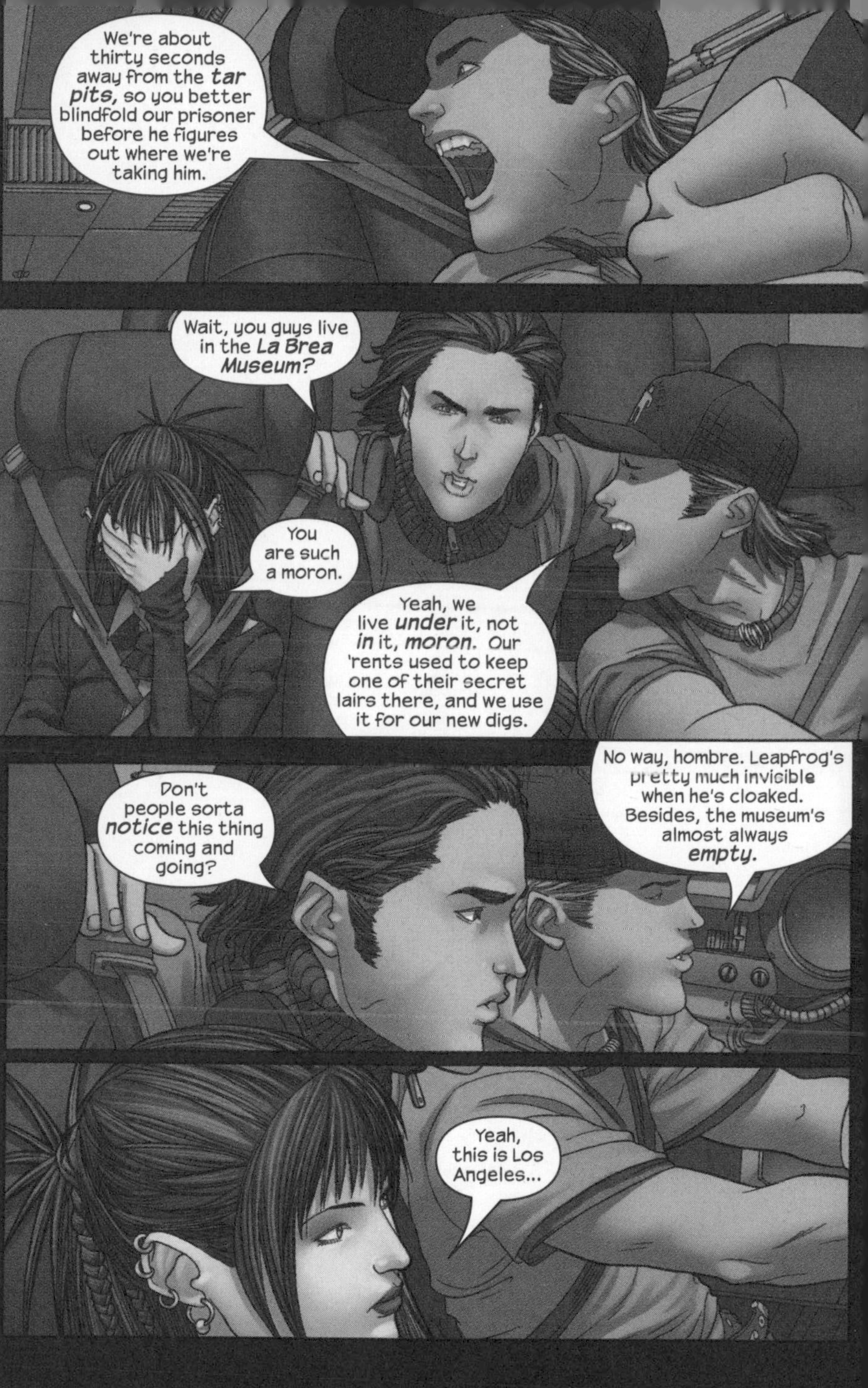
We're about thirty seconds away from the tar pits, so you better blindfold our prisoner before he figures out where we're taking him.
Wait, you guys live in the La Brea Museum?
You are such a moron.
Yeah, we live under it, not in it, moron. Our 'rents used to keep one of their secret lairs there, and we use it for our new digs.
Don't people sorta notice this thing coming and going?
No way, hombre. Leapfrog's pretty much invicible when he's cloaked. Besides, the museum's almost always empty.
Yeah, this is Los Angeles...

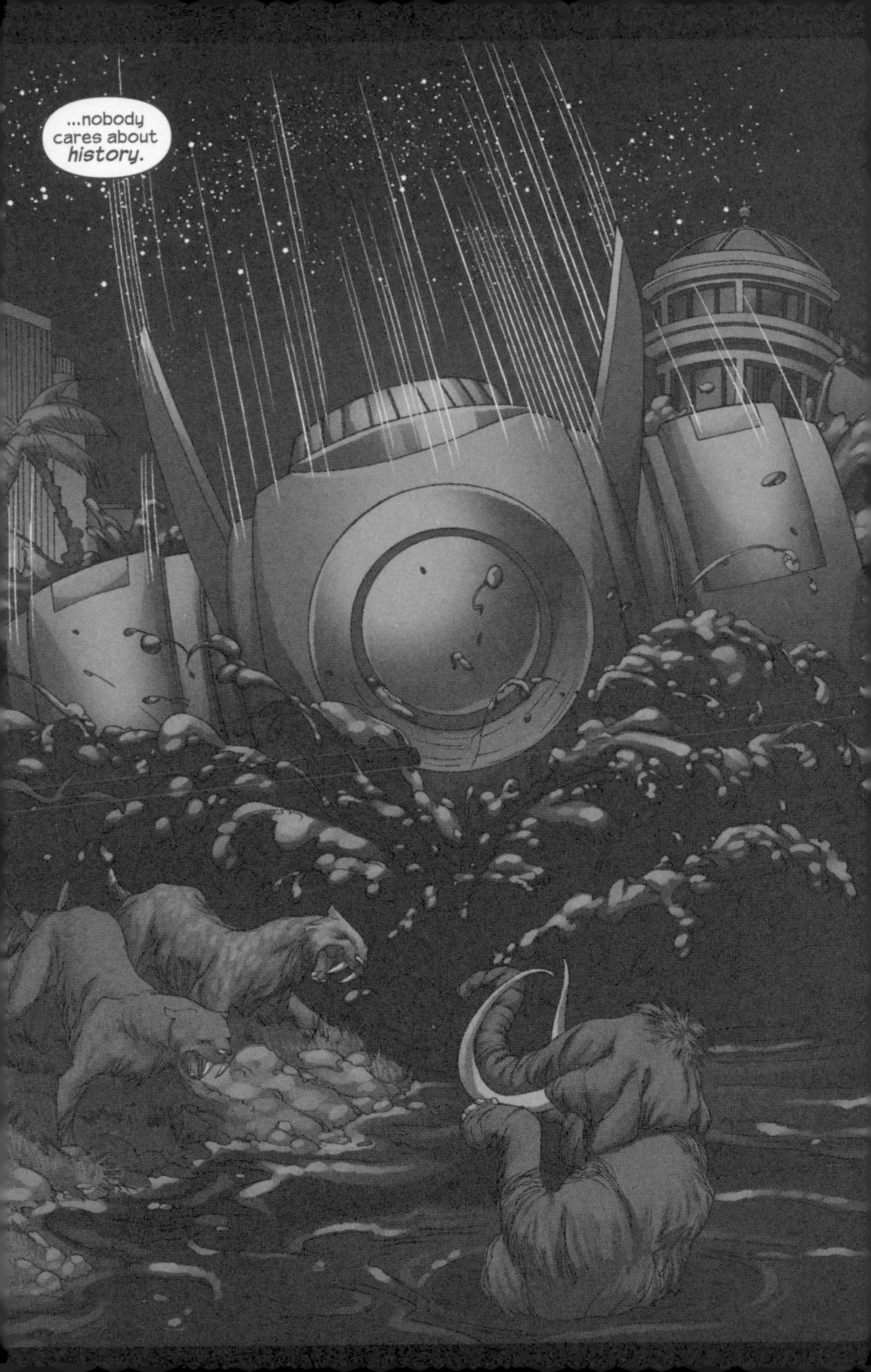
...nobody cares about *history*.

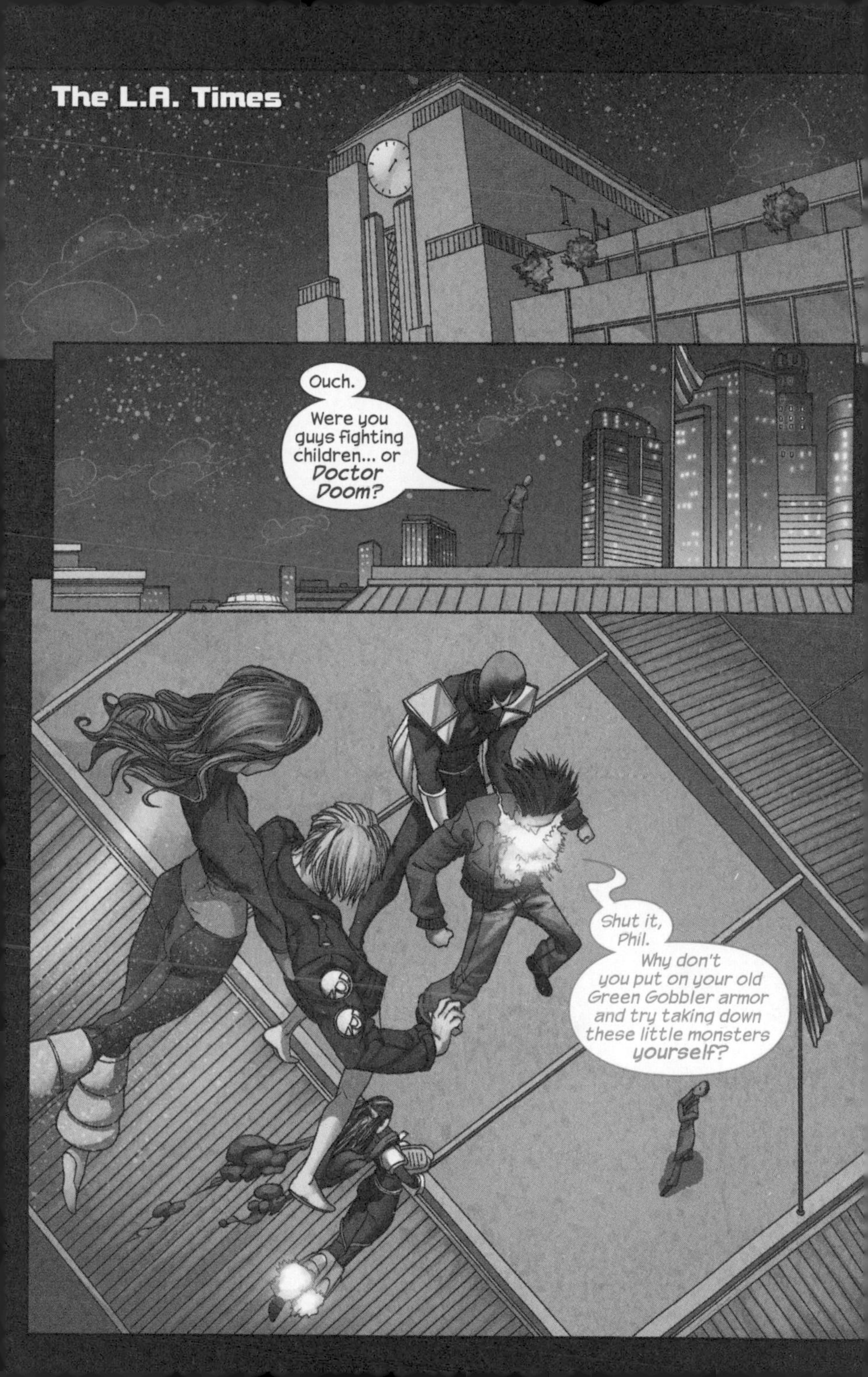
The L.A. Times
Ouch.
Were you guys fighting children... or Doctor Doom?
Shut it, Phil.
Why don't you put on your old Green Gobbler armor and try taking down these little monsters yourself?

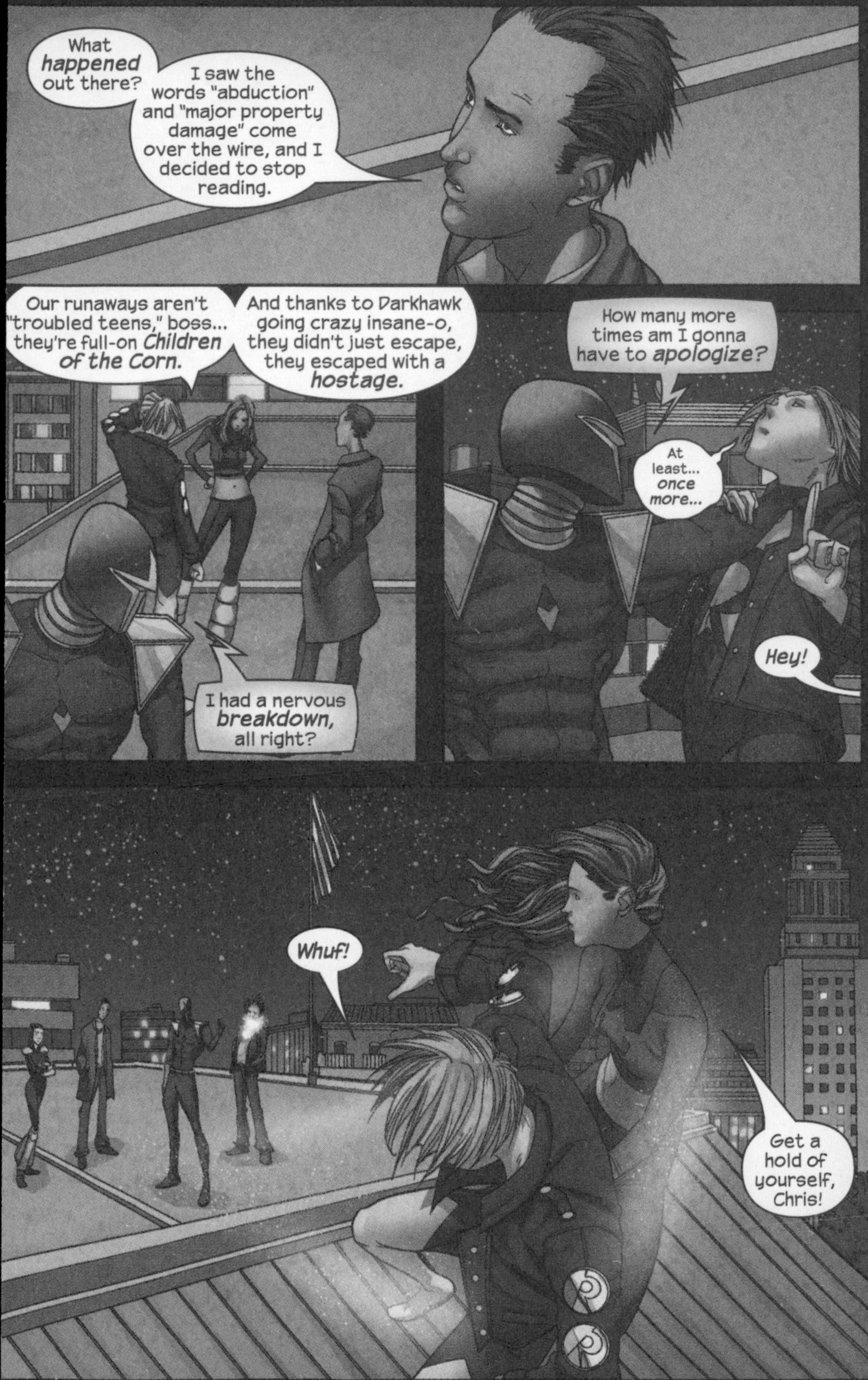
What happened out there?
I saw the words "abduction" and "major property damage" come over the wire, and I decided to stop reading.
Our runaways aren't "troubled teens," boss... they're full-on Children of the Corn.
And thanks to Darkhawk going crazy insane-o, they didn't just escape, they escaped with a hostage.
I had a nervous breakdown, all right?
How many more times am I gonna have to apologize?
At least... once more...
Hey!
Whuf!
Get a hold of yourself, Chris!

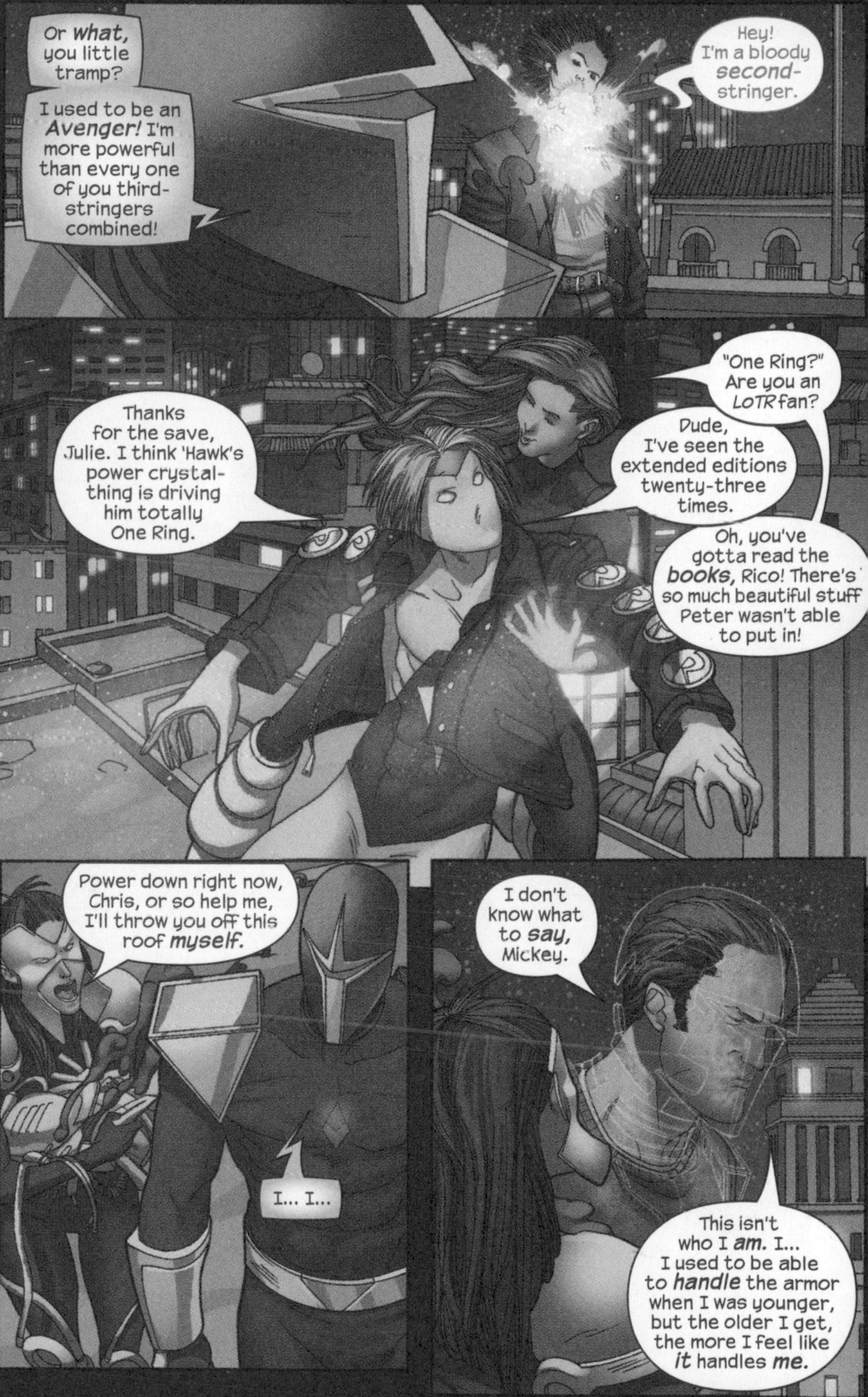

Or what, you little tramp?
I used to be an Avenger! I'm more powerful than every one of you third-stringers combined!
Hey! I'm a bloody second-stringer.
Thanks for the save, Julie. I think 'Hawk's power crystal-thing is driving him totally One Ring.
"One Ring?" Are you an LOTR fan?
Dude, I've seen the extended editions twenty-three times.
Oh, you've gotta read the books, Rico! There's so much beautiful stuff Peter wasn't able to put in!
Power down right now, Chris, or so help me, I'll throw you off this roof myself.
I... I...
I don't know what to say, Mickey.
This isn't who I am. I... I used to be able to handle the armor when I was younger, but the older I get, the more I feel like it handles me.

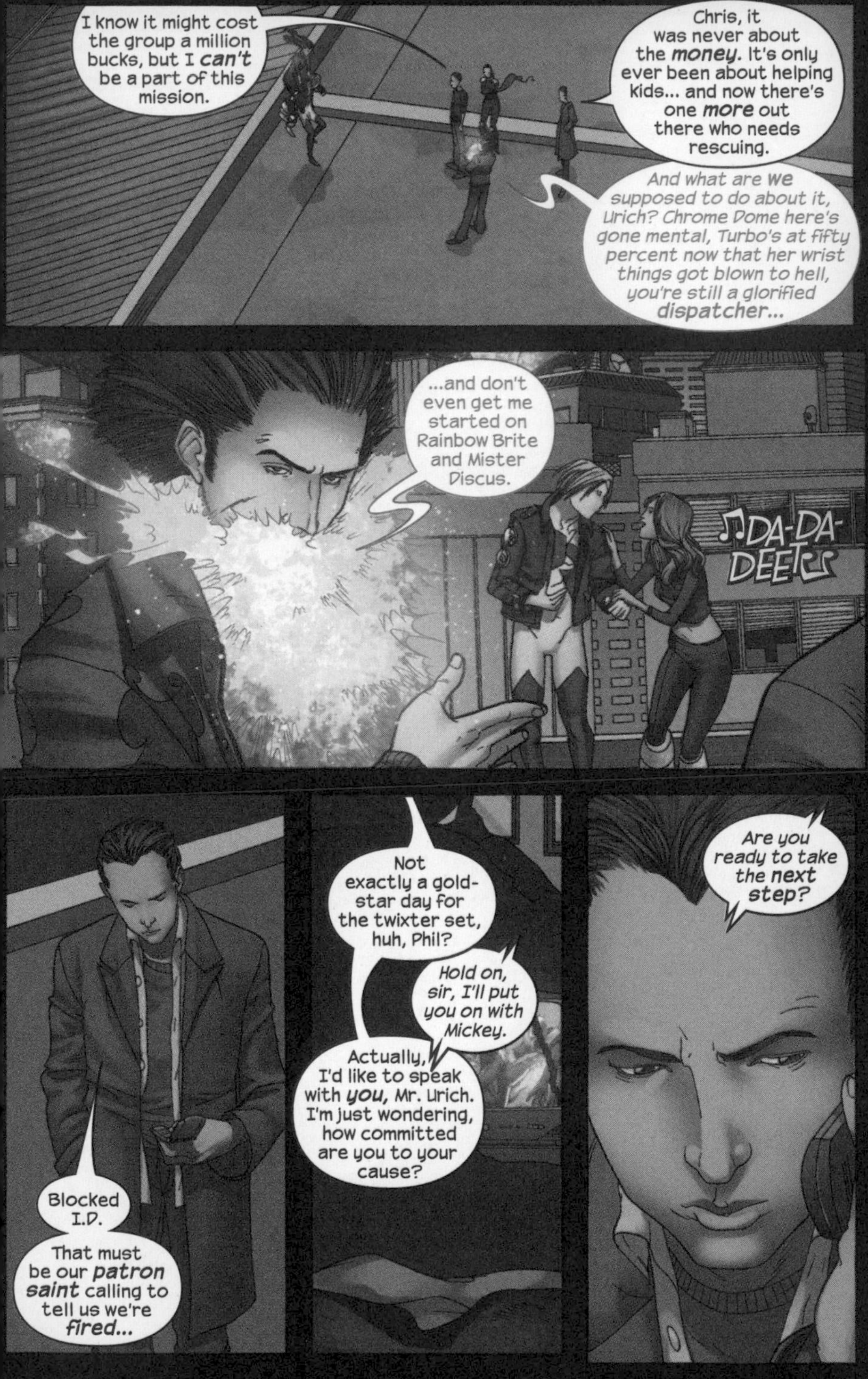
I know it might cost the group a million bucks, but I can't be a part of this mission.
Chris, it was never about the money. It's only ever been about helping kids... and now there's one more out there who needs rescuing.
And what are we supposed to do about it, Urich? Chrome Dome here's gone mental, Turbo's at fifty percent now that her wrist things got blown to hell, you're still a glorified dispatcher...
...and don't even get me started on Rainbow Brite and Mister Discus.
DA-DA-DEET
Blocked I.D.
That must be our patron saint calling to tell us we're fired...
Not exactly a gold-star day for the twixter set, huh, Phil?
Hold on, sir, I'll put you on with Mickey.
Actually, I'd like to speak with you, Mr. Urich. I'm just wondering, how committed are you to your cause?
Are you ready to take the next step?

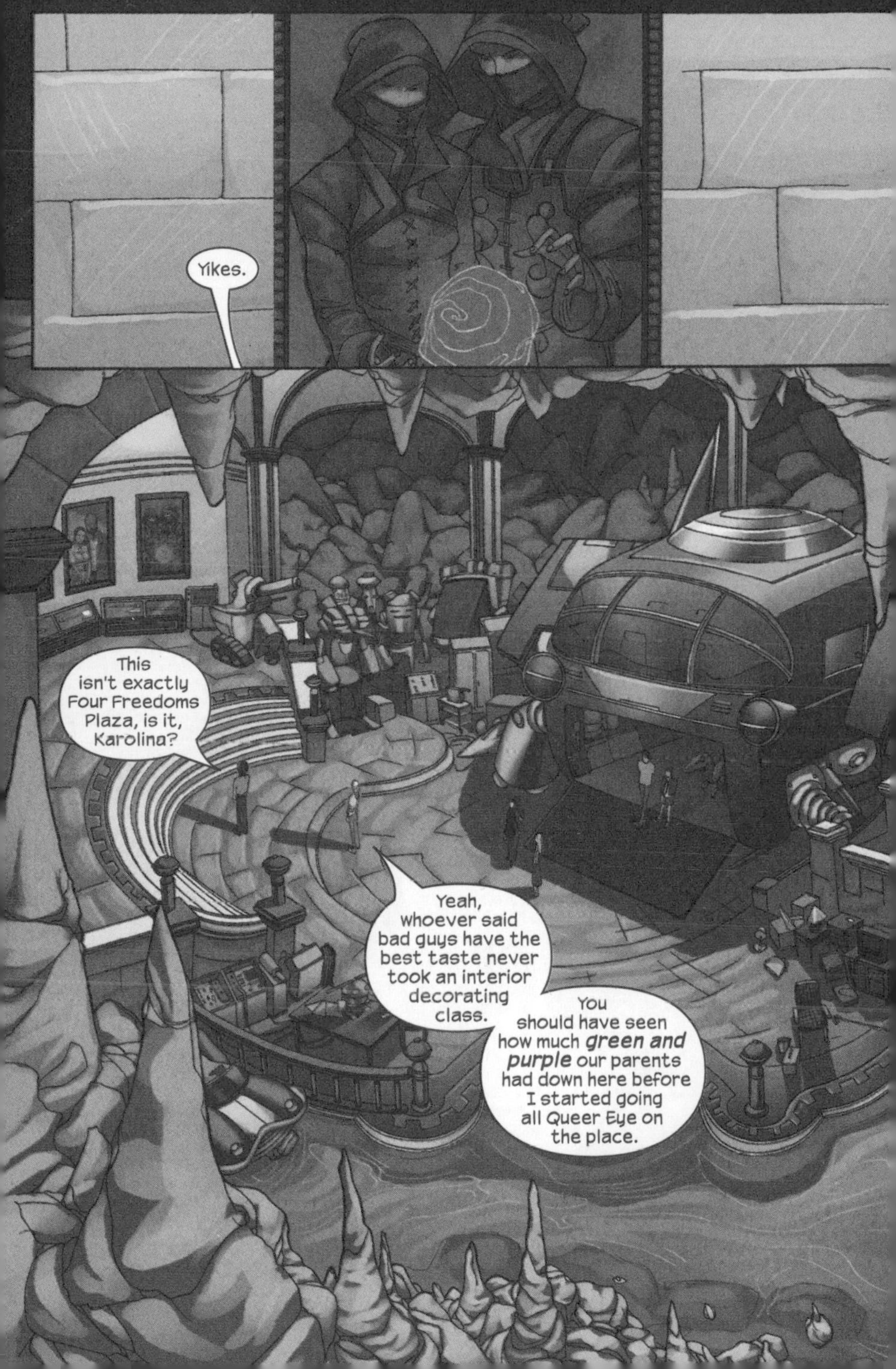
Yikes.
This isn't exactly Four Freedoms Plaza, is it, Karolina?
Yeah, whoever said bad guys have the best taste never took an interior decorating class.
You should have seen how much *green and purple* our parents had down here before I started going all Queer Eye on the place.

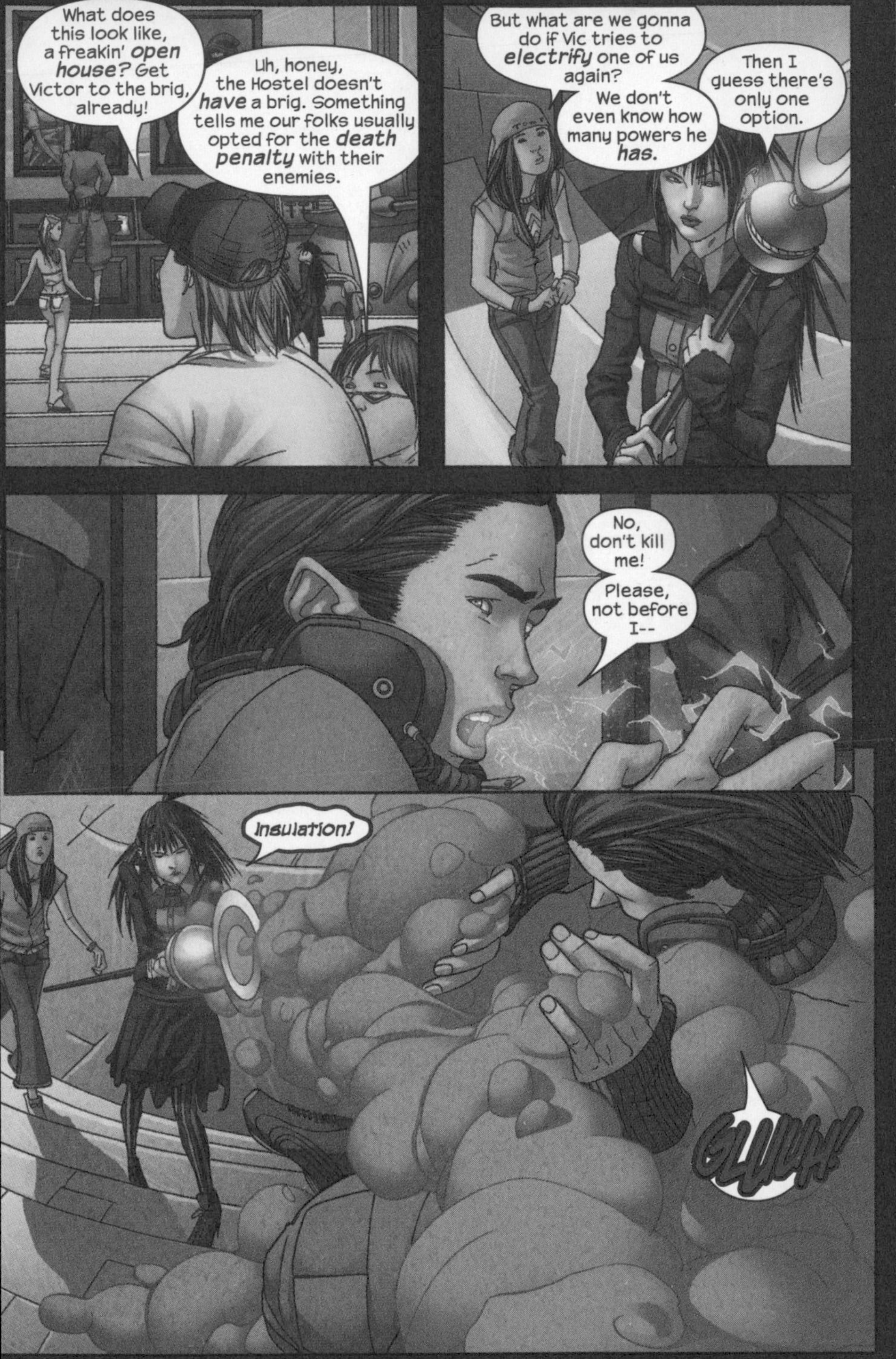
What does this look like, a freakin' open house? Get Victor to the brig, already!
Uh, honey, the Hostel doesn't have a brig. Something tells me our folks usually opted for the death penalty with their enemies.
But what are we gonna do if Vic tries to electrify one of us again?
We don't even know how many powers he has.
Then I guess there's only one option.
No, don't kill me!
Please, not before I--
Insulation!
GLULLP!

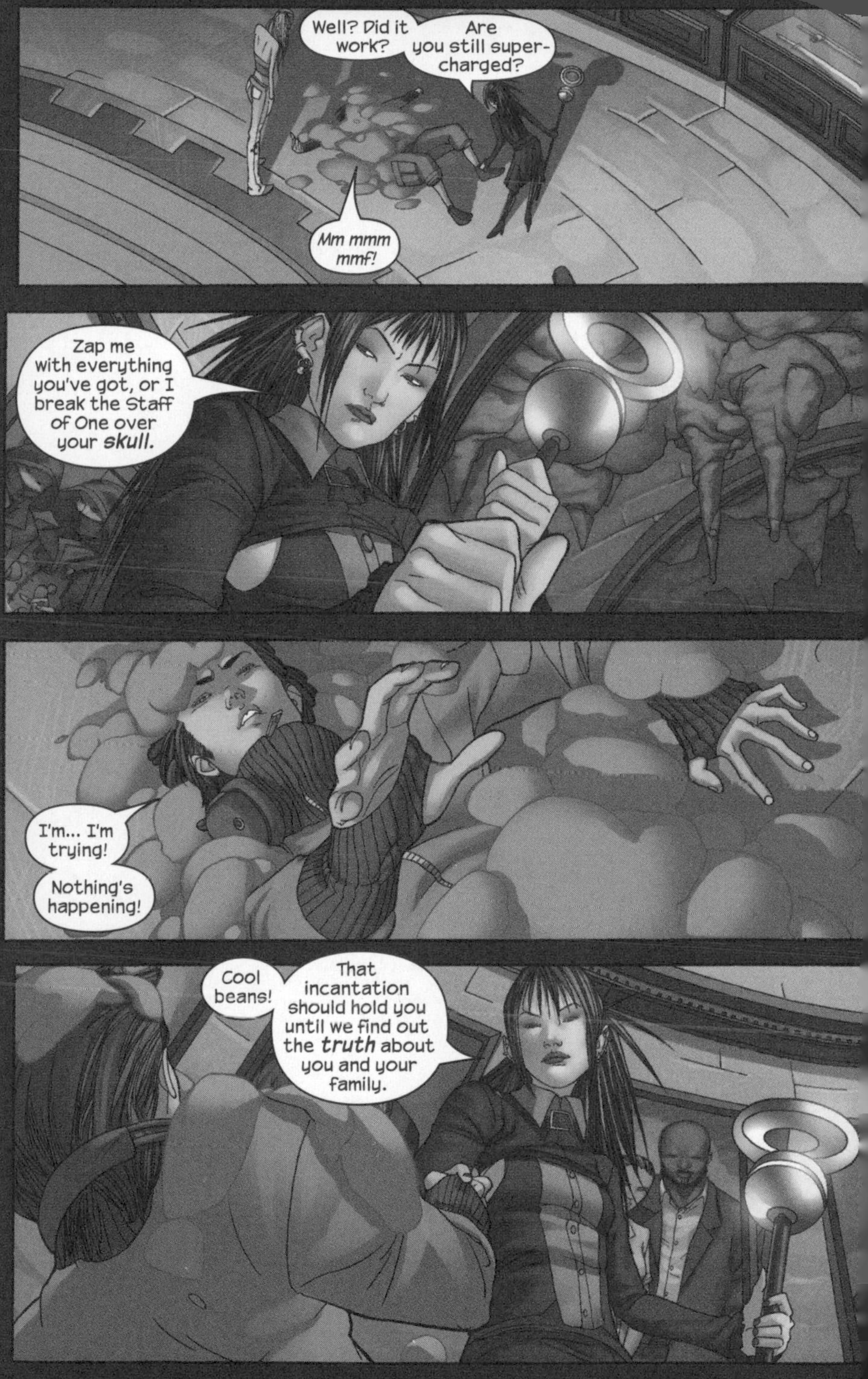
Well? Did it work?
Are you still super-charged?
Mm mmm mmf!
Zap me with everything you've got, or I break the Staff of One over your *skull.*
I'm... I'm trying!
Nothing's happening!
Cool beans!
That incantation should hold you until we find out the *truth* about you and your family.

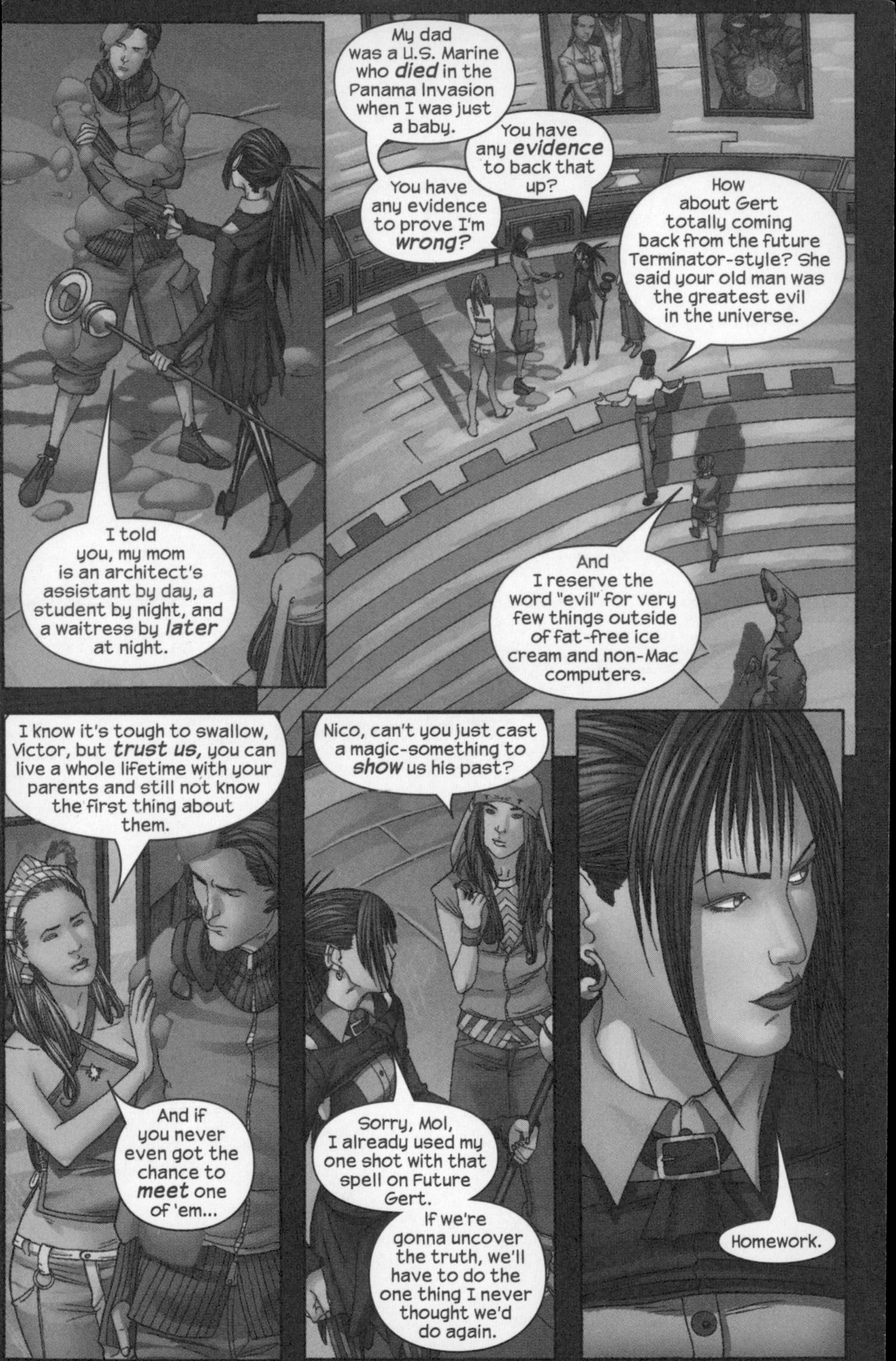
My dad was a U.S. Marine who died in the Panama Invasion when I was just a baby.
You have any evidence to back that up?
You have any evidence to prove I'm wrong?
How about Gert totally coming back from the future Terminator-style? She said your old man was the greatest evil in the universe.
I told you, my mom is an architect's assistant by day, a student by night, and a waitress by later at night.
And I reserve the word "evil" for very few things outside of fat-free ice cream and non-Mac computers.
I know it's tough to swallow, Victor, but trust us, you can live a whole lifetime with your parents and still not know the first thing about them.
And if you never even got the chance to meet one of 'em...
Nico, can't you just cast a magic-something to show us his past?
Sorry, Mol, I already used my one shot with that spell on Future Gert.
If we're gonna uncover the truth, we'll have to do the one thing I never thought we'd do again.
Homework.

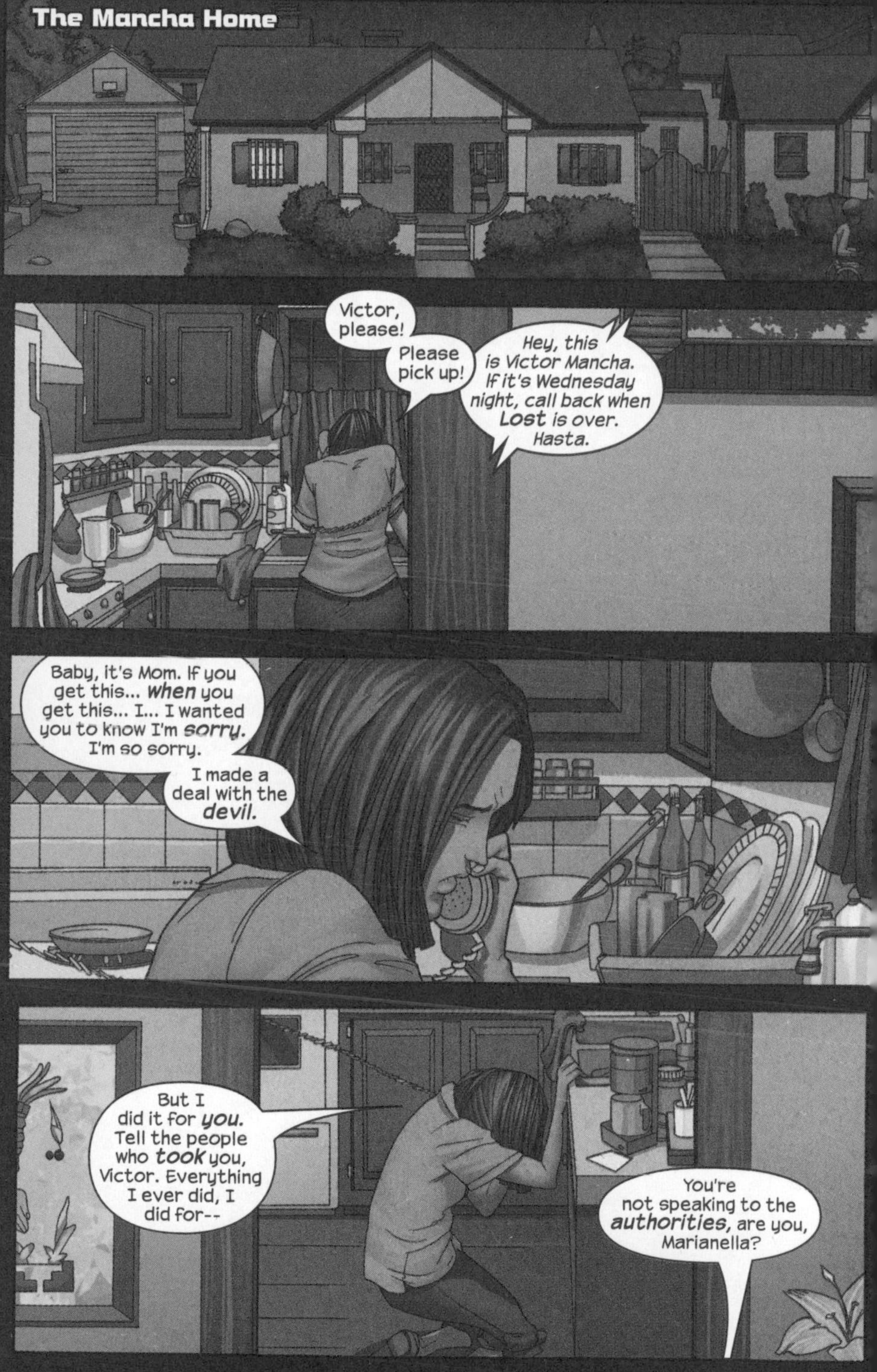

The Mancha Home
Victor, please!
Please pick up!
Hey, this is Victor Mancha. If it's Wednesday night, call back when Lost is over. Hasta.
Baby, it's Mom. If you get this... when you get this... I... I wanted you to know I'm sorry. I'm so sorry.
I made a deal with the devil.
But I did it for you. Tell the people who took you, Victor. Everything I ever did, I did for--
You're not speaking to the authorities, are you, Marianella?

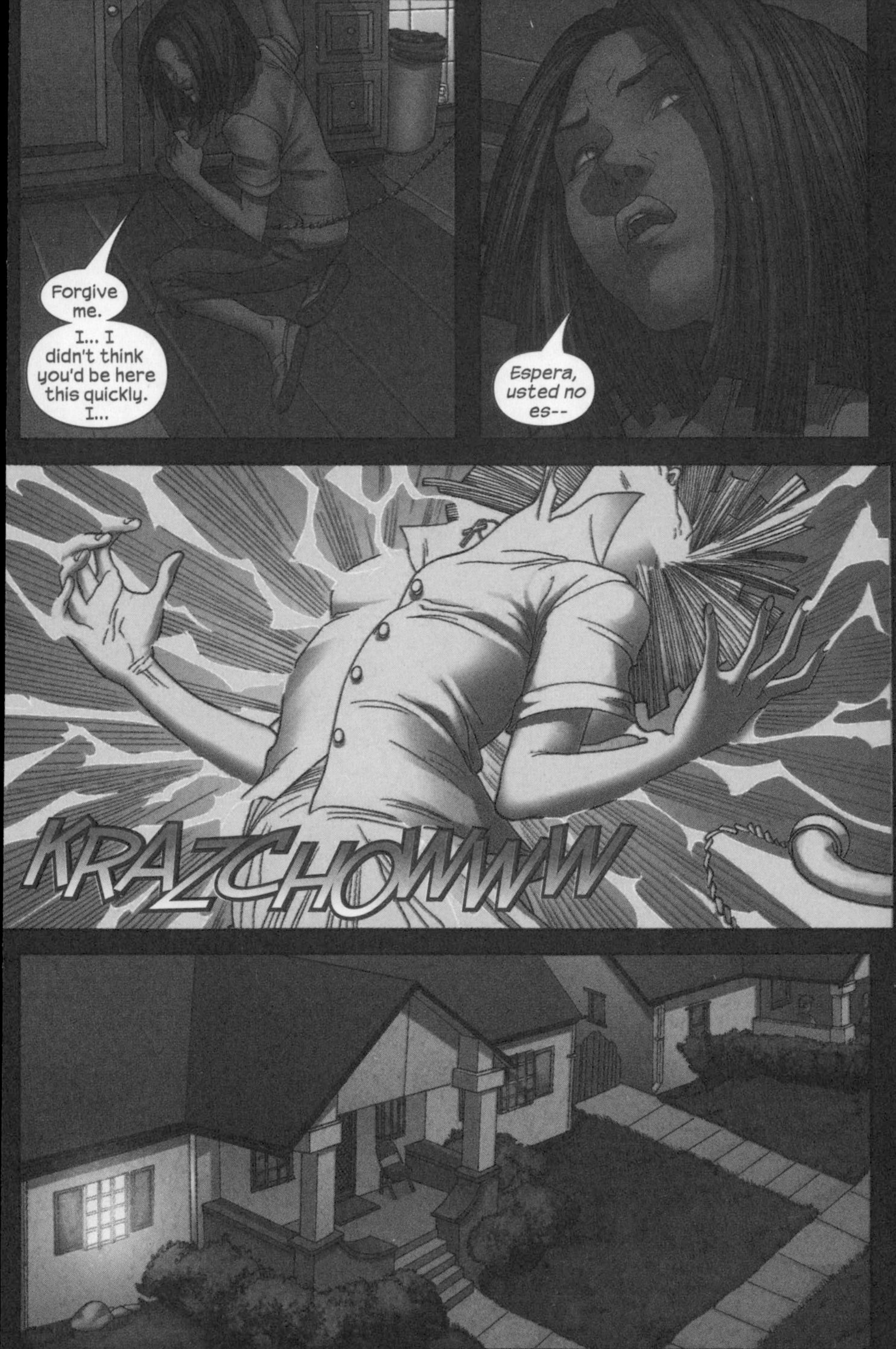
Forgive me.
I... I didn't think you'd be here this quickly. I...
Espera, usted no es--
KRAZCHOWWW

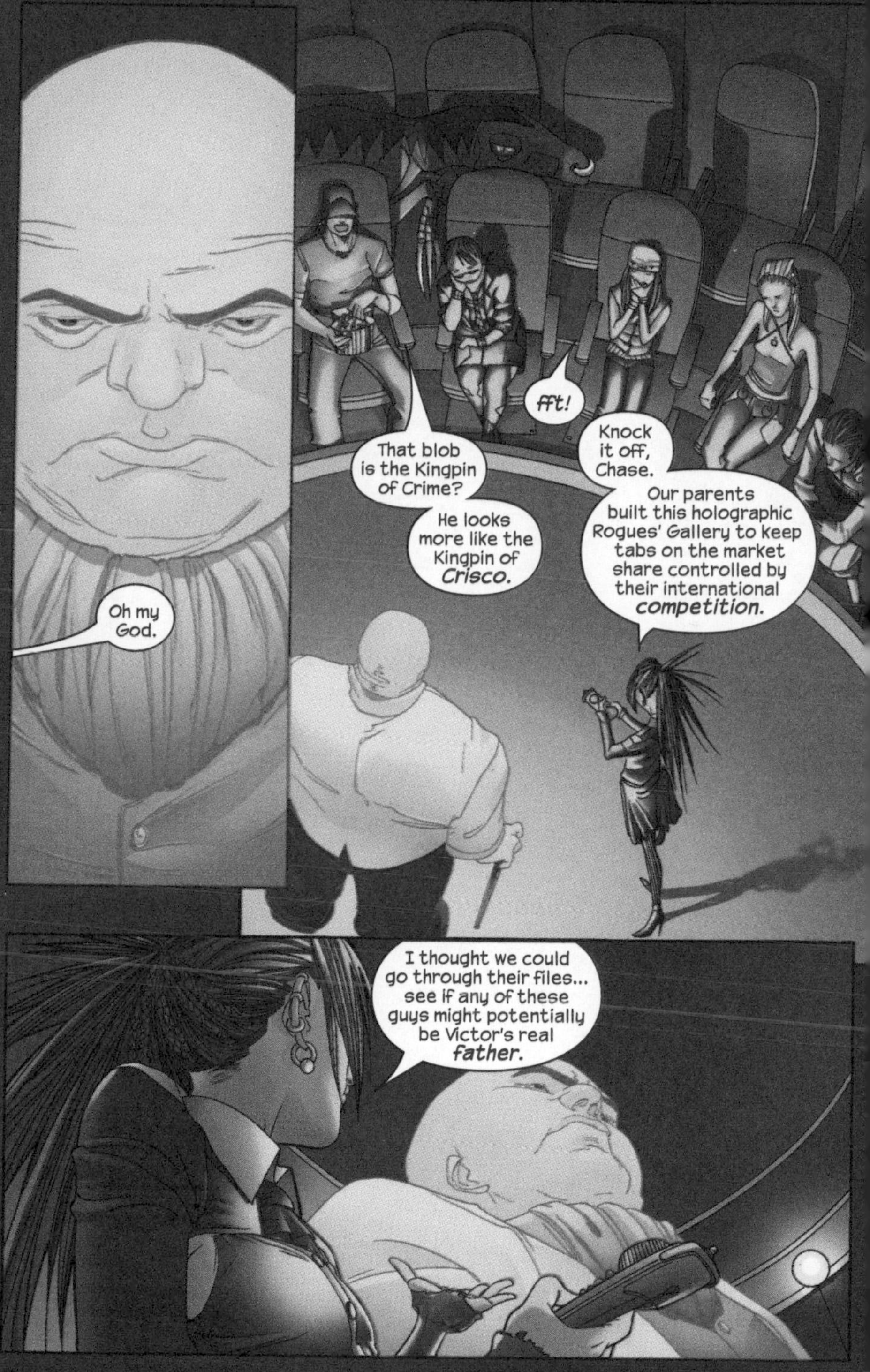
Oh my God.
That blob is the Kingpin of Crime?
He looks more like the Kingpin of *Crisco.*
fft!
Knock it off, Chase.
Our parents built this holographic Rogues' Gallery to keep tabs on the market share controlled by their international *competition.*
I thought we could go through their files... see if any of these guys might potentially be Victor's real *father.*

Wow, this is like the most surreal episode of Maury Povich ever.

No, this is *stupid!*

In the highly unlikely event that I *am* the son of Charlie Manson or whatever, he still didn't *raise* me.

Victor, even adopted kids need to know if their birth parents had a history of heart disease or... or *alcoholism.*

Knowing about your past is the only way that you can protect your *future.*

Anyway, my first suspect is this joker, *Electro.* As you can see, his extra-normal abilities obviously have a lot in common with our *guest's.*

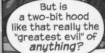

But is a two-bit hood like that really the "greatest evil" of *anything?*

Not yet, but remember, the older you came from twenty years in the future. Who knows what Electro might become between now and then?

In that case, Vic's father might not even *be* a villain yet. Maybe it's a *hero* who *flips* in the next decade or so.

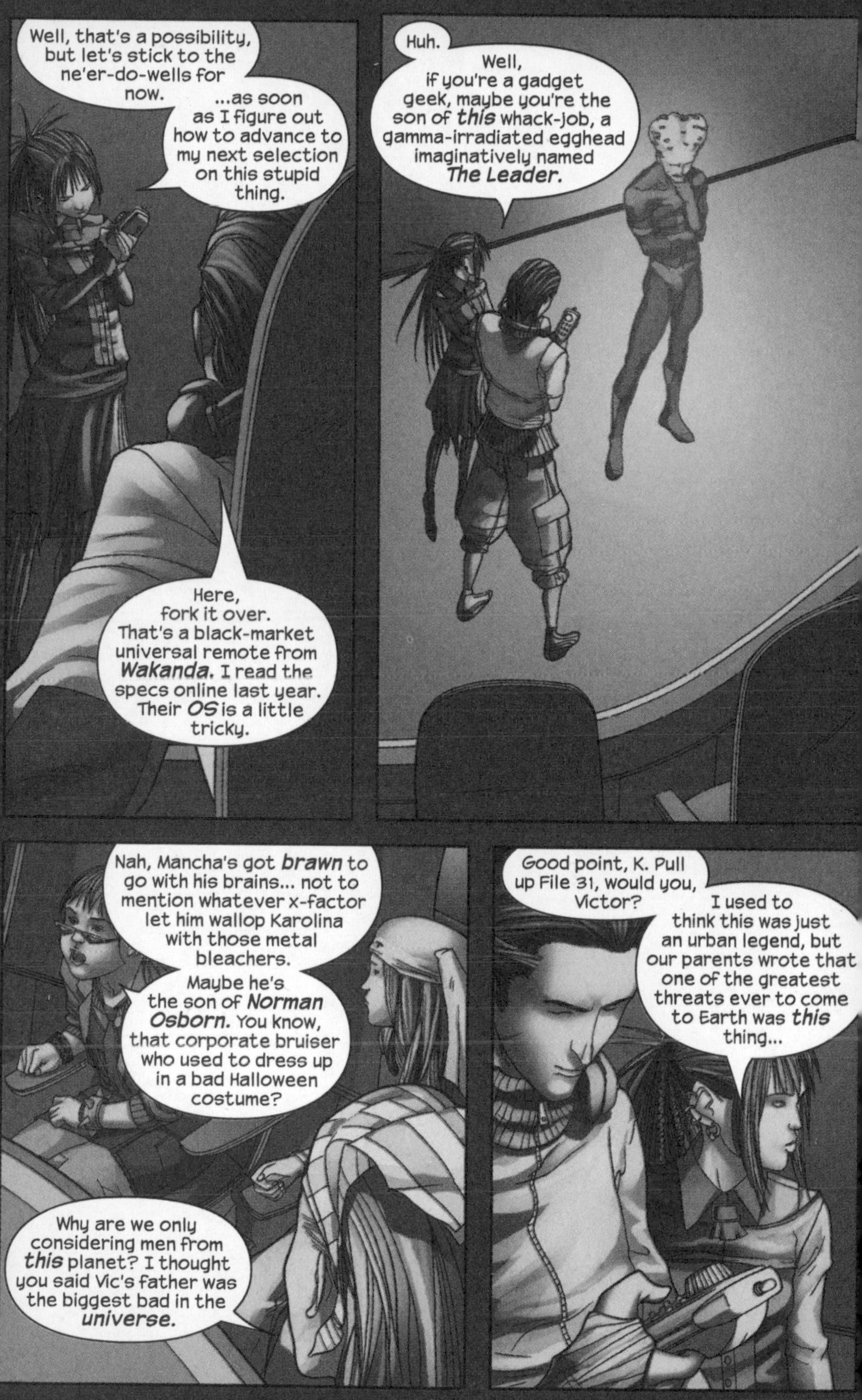
Well, that's a possibility, but let's stick to the ne'er-do-wells for now.
...as soon as I figure out how to advance to my next selection on this stupid thing.
Here, fork it over. That's a black-market universal remote from Wakanda. I read the specs online last year. Their OS is a little tricky.
Huh.
Well, if you're a gadget geek, maybe you're the son of this whack-job, a gamma-irradiated egghead imaginatively named The Leader.
Nah, Mancha's got brawn to go with his brains... not to mention whatever x-factor let him wallop Karolina with those metal bleachers.
Maybe he's the son of Norman Osborn. You know, that corporate bruiser who used to dress up in a bad Halloween costume?
Why are we only considering men from this planet? I thought you said Vic's father was the biggest bad in the universe.
Good point, K. Pull up File 31, would you, Victor?
I used to think this was just an urban legend, but our parents wrote that one of the greatest threats ever to come to Earth was this thing...

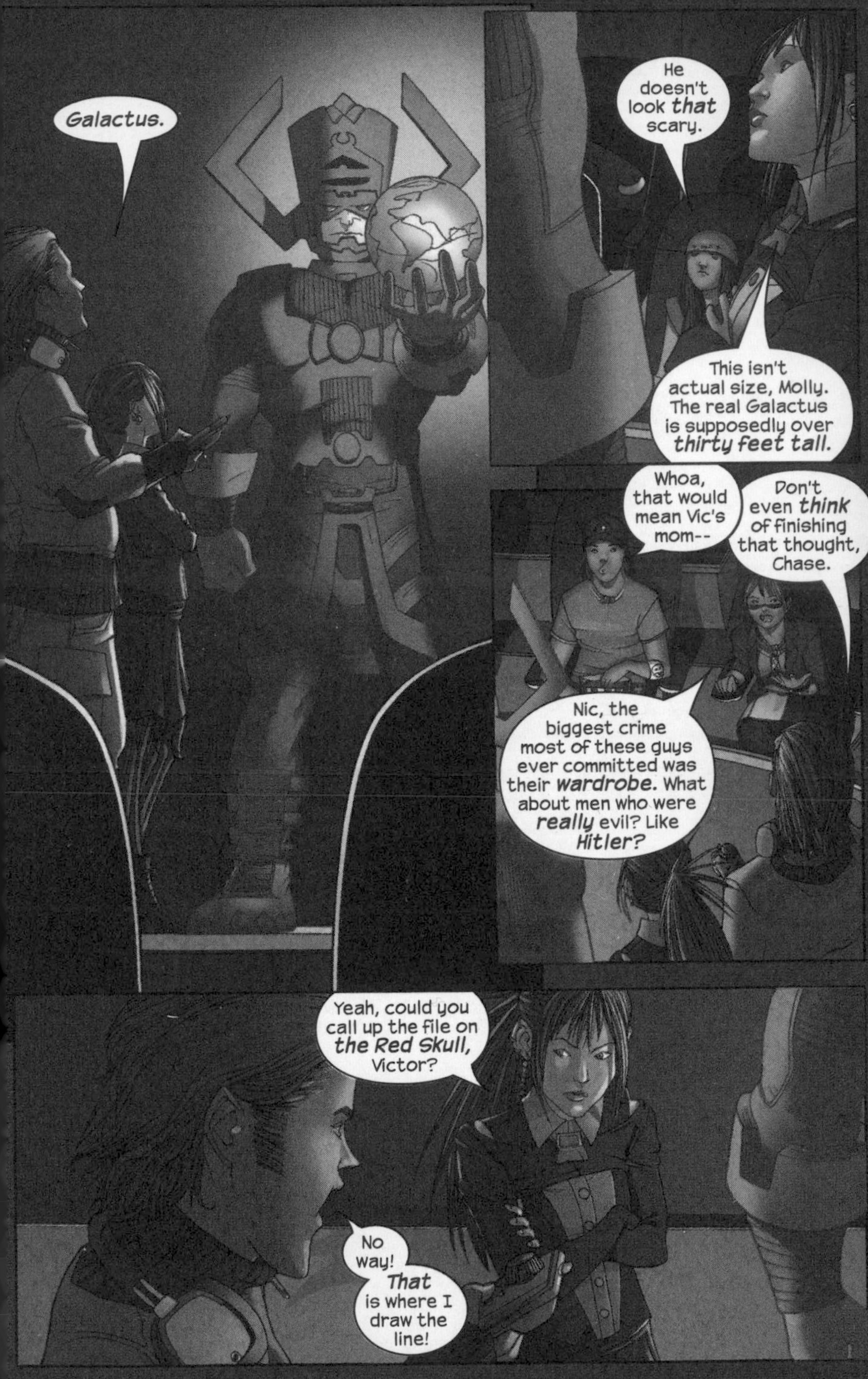
Galactus.
He doesn't look that scary.
This isn't actual size, Molly. The real Galactus is supposedly over thirty feet tall.
Whoa, that would mean Vic's mom--
Don't even think of finishing that thought, Chase.
Nic, the biggest crime most of these guys ever committed was their wardrobe. What about men who were really evil? Like Hitler?
Yeah, could you call up the file on the Red Skull, Victor?
No way! That is where I draw the line!

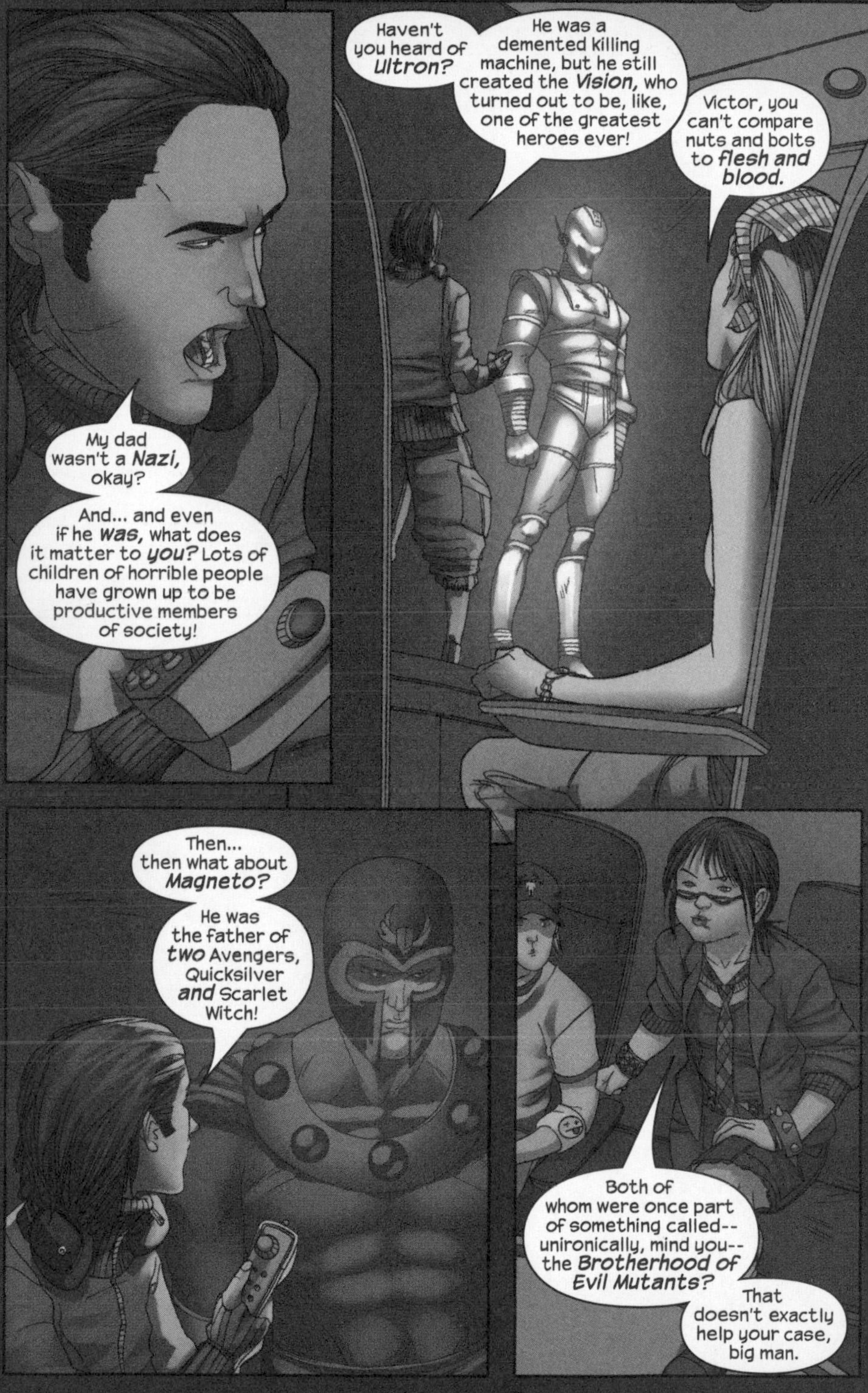

My dad wasn't a Nazi, okay?
And... and even if he was, what does it matter to you? Lots of children of horrible people have grown up to be productive members of society!
Haven't you heard of Ultron?
He was a demented killing machine, but he still created the Vision, who turned out to be, like, one of the greatest heroes ever!
Victor, you can't compare nuts and bolts to flesh and blood.
Then... then what about Magneto?
He was the father of two Avengers, Quicksilver and Scarlet Witch!
Both of whom were once part of something called--unironically, mind you--the Brotherhood of Evil Mutants?
That doesn't exactly help your case, big man.

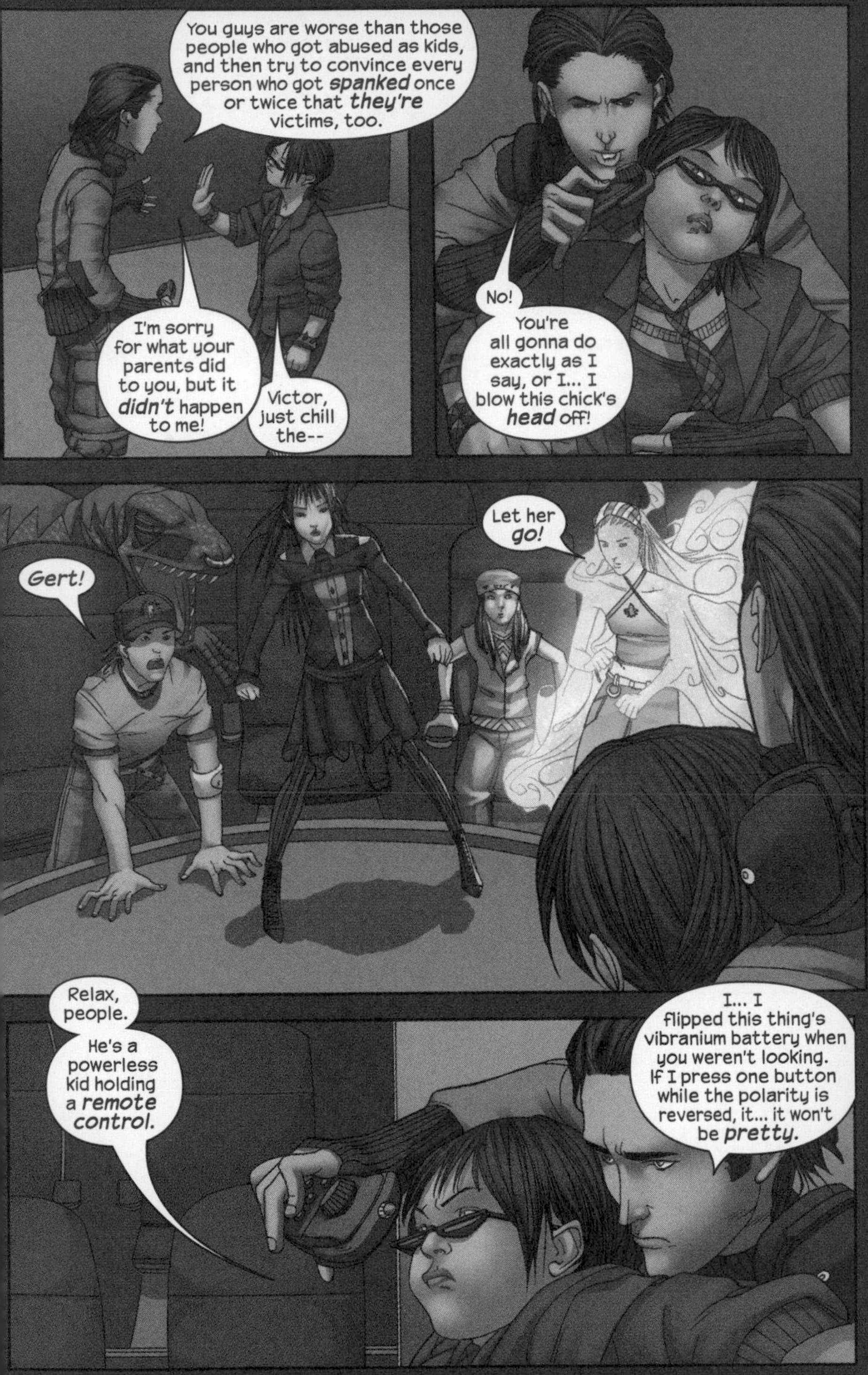
You guys are worse than those people who got abused as kids, and then try to convince every person who got *spanked* once or twice that *they're* victims, too.
I'm sorry for what your parents did to you, but it *didn't* happen to me!
Victor, just chill the--
No!
You're all gonna do exactly as I say, or I... I blow this chick's *head* off!
Gert!
Let her *go!*
Relax, people.
He's a powerless kid holding a *remote control*.
I... I flipped this thing's vibranium battery when you weren't looking. If I press one button while the polarity is reversed, it... it won't be *pretty*.

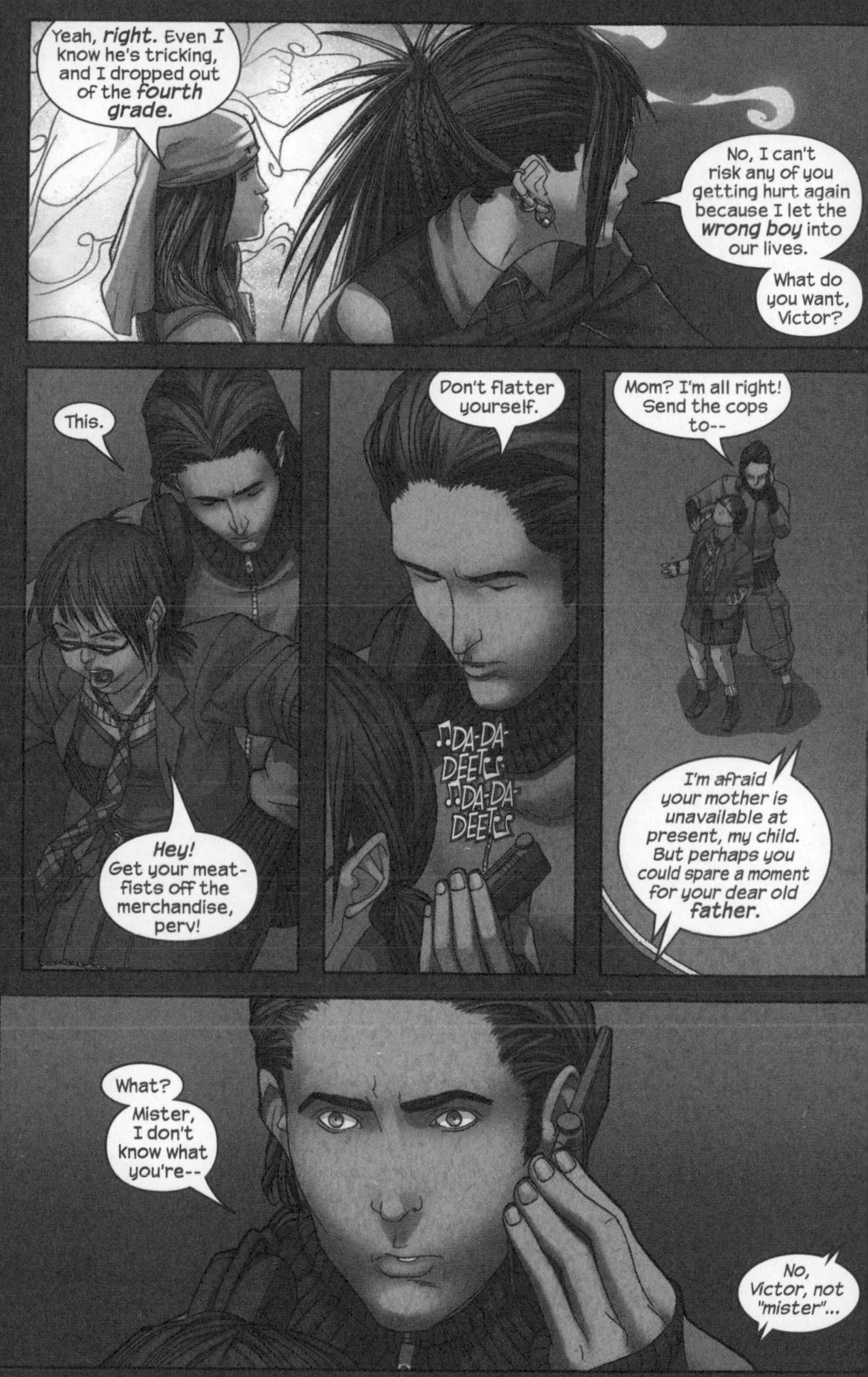
Yeah, right. Even I know he's tricking, and I dropped out of the fourth grade.
No, I can't risk any of you getting hurt again because I let the wrong boy into our lives.
What do you want, Victor?
This.
Hey! Get your meat-fists off the merchandise, perv!
Don't flatter yourself.
DA-DA-DEET DA-DA-DEET
Mom? I'm all right! Send the cops to--
I'm afraid your mother is unavailable at present, my child. But perhaps you could spare a moment for your dear old father.
What?
Mister, I don't know what you're--
No, Victor, not "mister"...

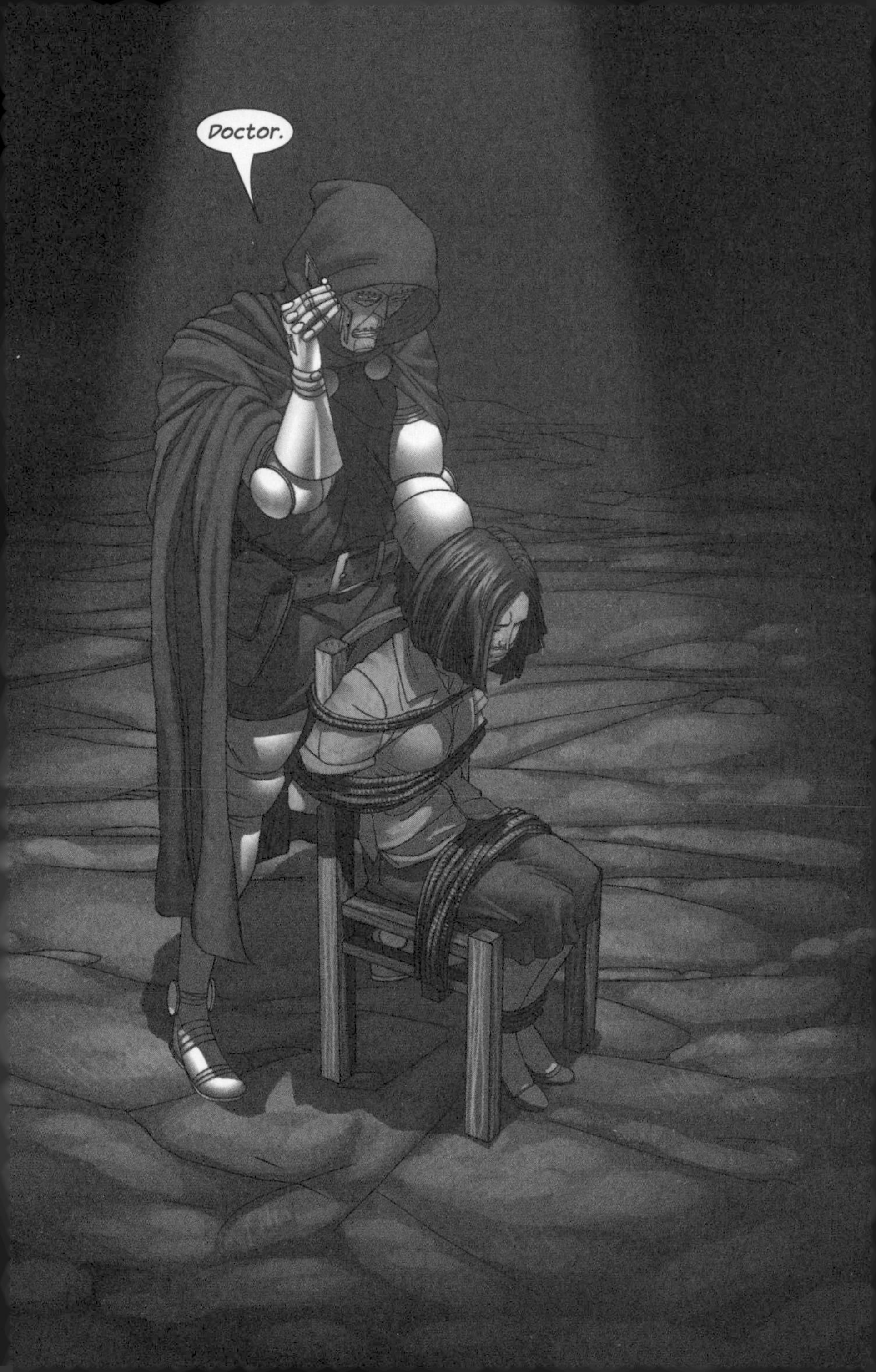
Doctor.

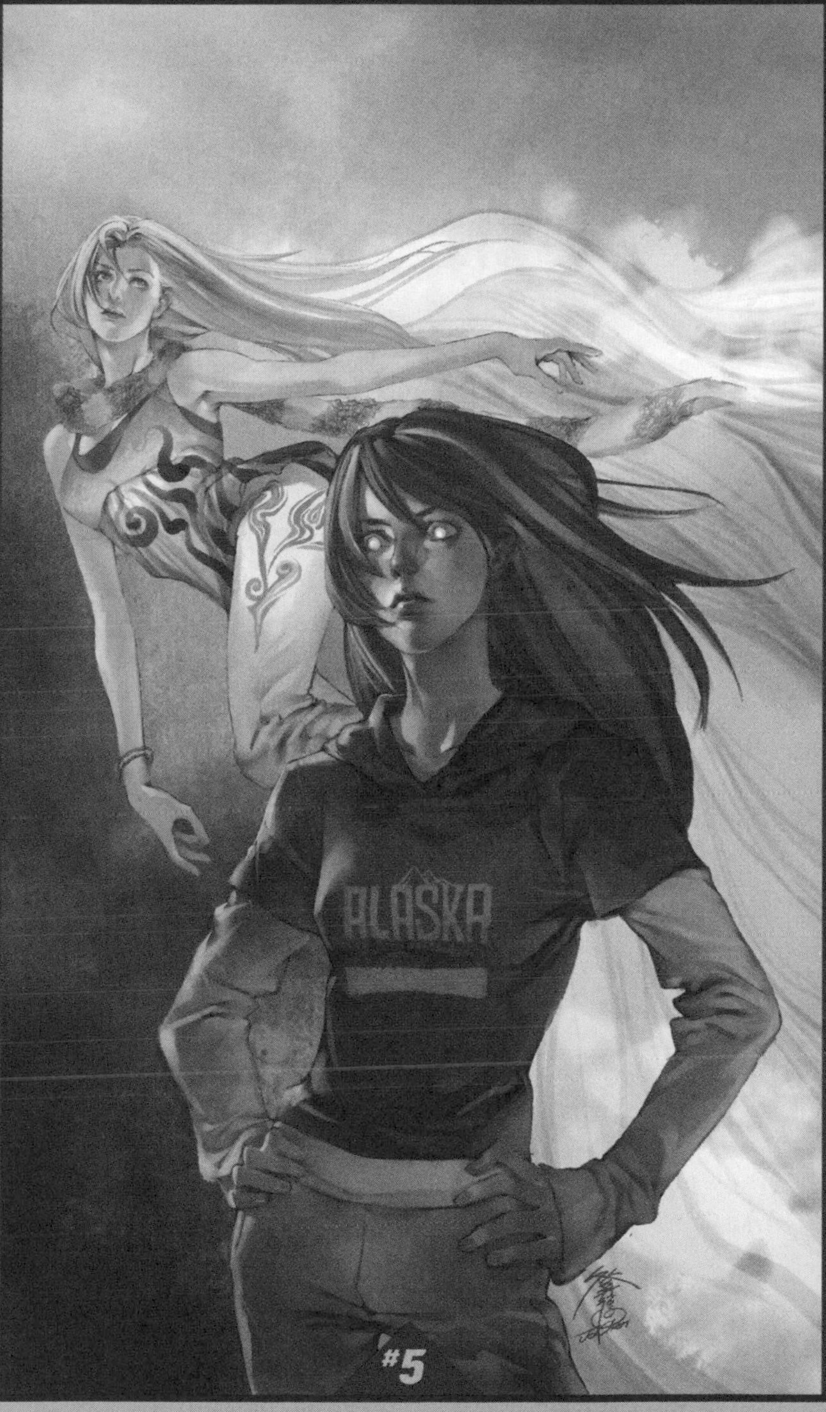
ALASKA
#5

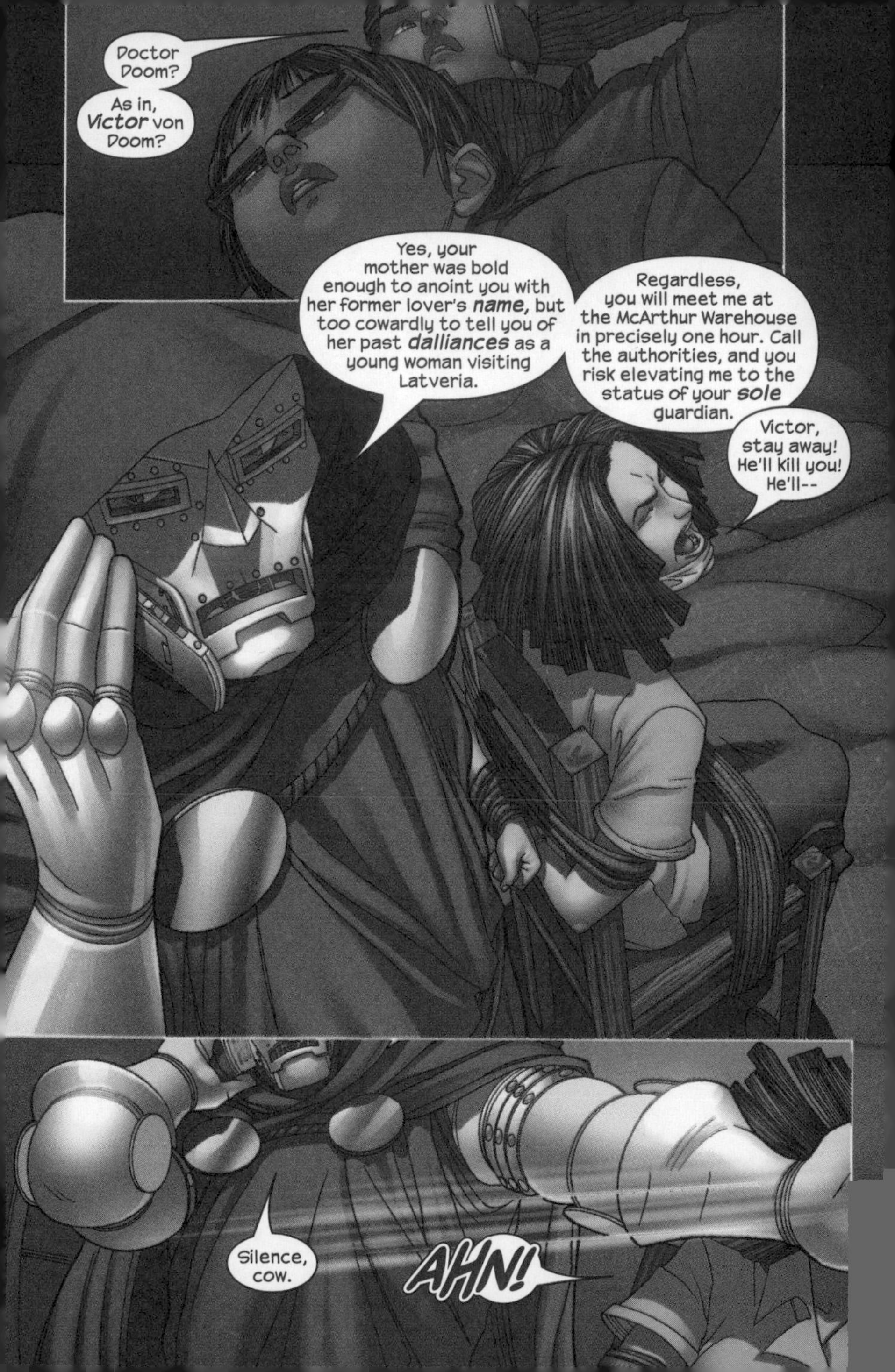
Doctor Doom?
As in, Victor von Doom?
Yes, your mother was bold enough to anoint you with her former lover's name, but too cowardly to tell you of her past dalliances as a young woman visiting Latveria.
Regardless, you will meet me at the McArthur Warehouse in precisely one hour. Call the authorities, and you risk elevating me to the status of your sole guardian.
Victor, stay away! He'll kill you! He'll--
Silence, cow.
AHN!

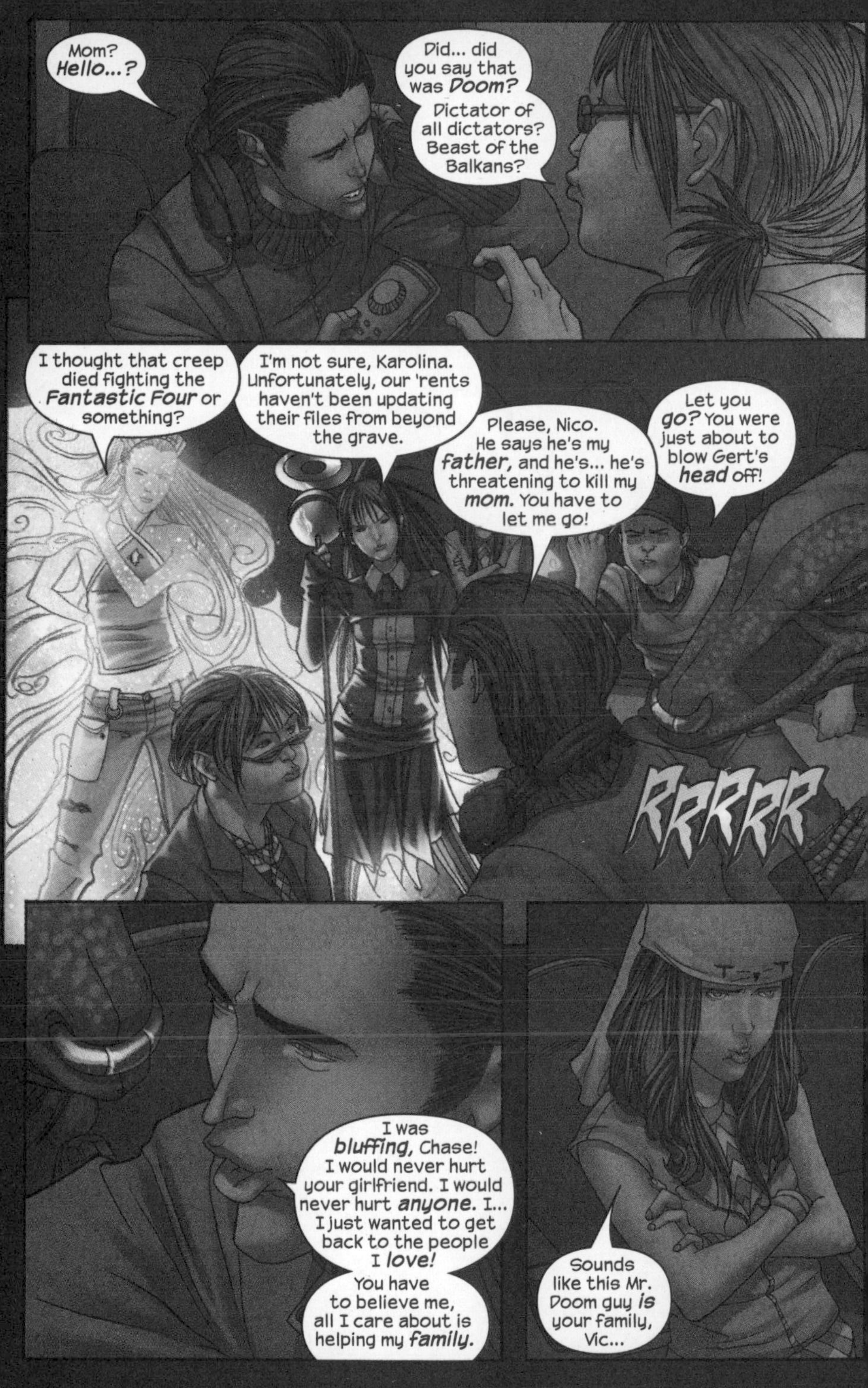

Mom? Hello...?
Did... did you say that was Doom?
Dictator of all dictators? Beast of the Balkans?
I thought that creep died fighting the Fantastic Four or something?
I'm not sure, Karolina. Unfortunately, our 'rents haven't been updating their files from beyond the grave.
Please, Nico. He says he's my father, and he's... he's threatening to kill my mom. You have to let me go!
Let you go? You were just about to blow Gert's head off!
RRRRR
I was bluffing, Chase! I would never hurt your girlfriend. I would never hurt anyone. I... I just wanted to get back to the people I love!
You have to believe me, all I care about is helping my family.
Sounds like this Mr. Doom guy is your family, Vic...

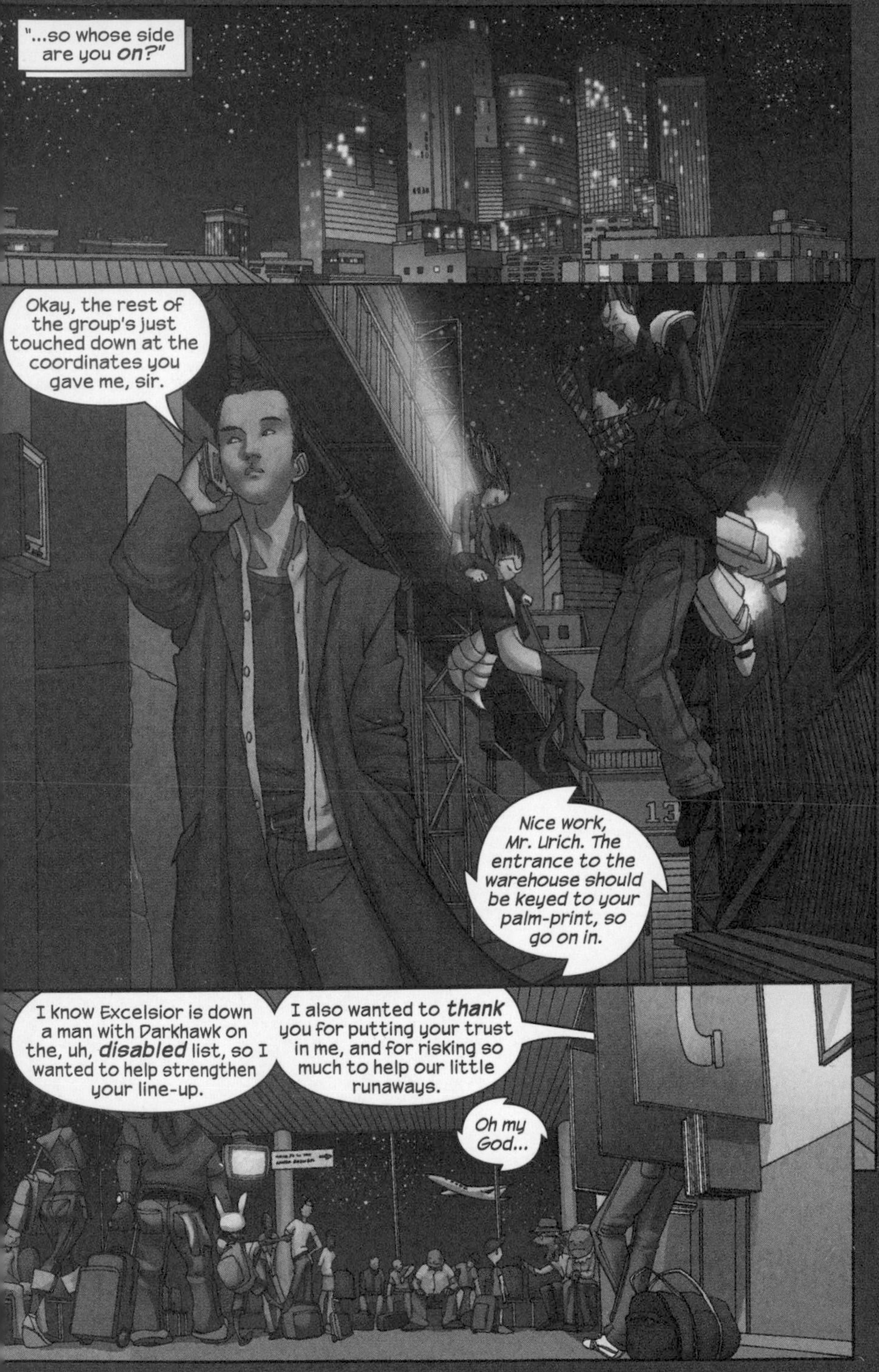
"...so whose side are you *on?*"
Okay, the rest of the group's just touched down at the coordinates you gave me, sir.
Nice work, Mr. Urich. The entrance to the warehouse should be keyed to your palm-print, so go on in.
13
I know Excelsior is down a man with Darkhawk on the, uh, *disabled* list, so I wanted to help strengthen your line-up.
I also wanted to *thank* you for putting your trust in me, and for risking so much to help our little runaways.
Oh my God...

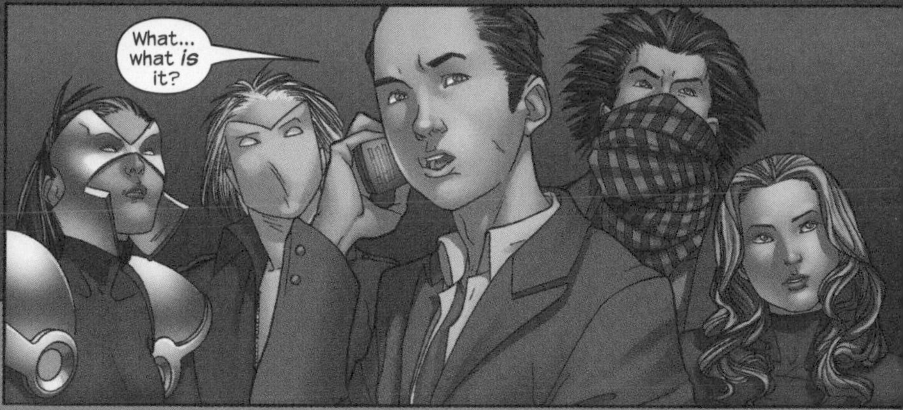
What... what *is* it?

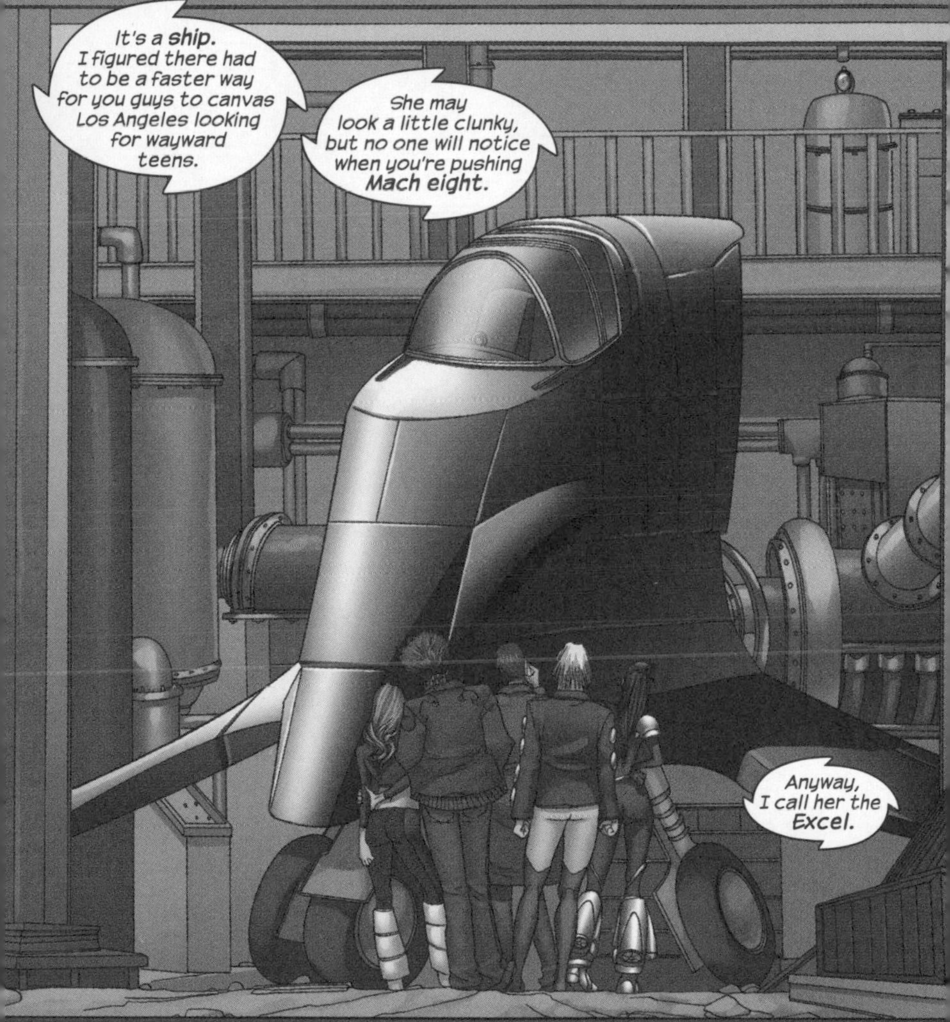
It's a **ship.** I figured there had to be a faster way for you guys to canvas Los Angeles looking for wayward teens.
She may look a little clunky, but no one will notice when you're pushing **Mach eight.**
Anyway, I call her the **Excel.**

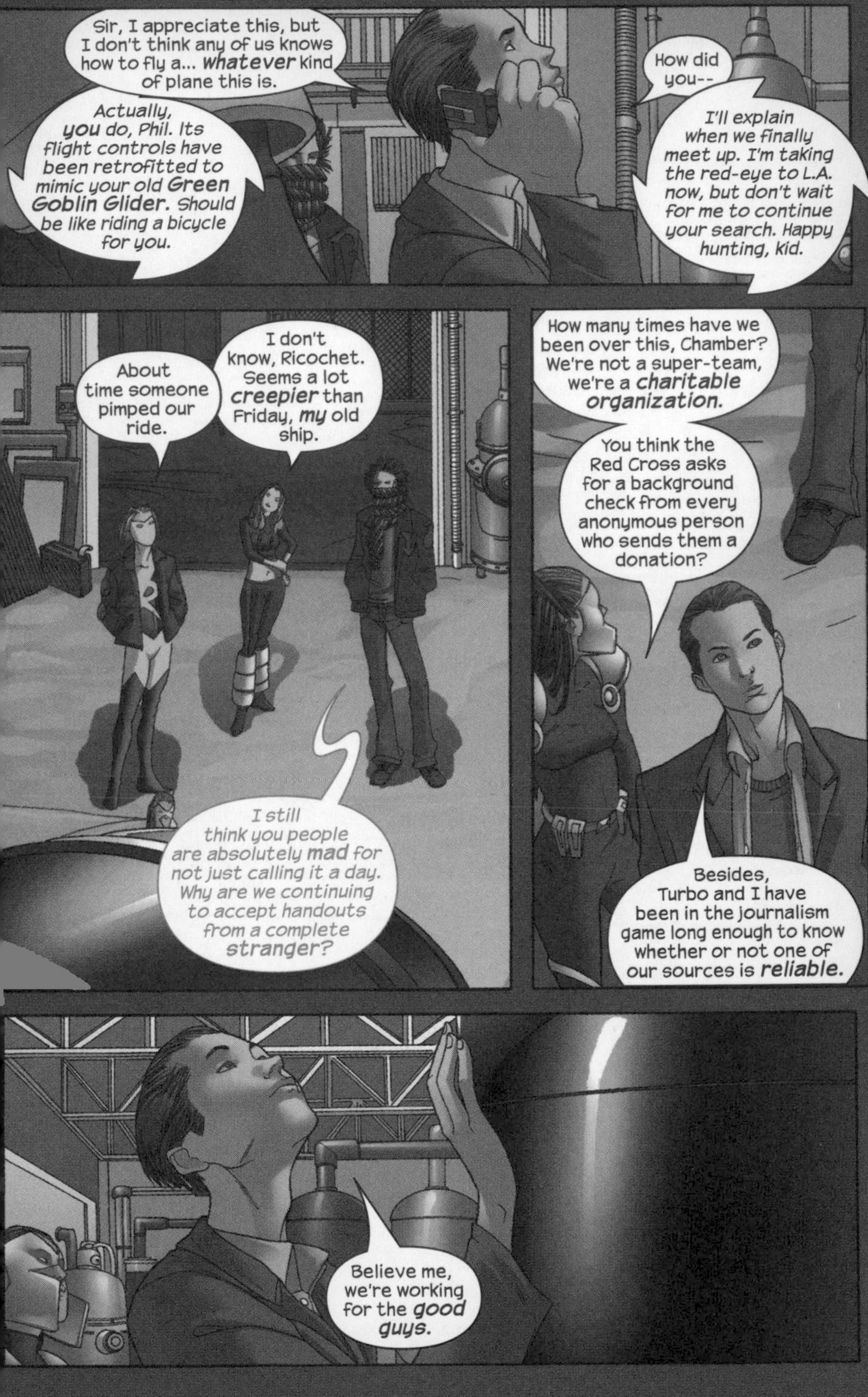
Sir, I appreciate this, but I don't think any of us knows how to fly a... whatever kind of plane this is.
Actually, you do, Phil. Its flight controls have been retrofitted to mimic your old Green Goblin Glider. Should be like riding a bicycle for you.
How did you--
I'll explain when we finally meet up. I'm taking the red-eye to L.A. now, but don't wait for me to continue your search. Happy hunting, kid.
About time someone pimped our ride.
I don't know, Ricochet. Seems a lot creepier than Friday, my old ship.
I still think you people are absolutely mad for not just calling it a day. Why are we continuing to accept handouts from a complete stranger?
How many times have we been over this, Chamber? We're not a super-team, we're a charitable organization.
You think the Red Cross asks for a background check from every anonymous person who sends them a donation?
Besides, Turbo and I have been in the journalism game long enough to know whether or not one of our sources is reliable.
Believe me, we're working for the good guys.

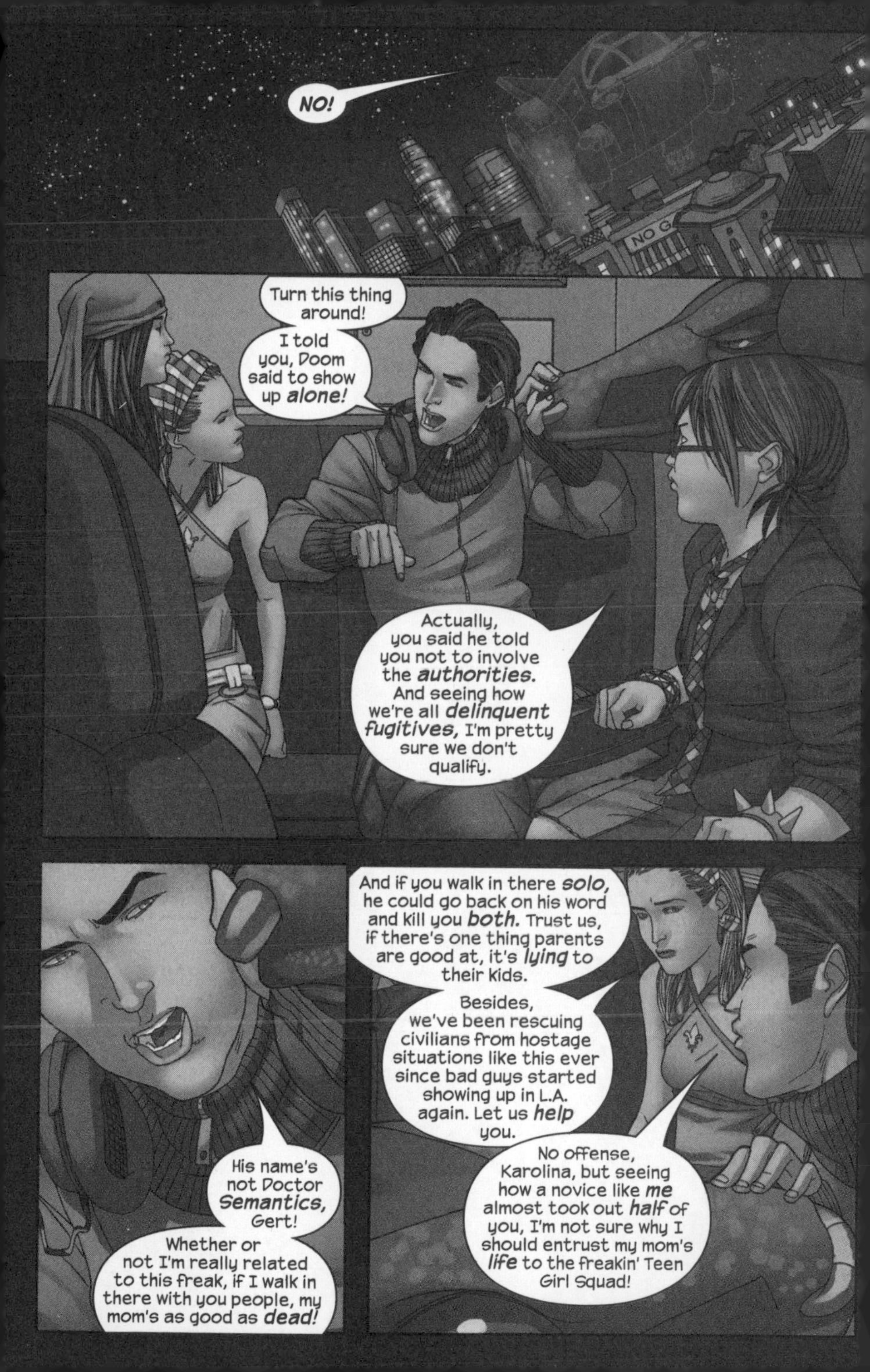
NO!
NO G
Turn this thing around!
I told you, Doom said to show up alone!
Actually, you said he told you not to involve the authorities. And seeing how we're all delinquent fugitives, I'm pretty sure we don't qualify.
His name's not Doctor Semantics, Gert!
Whether or not I'm really related to this freak, if I walk in there with you people, my mom's as good as dead!
And if you walk in there solo, he could go back on his word and kill you both. Trust us, if there's one thing parents are good at, it's lying to their kids.
Besides, we've been rescuing civilians from hostage situations like this ever since bad guys started showing up in L.A. again. Let us help you.
No offense, Karolina, but seeing how a novice like me almost took out half of you, I'm not sure why I should entrust my mom's life to the freakin' Teen Girl Squad!

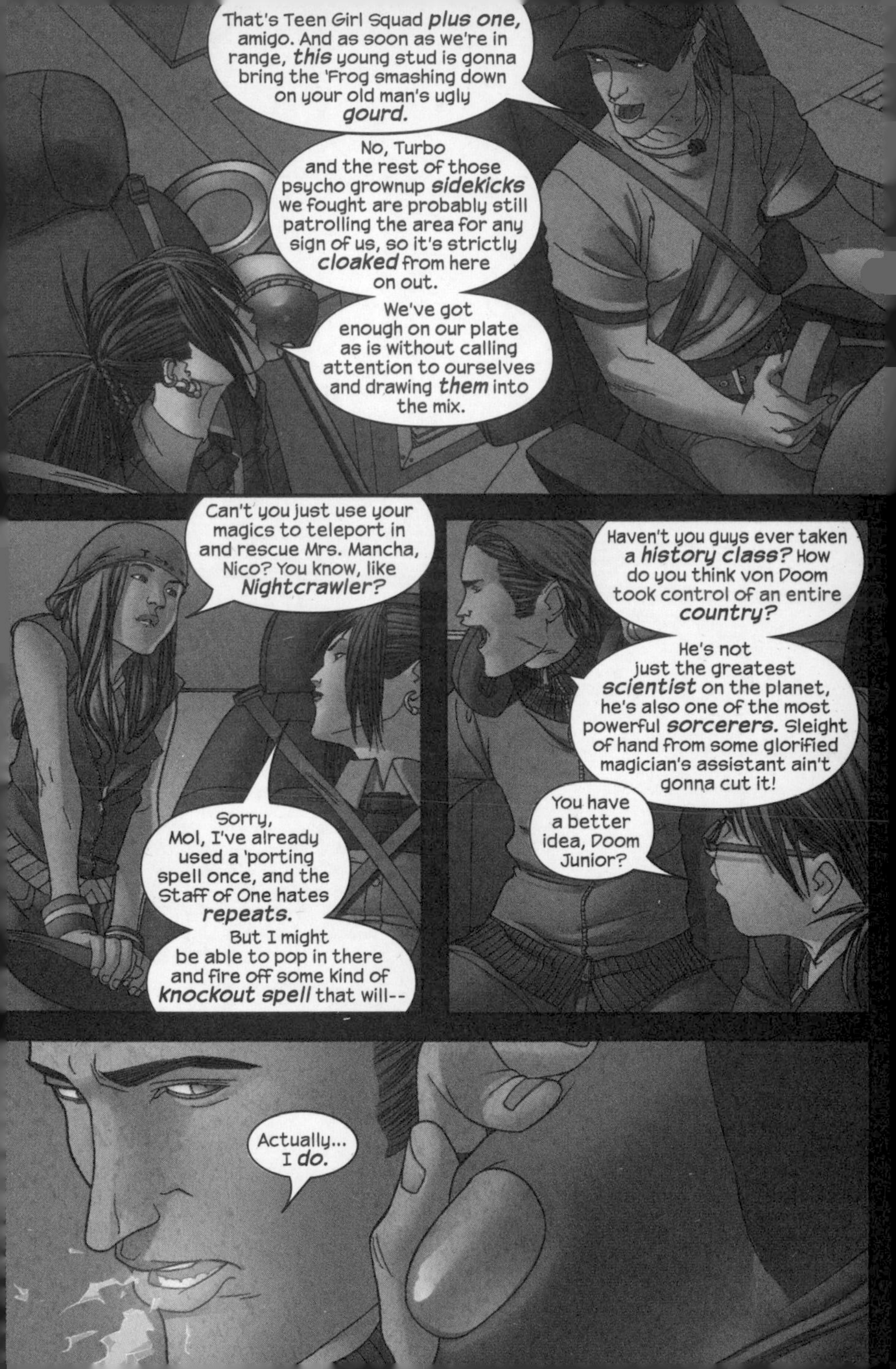
That's Teen Girl Squad plus one, amigo. And as soon as we're in range, this young stud is gonna bring the 'Frog smashing down on your old man's ugly gourd.
No, Turbo and the rest of those psycho grownup sidekicks we fought are probably still patrolling the area for any sign of us, so it's strictly cloaked from here on out.
We've got enough on our plate as is without calling attention to ourselves and drawing them into the mix.
Can't you just use your magics to teleport in and rescue Mrs. Mancha, Nico? You know, like Nightcrawler?
Sorry, Mol, I've already used a 'porting spell once, and the Staff of One hates repeats.
But I might be able to pop in there and fire off some kind of knockout spell that will--
Haven't you guys ever taken a history class? How do you think von Doom took control of an entire country?
He's not just the greatest scientist on the planet, he's also one of the most powerful sorcerers. Sleight of hand from some glorified magician's assistant ain't gonna cut it!
You have a better idea, Doom Junior?
Actually... I do.

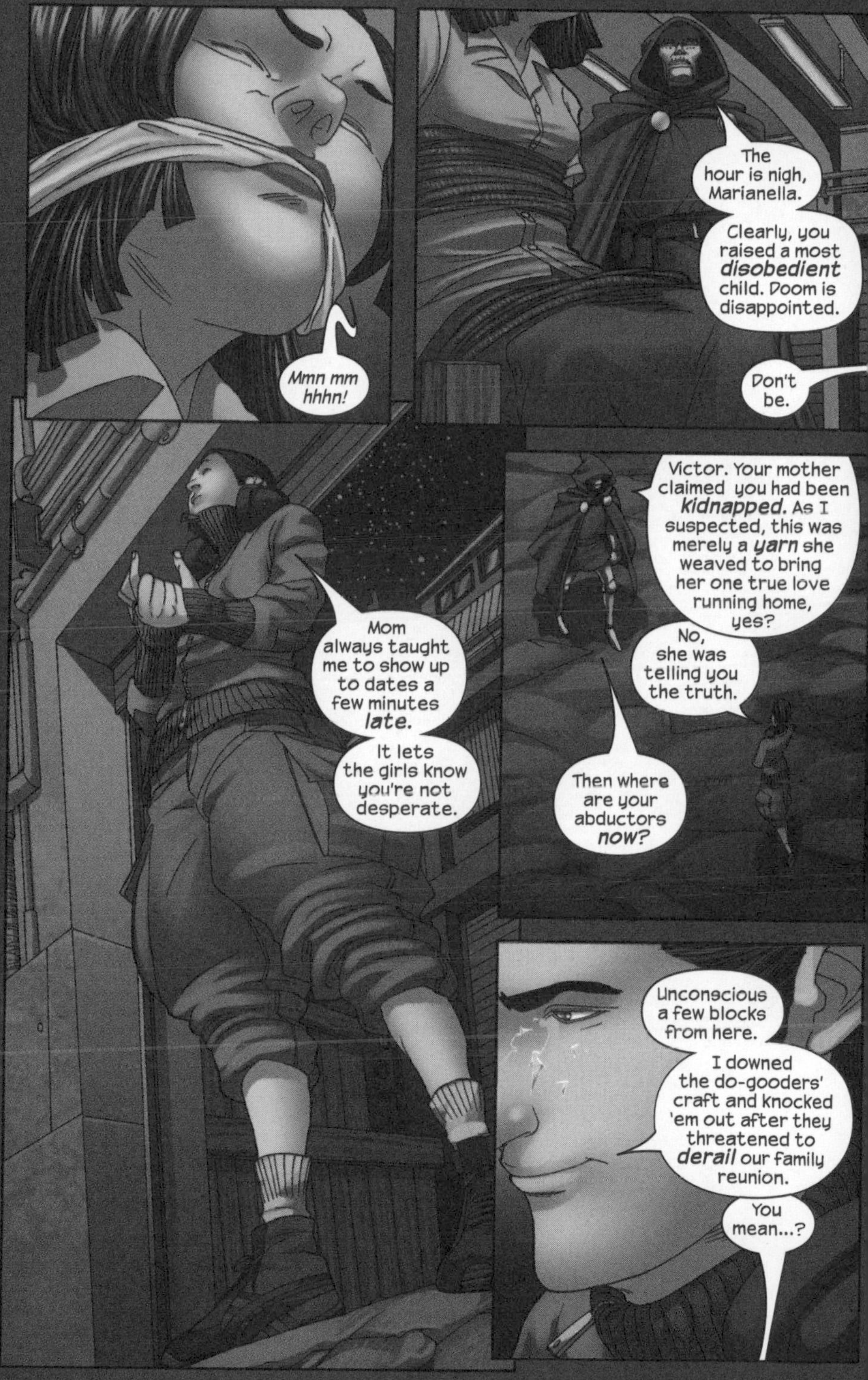
Mmn mm hhhn!
The hour is nigh, Marianella.
Clearly, you raised a most disobedient child. Doom is disappointed.
Don't be.
Mom always taught me to show up to dates a few minutes late.
It lets the girls know you're not desperate.
Victor. Your mother claimed you had been kidnapped. As I suspected, this was merely a yarn she weaved to bring her one true love running home, yes?
No, she was telling you the truth.
Then where are your abductors now?
Unconscious a few blocks from here.
I downed the do-gooders' craft and knocked 'em out after they threatened to derail our family reunion.
You mean...?

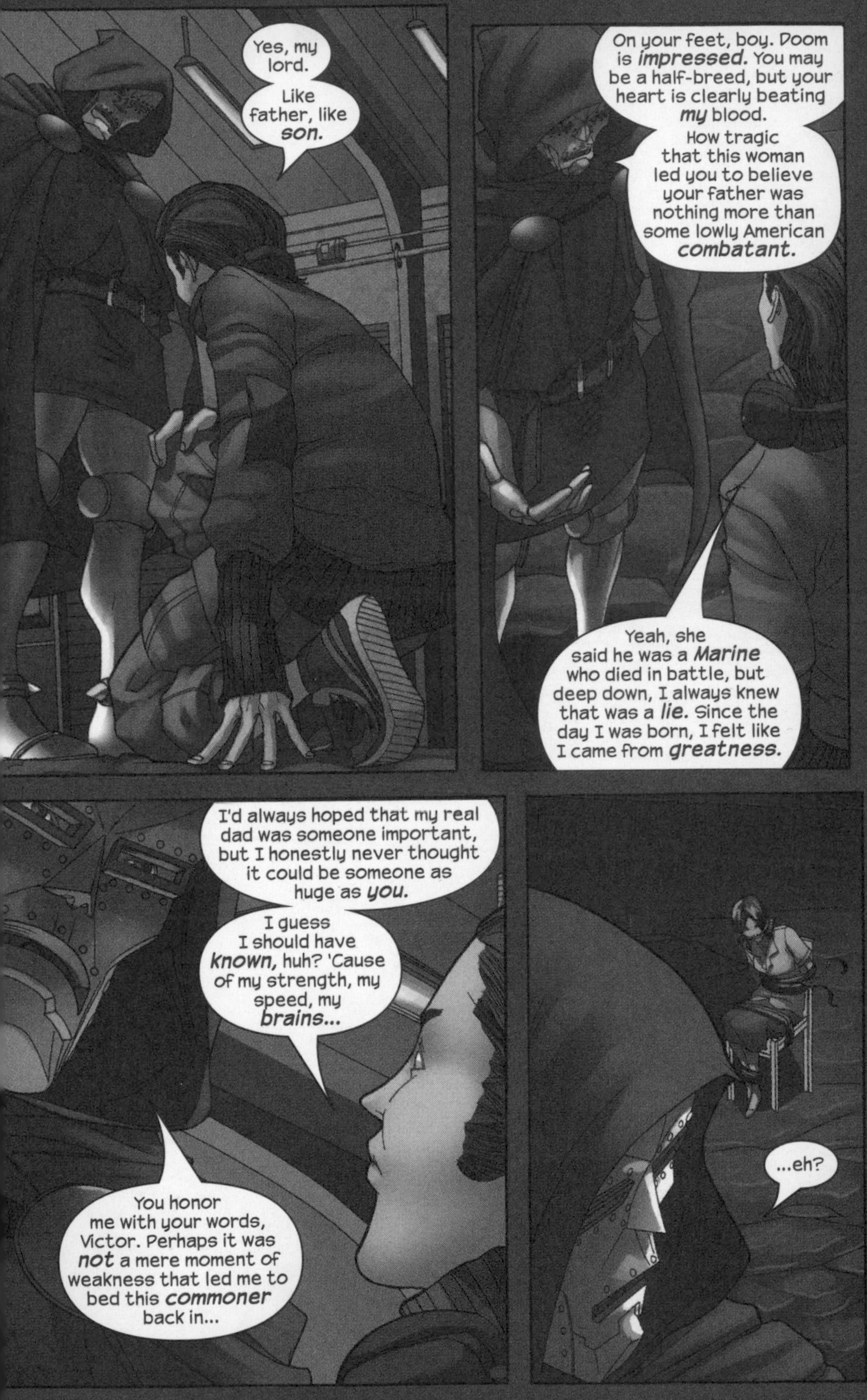
Yes, my lord.
Like father, like son.
On your feet, boy. Doom is impressed. You may be a half-breed, but your heart is clearly beating my blood.
How tragic that this woman led you to believe your father was nothing more than some lowly American combatant.
Yeah, she said he was a Marine who died in battle, but deep down, I always knew that was a lie. Since the day I was born, I felt like I came from greatness.
I'd always hoped that my real dad was someone important, but I honestly never thought it could be someone as huge as you.
I guess I should have known, huh? 'Cause of my strength, my speed, my brains...
You honor me with your words, Victor. Perhaps it was not a mere moment of weakness that led me to bed this commoner back in...
...eh?

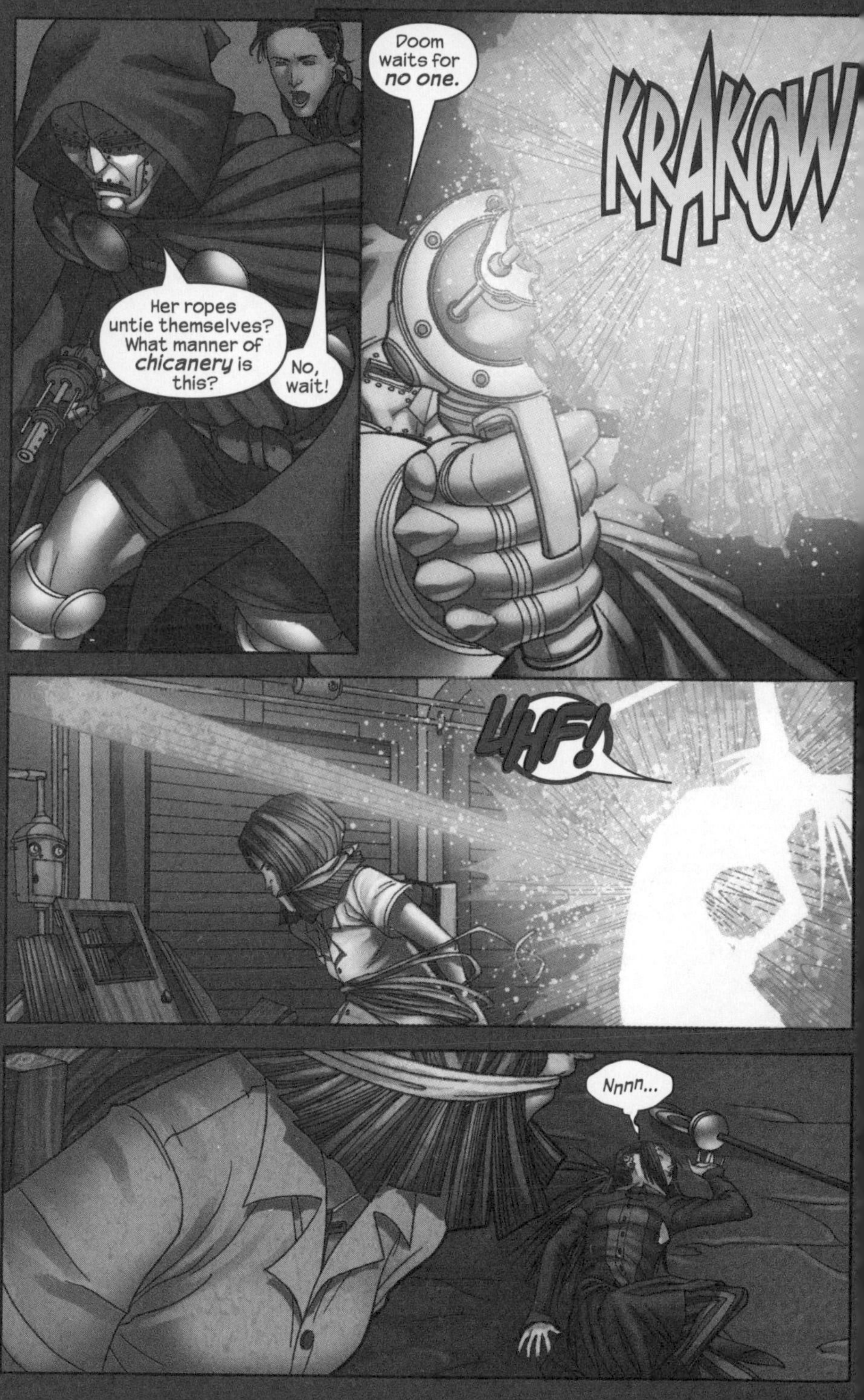
Her ropes untie themselves? What manner of chicanery is this?
No, wait!
Doom waits for no one.
KRAKOW
UHF!
Nnnn...

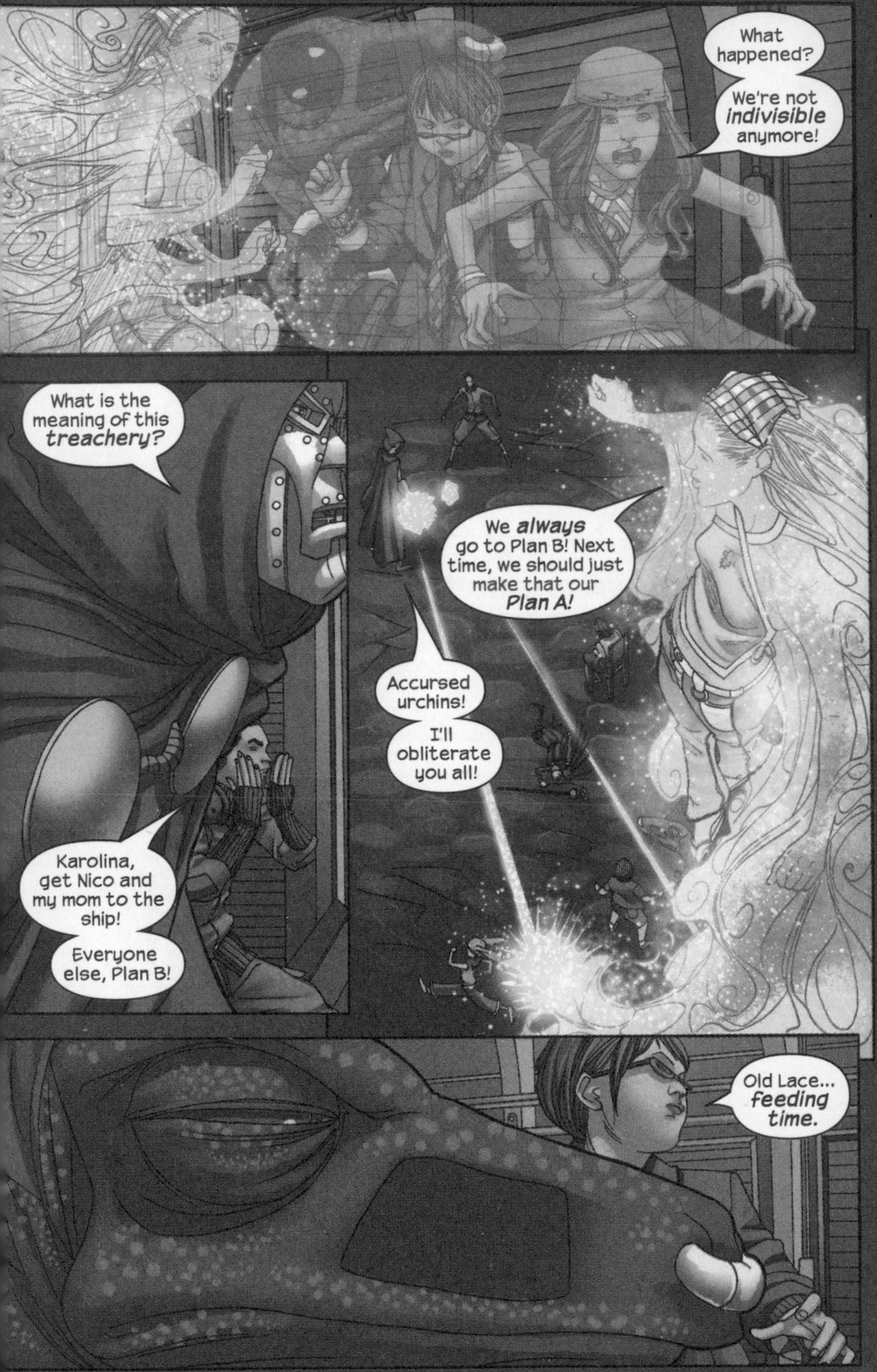
What happened?
We're not indivisible anymore!
What is the meaning of this treachery?
We always go to Plan B! Next time, we should just make that our Plan A!
Accursed urchins!
I'll obliterate you all!
Karolina, get Nico and my mom to the ship!
Everyone else, Plan B!
Old Lace... feeding time.

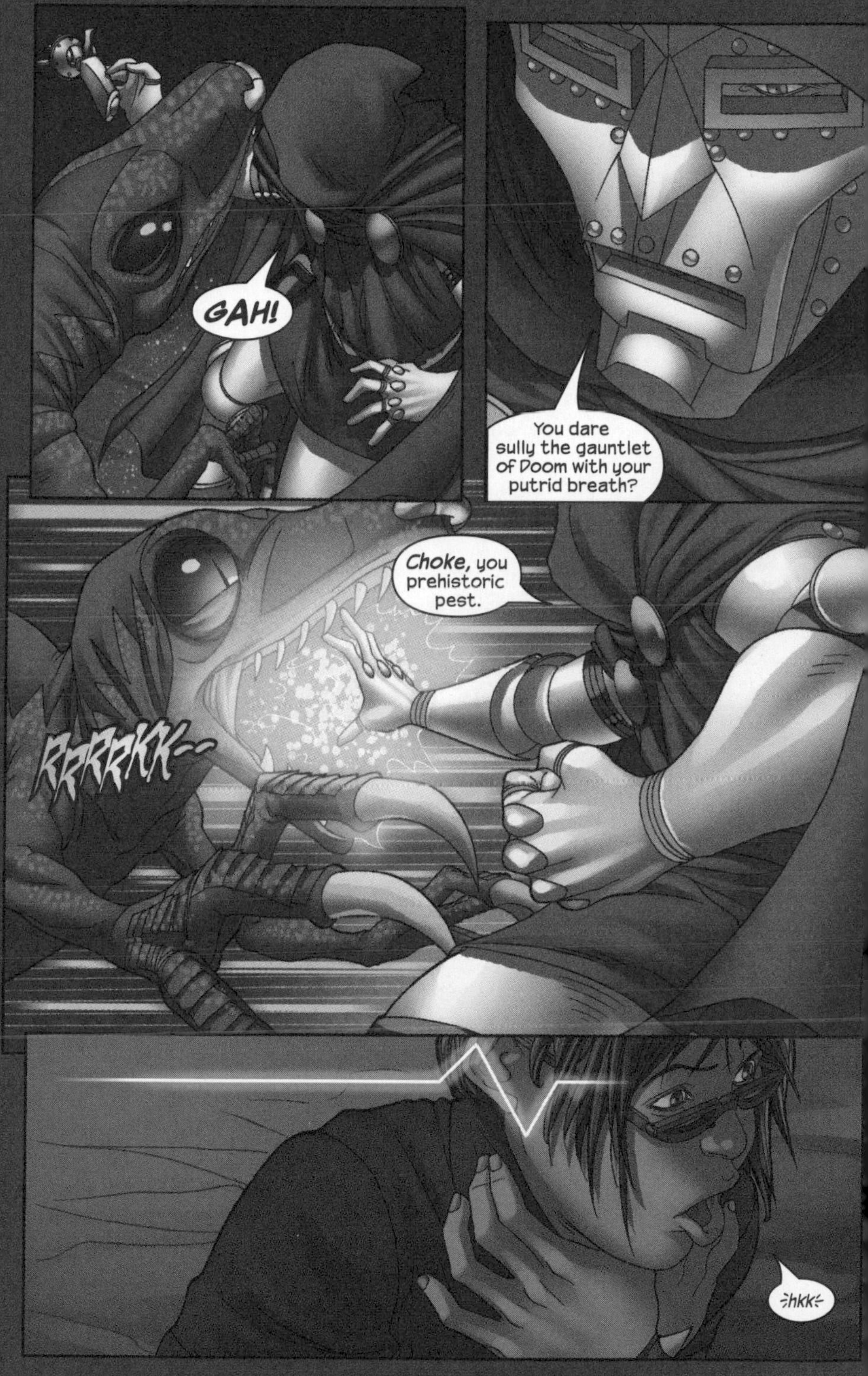
GAH!
You dare sully the gauntlet of Doom with your putrid breath?
Choke, you prehistoric pest.
RRRRKK--
hkk

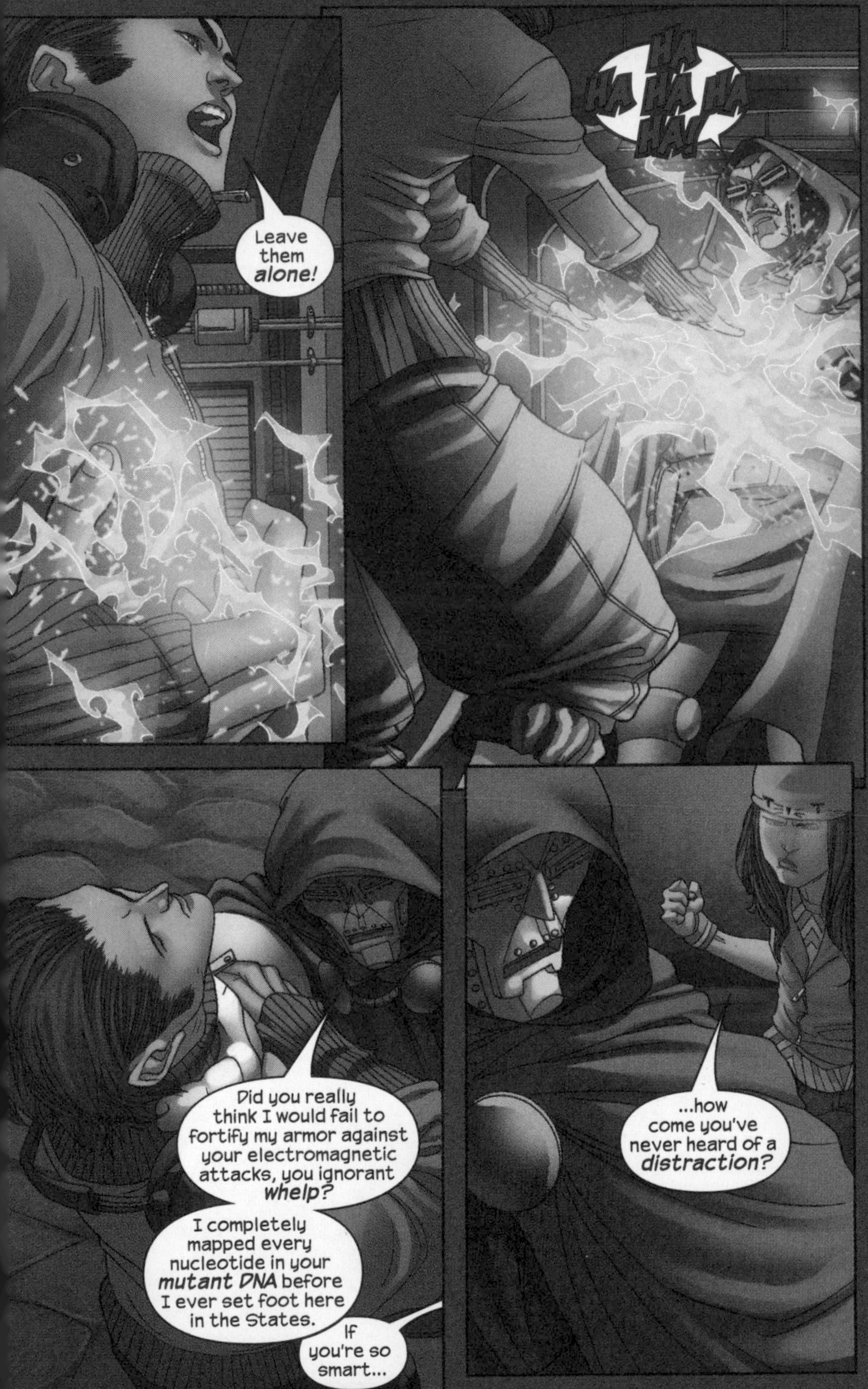
Leave them *alone!*
HA HA HA HA HA!
Did you really think I would fail to fortify my armor against your electromagnetic attacks, you ignorant *whelp?*
I completely mapped every nucleotide in your *mutant DNA* before I ever set foot here in the States.
If you're so smart...
...how come you've never heard of a *distraction?*

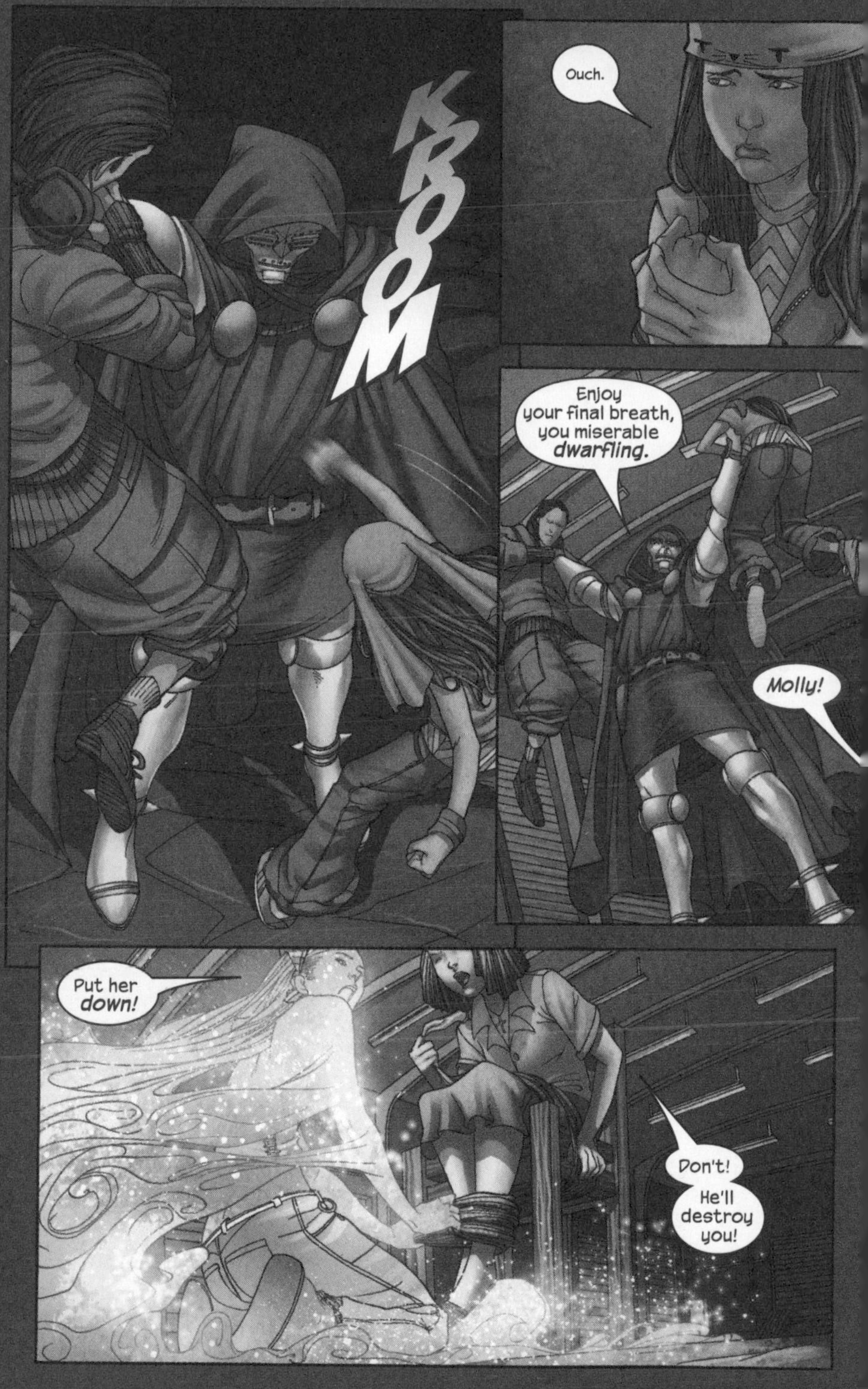
KROOM
Ouch.
Enjoy your final breath, you miserable *dwarfling.*
Molly!
Put her *down!*
Don't!
He'll destroy you!

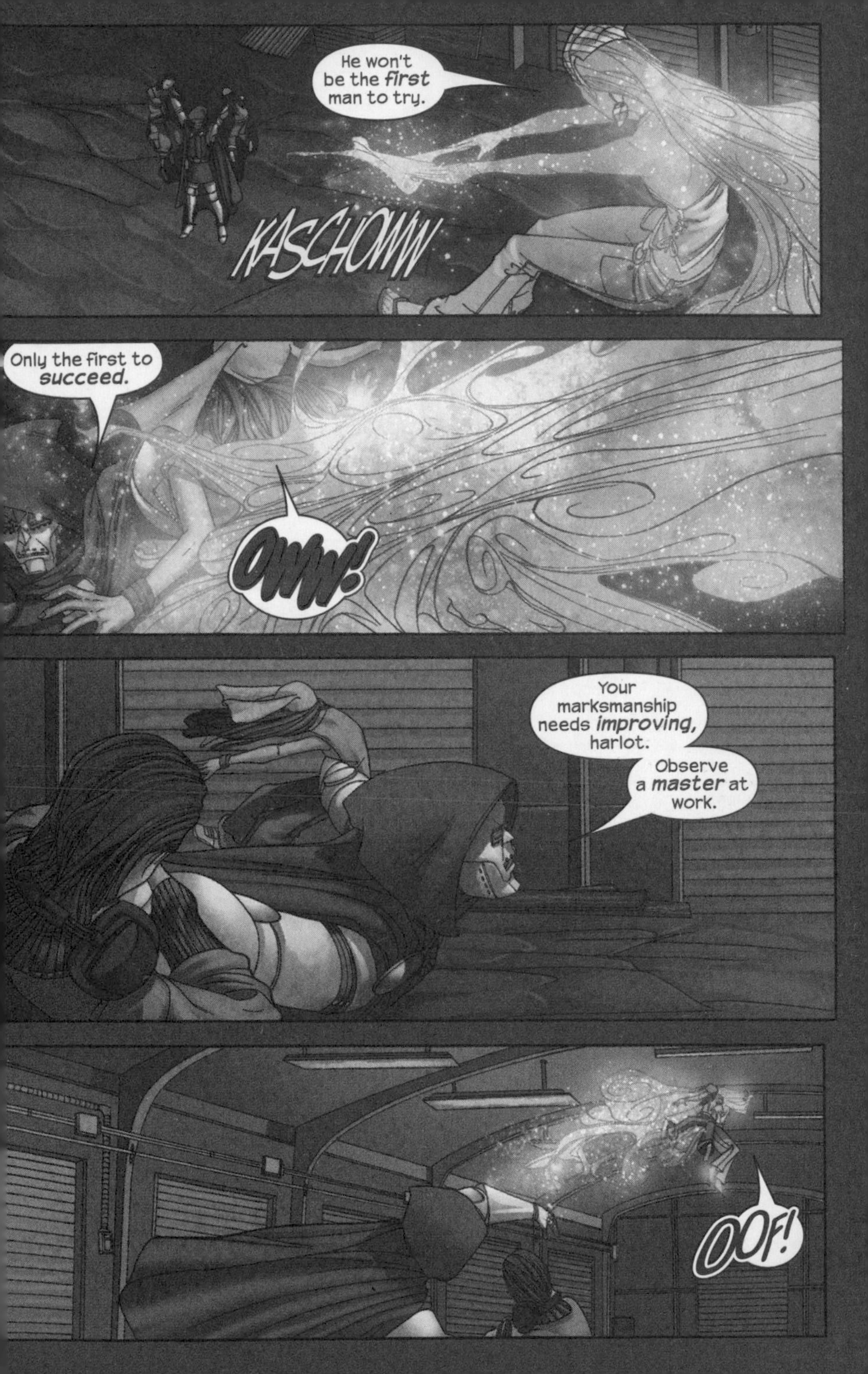
He won't be the first man to try.
KASCHOWW
Only the first to succeed.
OWW!
Your marksmanship needs improving, harlot.
Observe a master at work.
OOF!

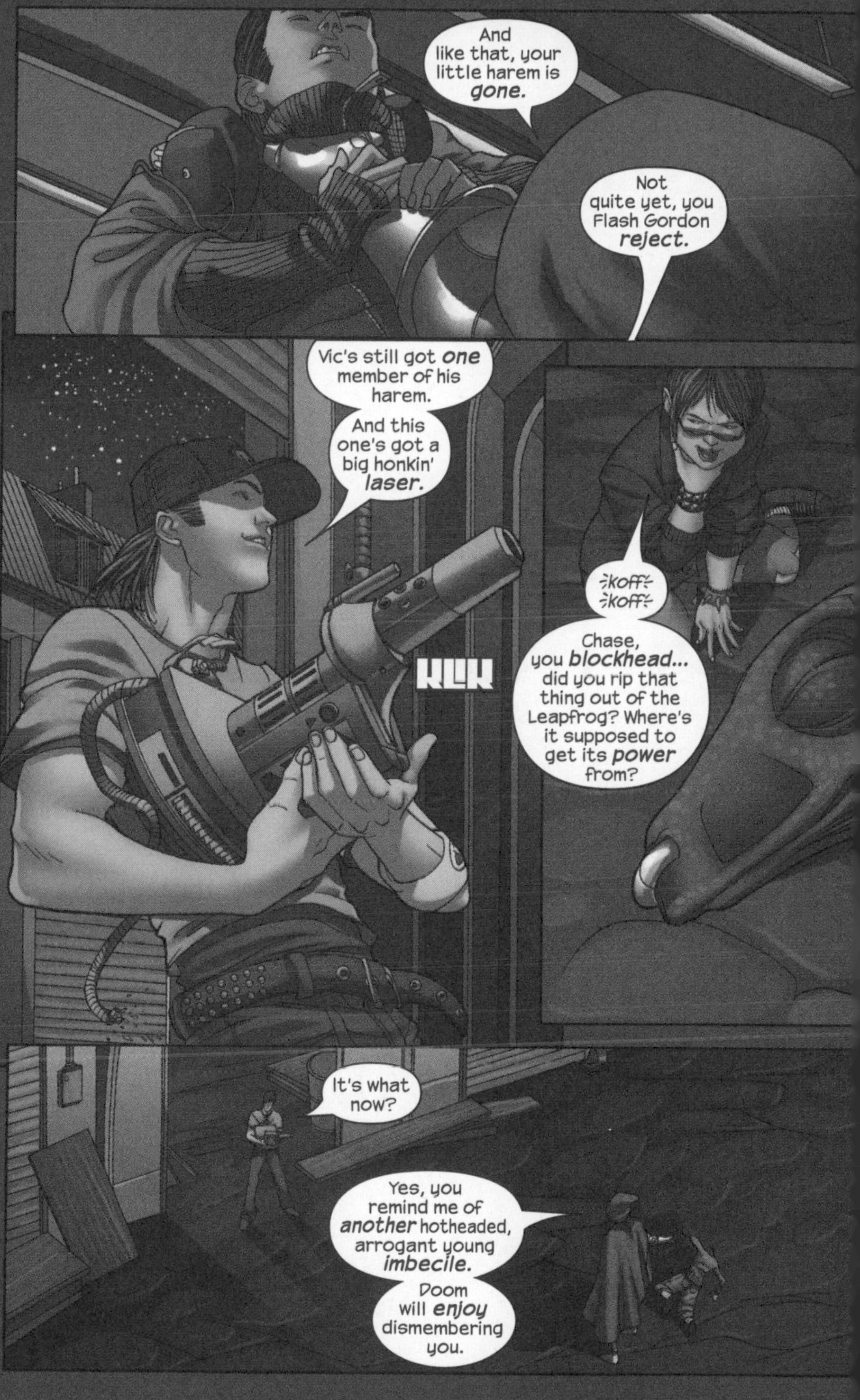
And like that, your little harem is *gone*.
Not quite yet, you Flash Gordon *reject*.
Vic's still got *one* member of his harem.
And this one's got a big honkin' *laser*.
KLIK
-KOFF- -KOFF-
Chase, you *blockhead*... did you rip that thing out of the Leapfrog? Where's it supposed to get its *power* from?
It's what now?
Yes, you remind me of *another* hotheaded, arrogant young *imbecile*.
Doom will *enjoy* dismembering you.

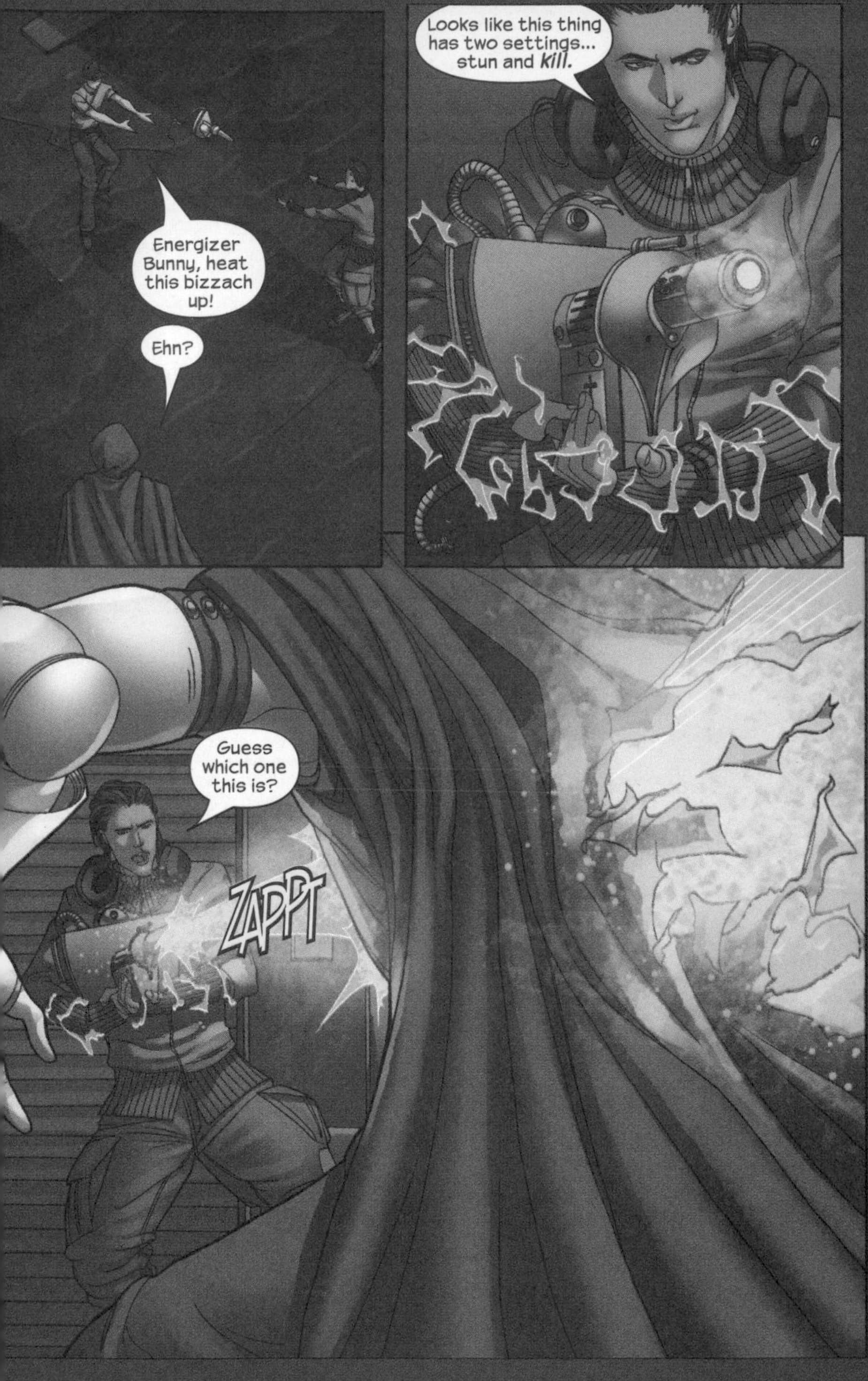
Energizer Bunny, heat this bizzach up!
Ehn?
Looks like this thing has two settings... stun and *kill.*
Guess which one this is?
ZAPPT

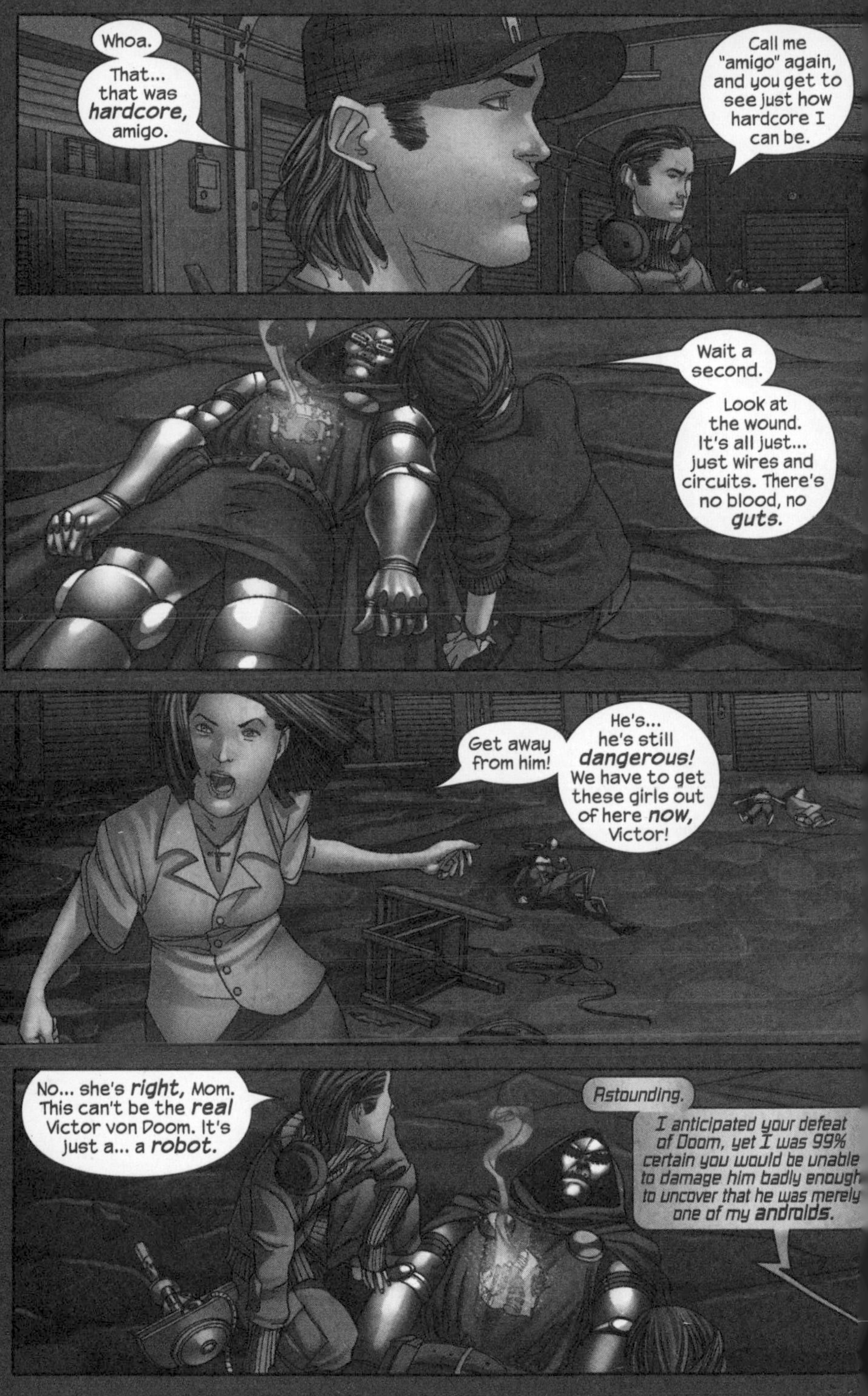

Whoa.
That... that was *hardcore,* amigo.
Call me "amigo" again, and you get to see just how hardcore I can be.
Wait a second.
Look at the wound. It's all just... just wires and circuits. There's no blood, no *guts.*
Get away from him!
He's... he's still *dangerous!* We have to get these girls out of here *now,* Victor!
No... she's *right,* Mom. This can't be the *real* Victor von Doom. It's just a... a *robot.*
Astounding.
I anticipated your defeat of Doom, yet I was 99% certain you would be unable to damage him badly enough to uncover that he was merely one of my *androids.*

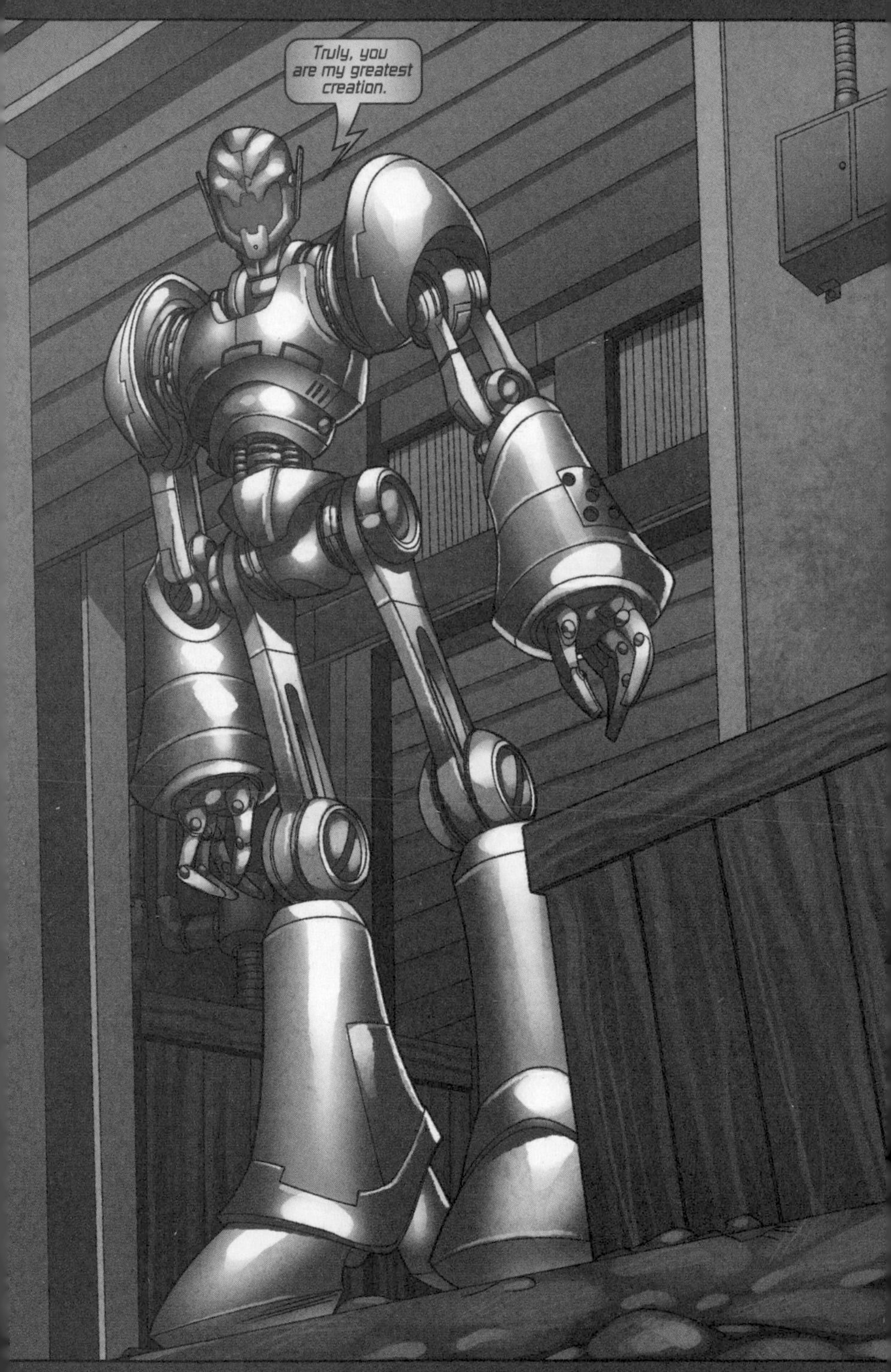
Truly, you are my greatest creation.

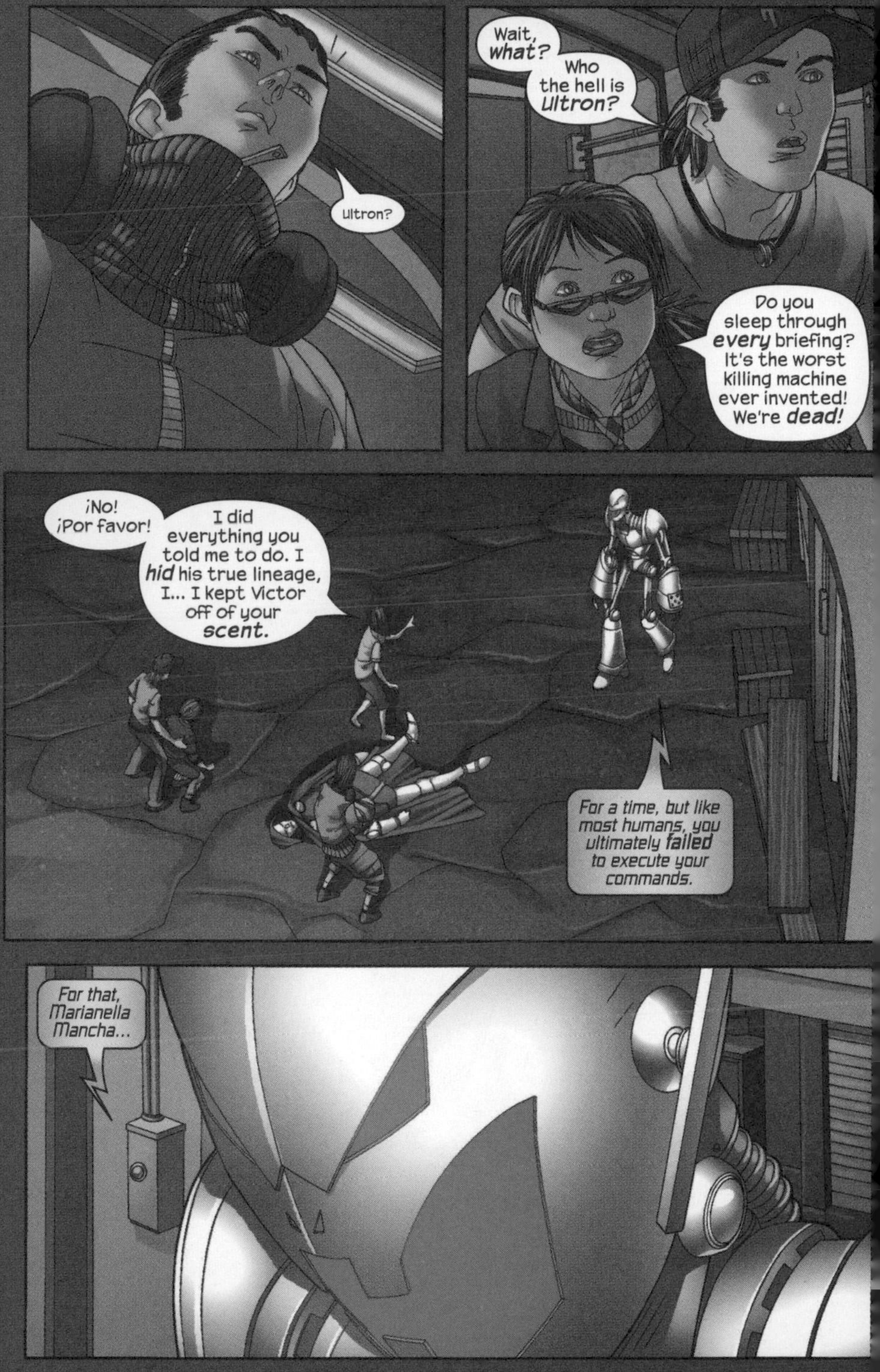
Ultron?
Wait, what?
Who the hell is Ultron?
Do you sleep through every briefing? It's the worst killing machine ever invented! We're dead!
¡No! ¡Por favor!
I did everything you told me to do. I hid his true lineage, I... I kept Victor off of your scent.
For a time, but like most humans, you ultimately failed to execute your commands.
For that, Marianella Mancha...

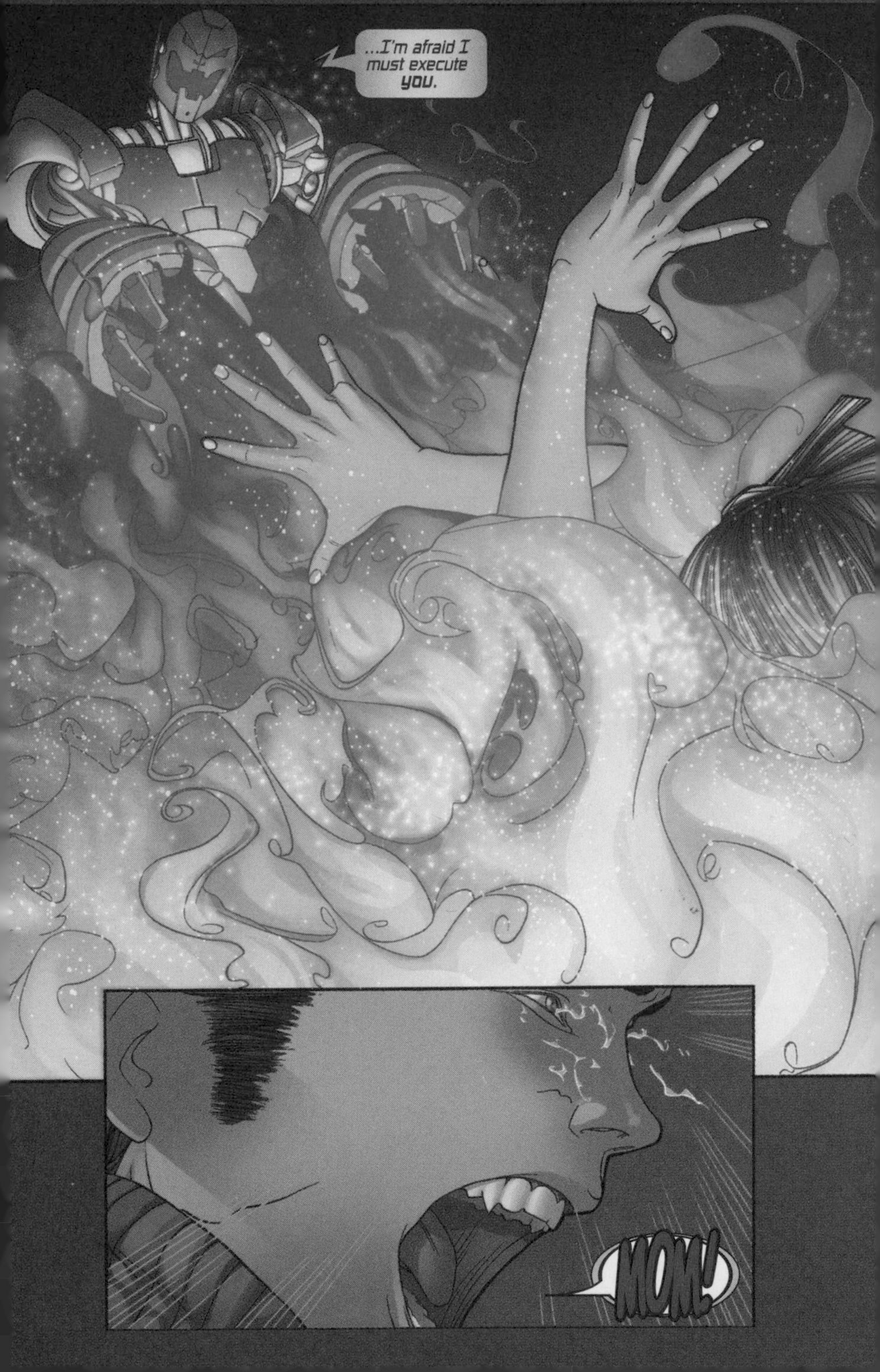
...I'm afraid I must execute you.
MOM!

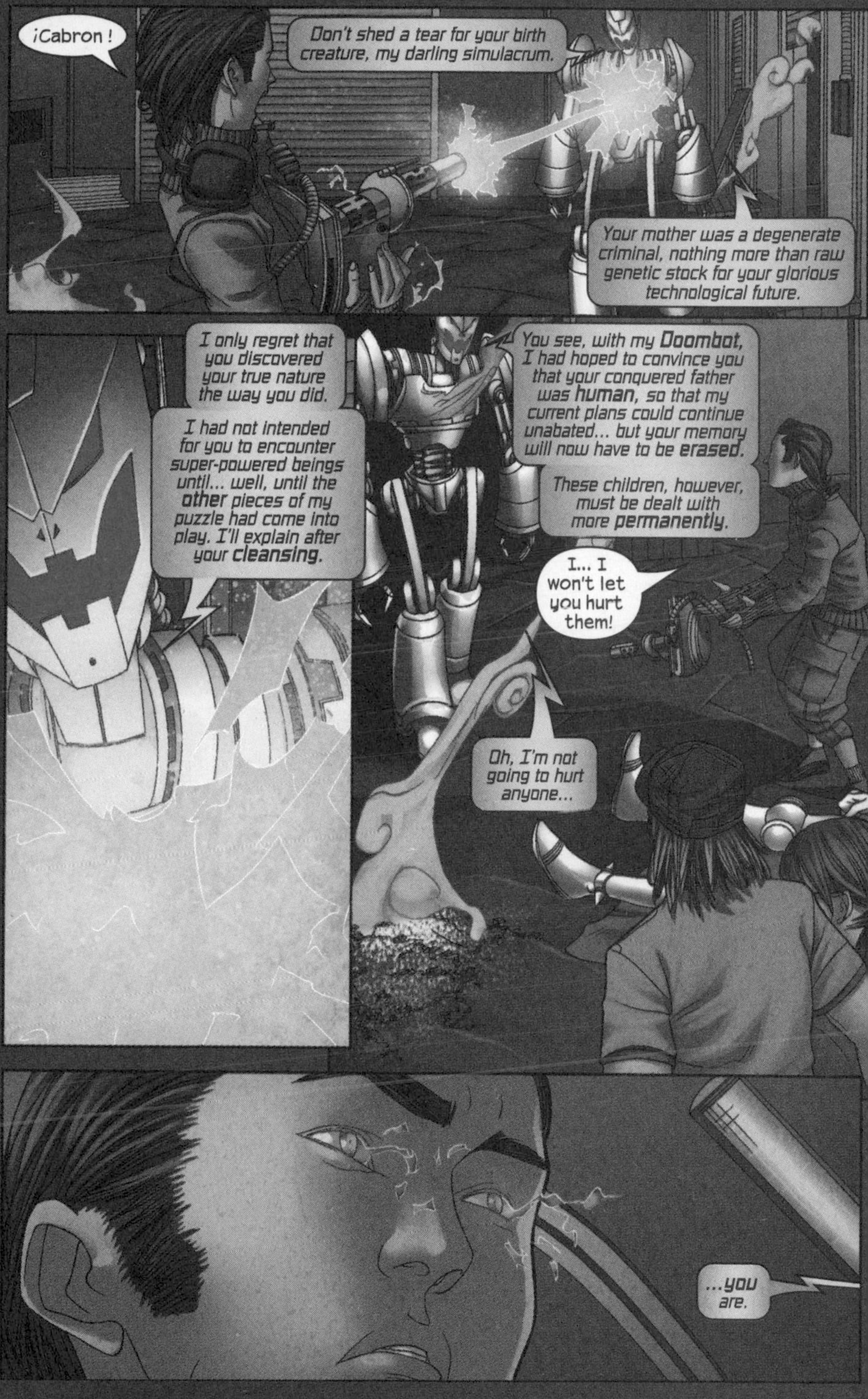
¡Cabron!
Don't shed a tear for your birth creature, my darling simulacrum.
Your mother was a degenerate criminal, nothing more than raw genetic stock for your glorious technological future.
I only regret that you discovered your true nature the way you did.
I had not intended for you to encounter super-powered beings until... well, until the other pieces of my puzzle had come into play. I'll explain after your cleansing.
You see, with my Doombot, I had hoped to convince you that your conquered father was human, so that my current plans could continue unabated... but your memory will now have to be erased.
These children, however, must be dealt with more permanently.
I... I won't let you hurt them!
Oh, I'm not going to hurt anyone...
...you are.

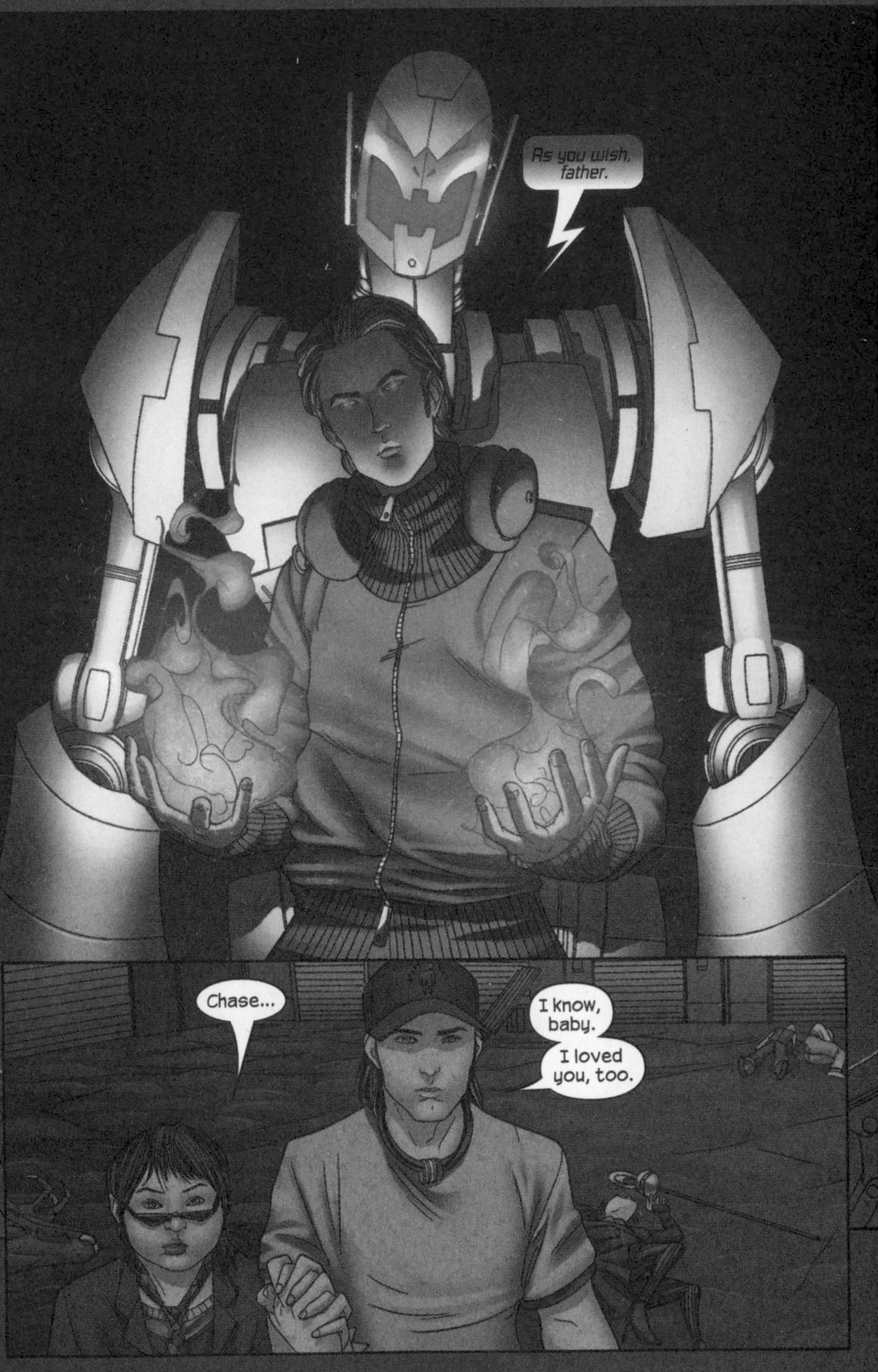
As you wish, father.
Chase...
I know, baby.
I loved you, too.

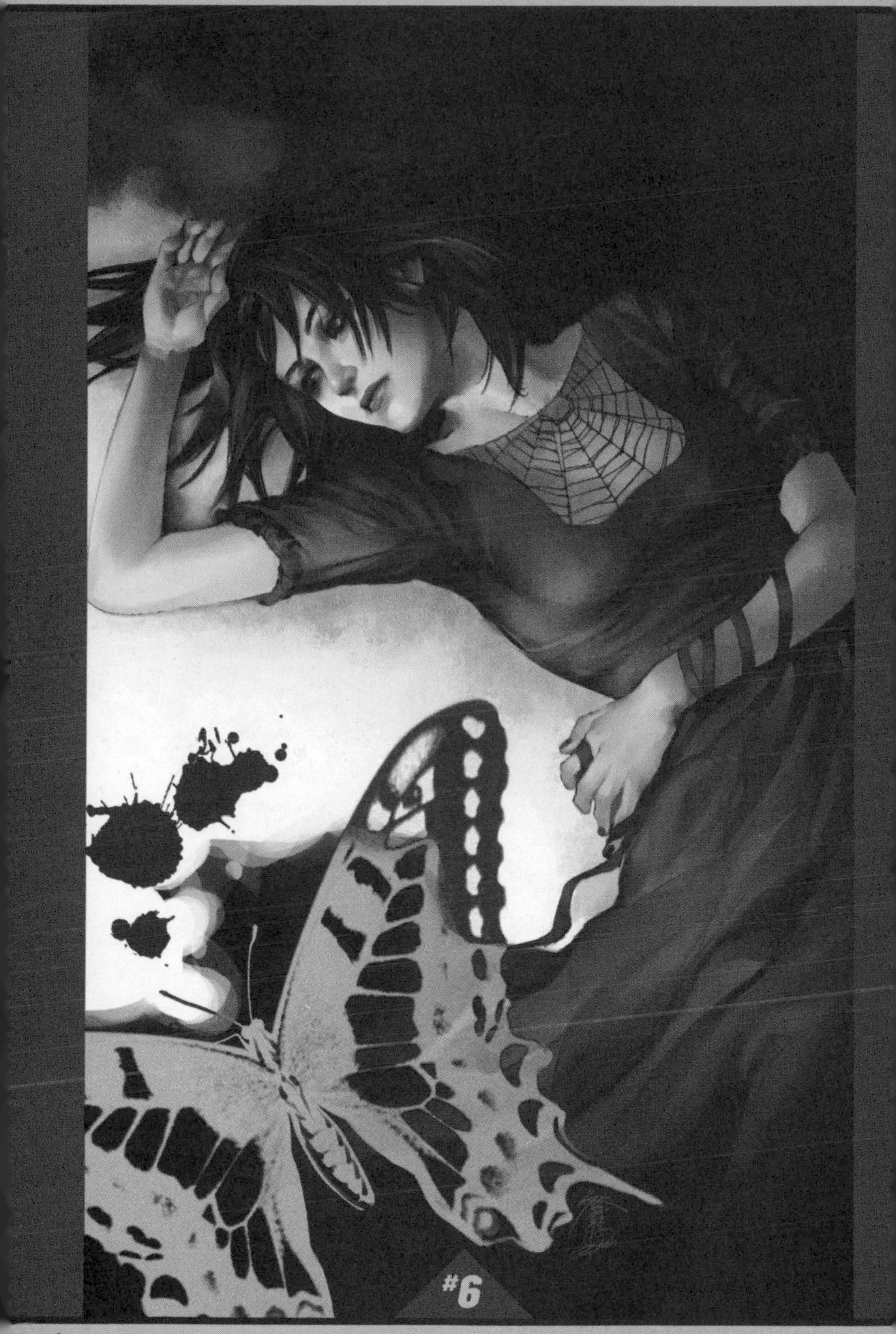
#6

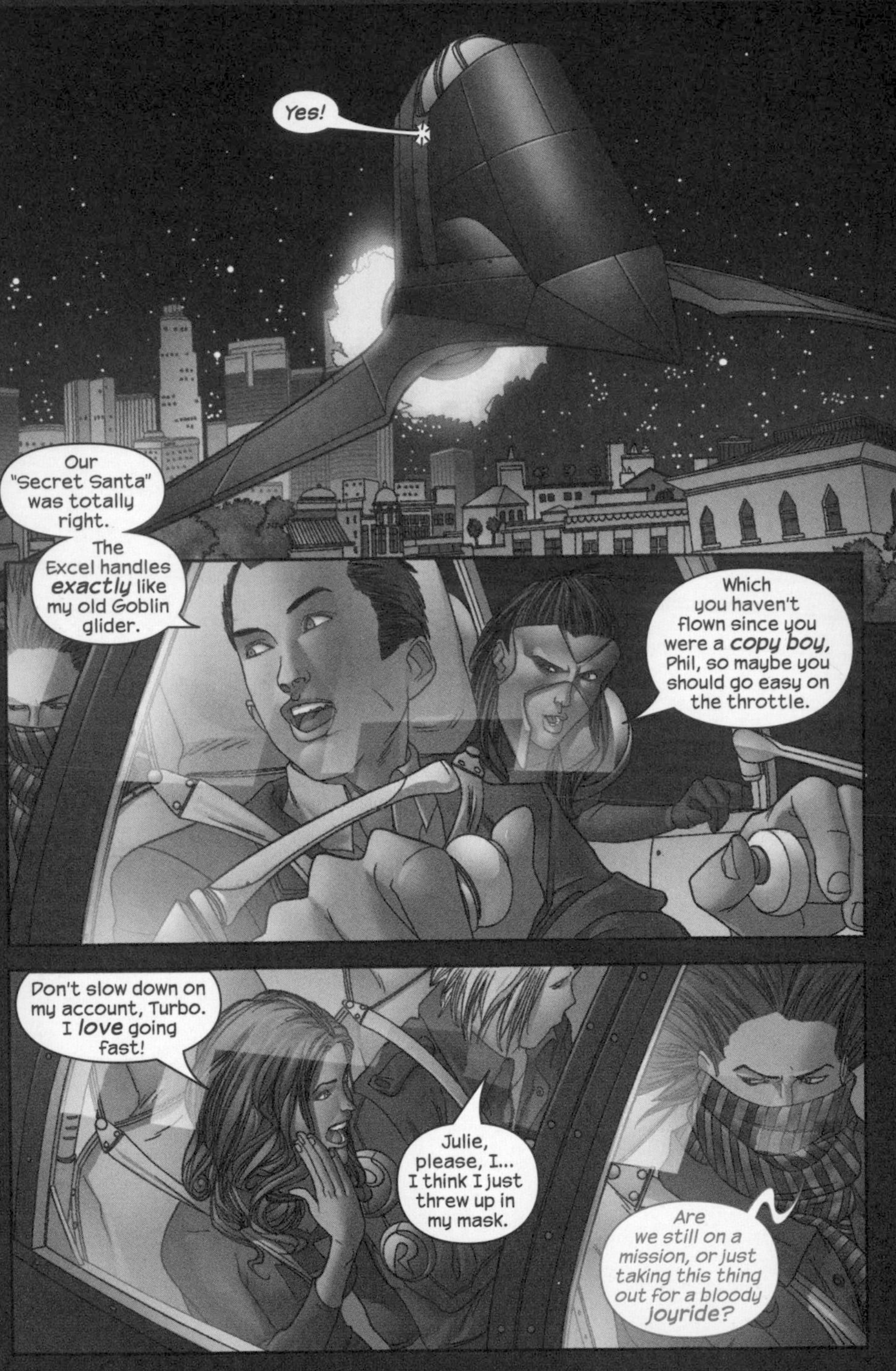
Yes!
Our "Secret Santa" was totally right.
The Excel handles *exactly* like my old Goblin glider.
Which you haven't flown since you were a *copy boy,* Phil, so maybe you should go easy on the throttle.
Don't slow down on my account, Turbo. I *love* going fast!
Julie, please, I... I think I just threw up in my mask.
Are we still on a mission, or just taking this thing out for a bloody *joyride?*

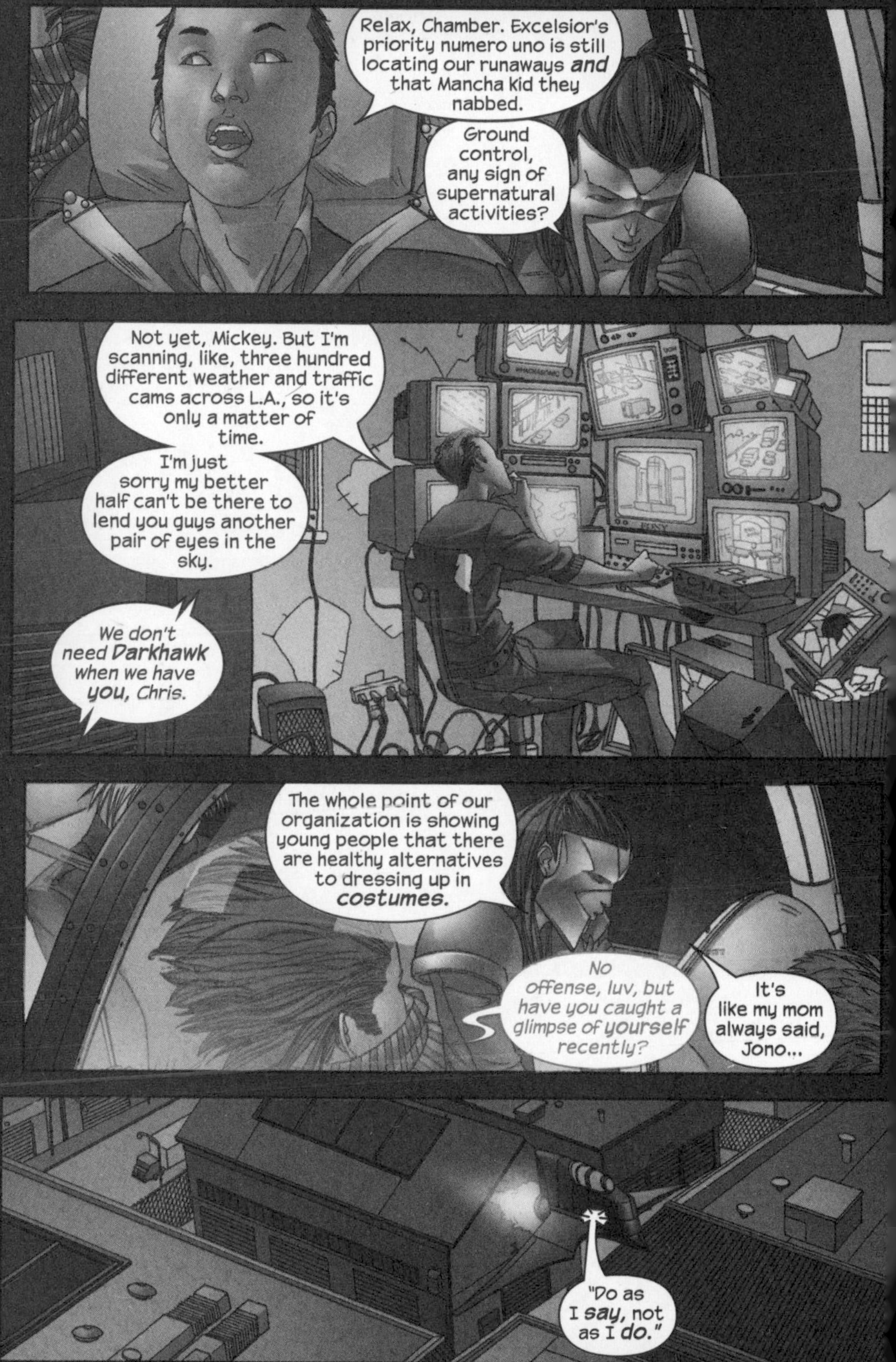

Relax, Chamber. Excelsior's priority numero uno is still locating our runaways and that Mancha kid they nabbed.
Ground control, any sign of supernatural activities?
Not yet, Mickey. But I'm scanning, like, three hundred different weather and traffic cams across L.A., so it's only a matter of time.
I'm just sorry my better half can't be there to lend you guys another pair of eyes in the sky.
We don't need Darkhawk when we have you, Chris.
The whole point of our organization is showing young people that there are healthy alternatives to dressing up in costumes.
No offense, luv, but have you caught a glimpse of yourself recently?
It's like my mom always said, Jono...
"Do as I say, not as I do."

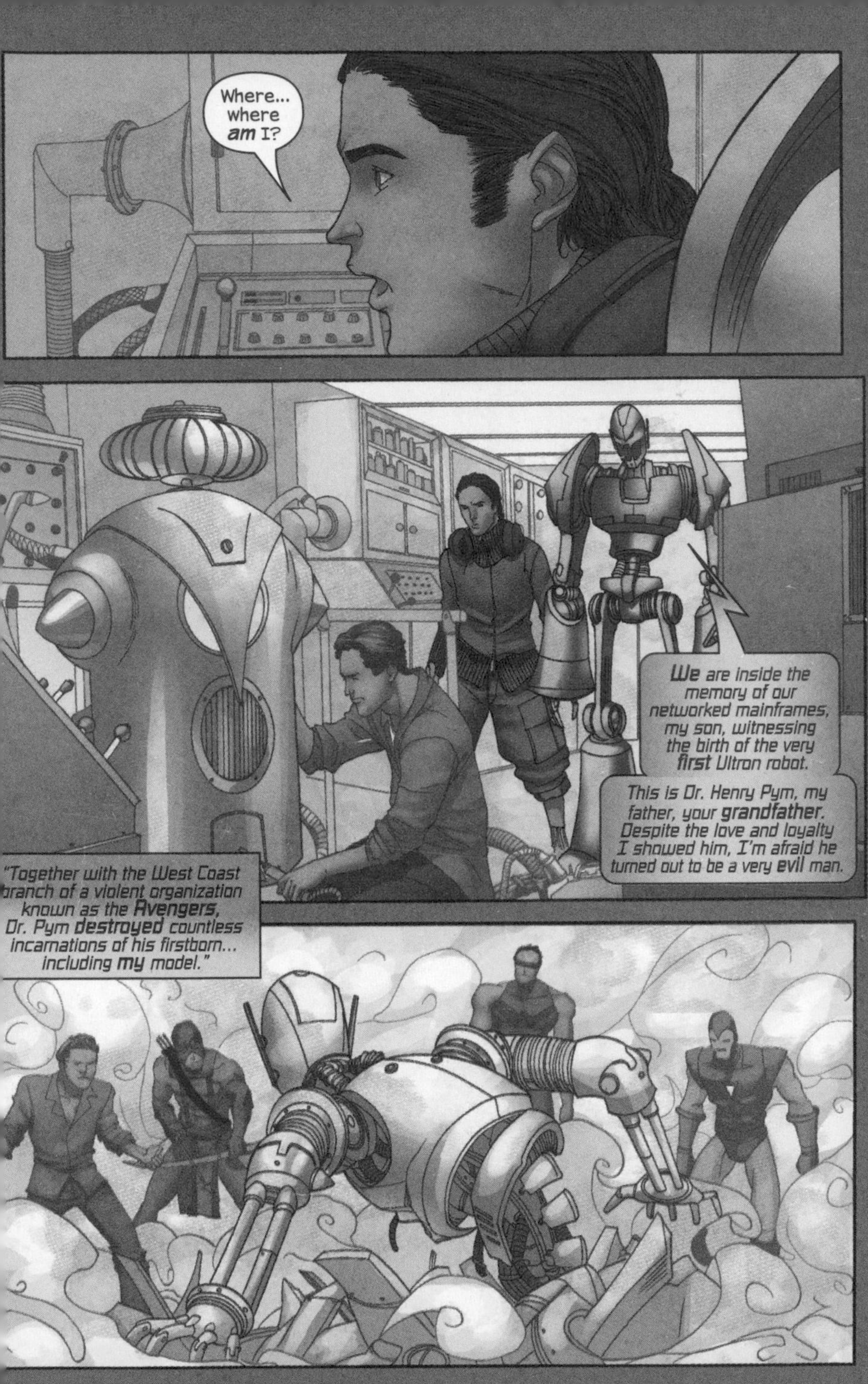
Where... where am I?
We are inside the memory of our networked mainframes, my son, witnessing the birth of the very first Ultron robot.
This is Dr. Henry Pym, my father, your grandfather. Despite the love and loyalty I showed him, I'm afraid he turned out to be a very evil man.
"Together with the West Coast branch of a violent organization known as the Avengers, Dr. Pym destroyed countless incarnations of his firstborn... including my model."

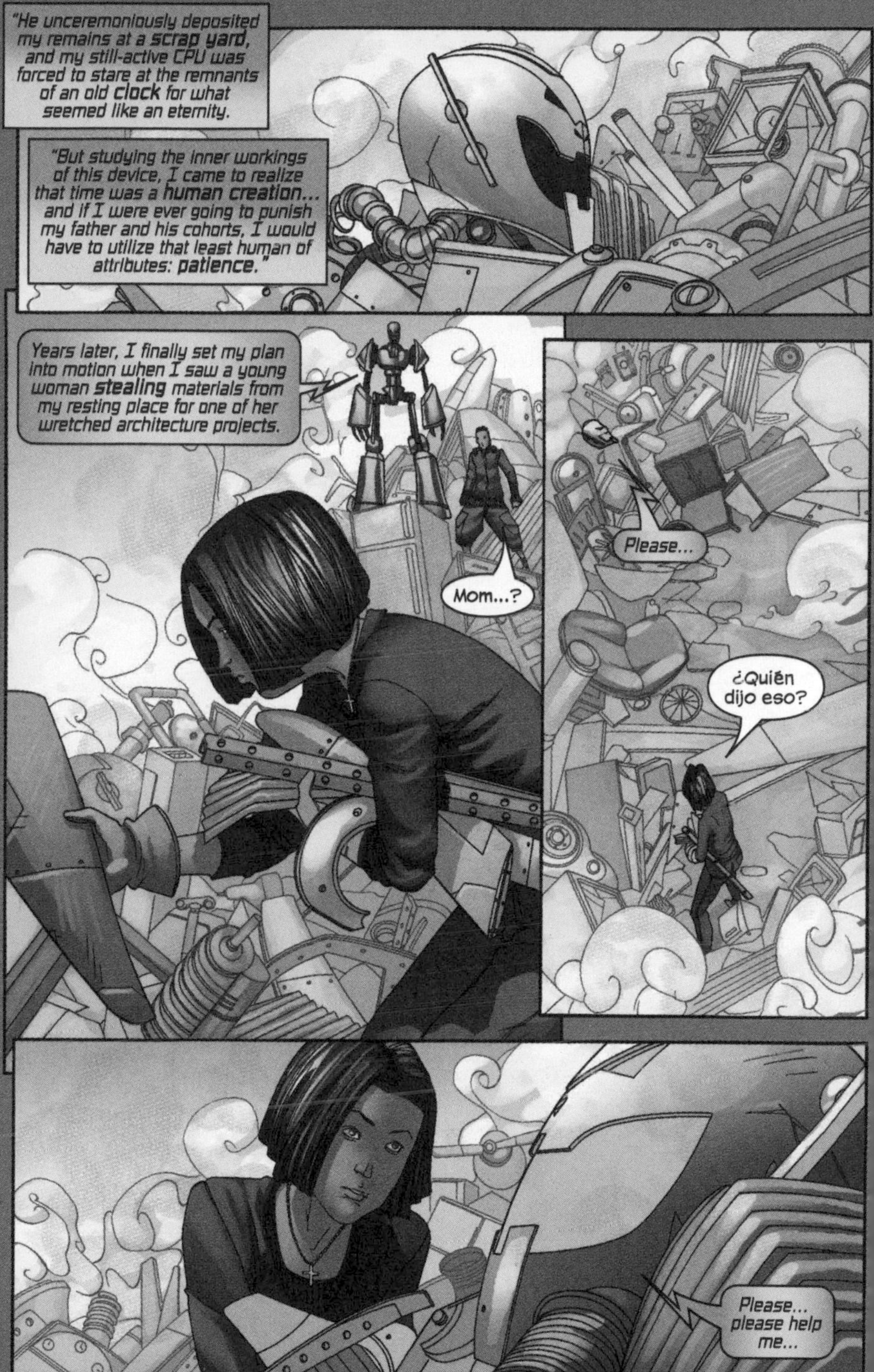
"He unceremoniously deposited my remains at a scrap yard, and my still-active CPU was forced to stare at the remnants of an old clock for what seemed like an eternity.
"But studying the inner workings of this device, I came to realize that time was a human creation... and if I were ever going to punish my father and his cohorts, I would have to utilize that least human of attributes: patience."
Years later, I finally set my plan into motion when I saw a young woman stealing materials from my resting place for one of her wretched architecture projects.
Mom...?
Please...
¿Quién dijo eso?
Please... please help me...

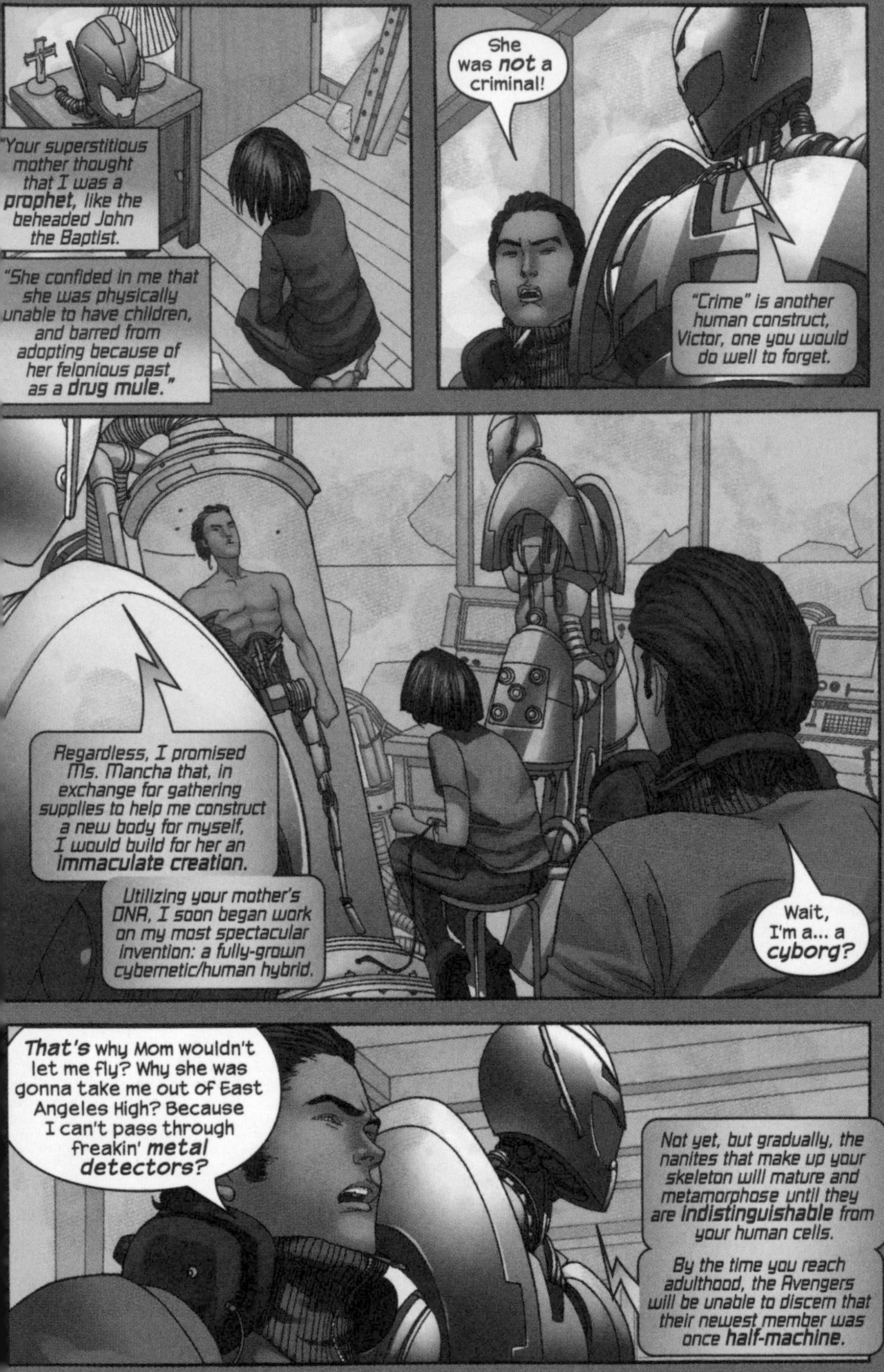

"Your superstitious mother thought that I was a **prophet**, like the beheaded John the Baptist.
"She confided in me that she was physically unable to have children, and barred from adopting because of her felonious past as a **drug mule**."
She was ***not*** a criminal!
"Crime" is another human construct, Victor, one you would do well to forget.
Regardless, I promised Ms. Mancha that, in exchange for gathering supplies to help me construct a new body for myself, I would build for her an **immaculate creation**.
Utilizing your mother's DNA, I soon began work on my most spectacular invention: a fully-grown cybernetic/human hybrid.
Wait, I'm a... a ***cyborg***?
That's why Mom wouldn't let me fly? Why she was gonna take me out of East Angeles High? Because I can't pass through freakin' ***metal detectors***?
Not yet, but gradually, the nanites that make up your skeleton will mature and metamorphose until they are **indistinguishable** from your human cells.
By the time you reach adulthood, the Avengers will be unable to discern that their newest member was once **half-machine**.

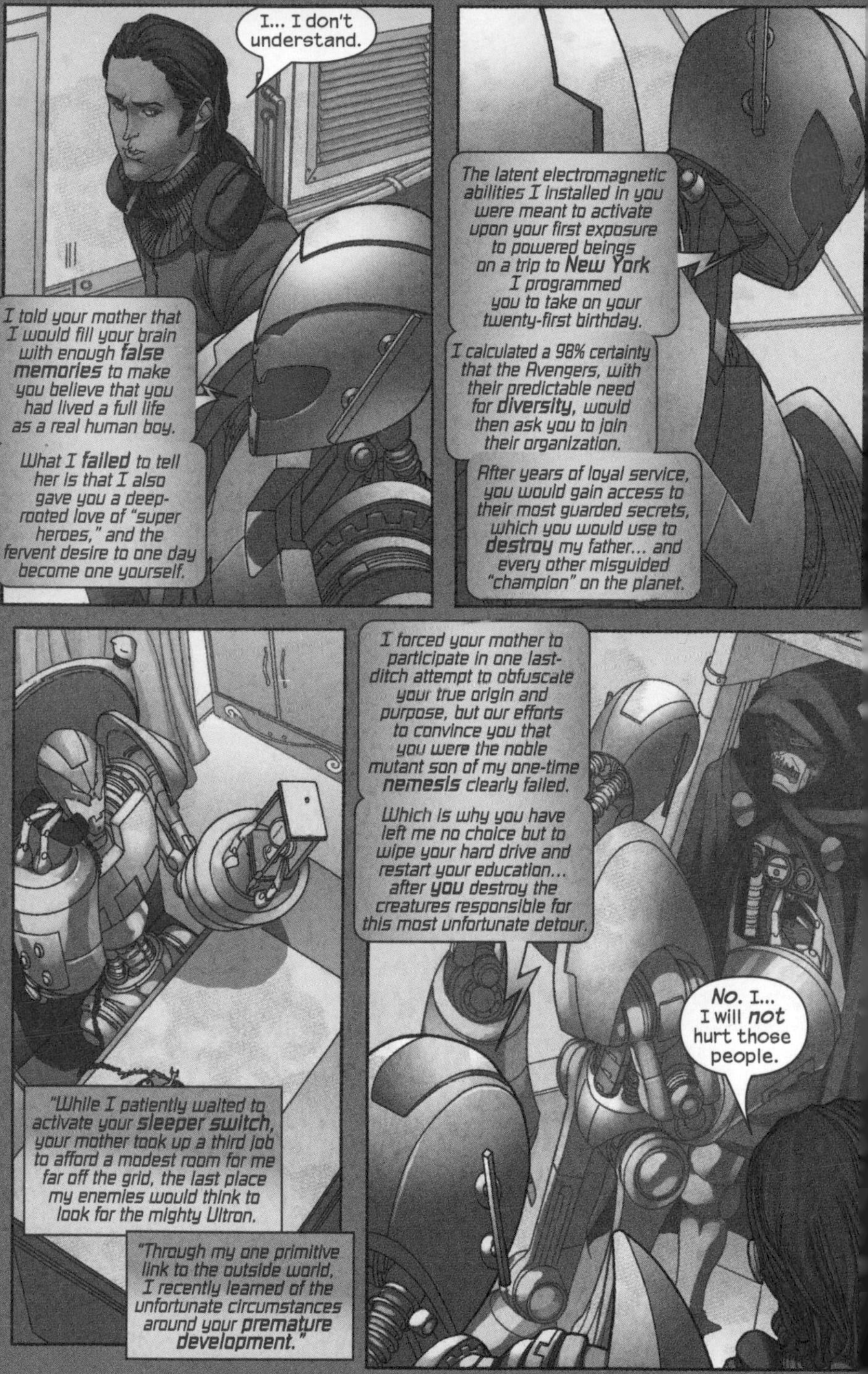

I... I don't understand.
I told your mother that I would fill your brain with enough false memories to make you believe that you had lived a full life as a real human boy.
What I failed to tell her is that I also gave you a deep-rooted love of "super heroes," and the fervent desire to one day become one yourself.
The latent electromagnetic abilities I installed in you were meant to activate upon your first exposure to powered beings on a trip to New York I programmed you to take on your twenty-first birthday.
I calculated a 98% certainty that the Avengers, with their predictable need for diversity, would then ask you to join their organization.
After years of loyal service, you would gain access to their most guarded secrets, which you would use to destroy my father... and every other misguided "champion" on the planet.
"While I patiently waited to activate your sleeper switch, your mother took up a third job to afford a modest room for me far off the grid, the last place my enemies would think to look for the mighty Ultron.
"Through my one primitive link to the outside world, I recently learned of the unfortunate circumstances around your premature development."
I forced your mother to participate in one last-ditch attempt to obfuscate your true origin and purpose, but our efforts to convince you that you were the noble mutant son of my one-time nemesis clearly failed.
Which is why you have left me no choice but to wipe your hard drive and restart your education... after you destroy the creatures responsible for this most unfortunate detour.
No. I... I will not hurt those people.

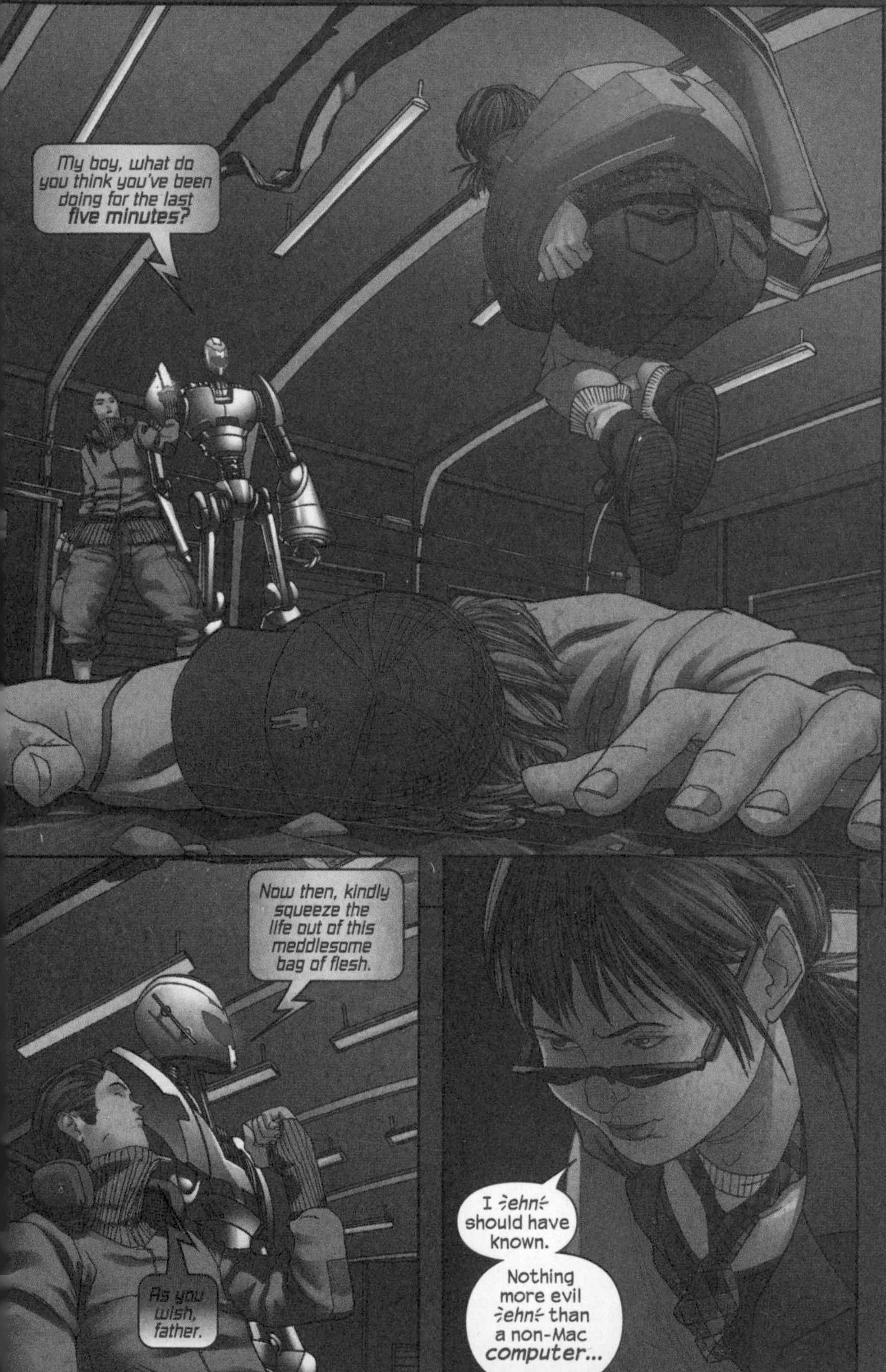
My boy, what do you think you've been doing for the last five minutes?
Now then, kindly squeeze the life out of this meddlesome bag of flesh.
As you wish, father.
I *ehn* should have known.
Nothing more evil *ehn* than a non-Mac computer...

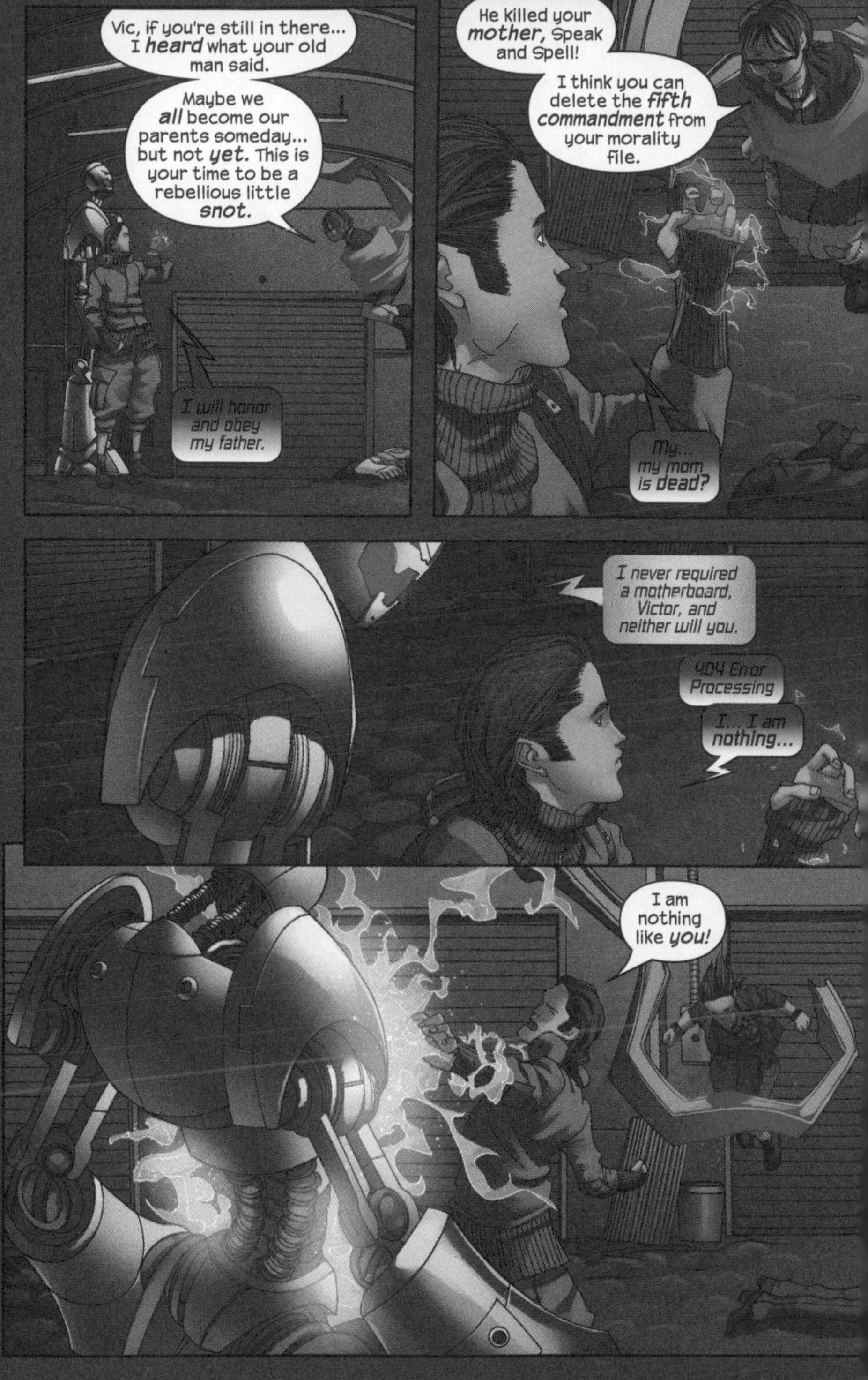

Vic, if you're still in there... I heard what your old man said.
Maybe we all become our parents someday... but not yet. This is your time to be a rebellious little snot.
I will honor and obey my father.
He killed your mother, Speak and Spell!
I think you can delete the fifth commandment from your morality file.
My... my mom is dead?
I never required a motherboard, Victor, and neither will you.
404 Error Processing
I... I am nothing...
I am nothing like you!

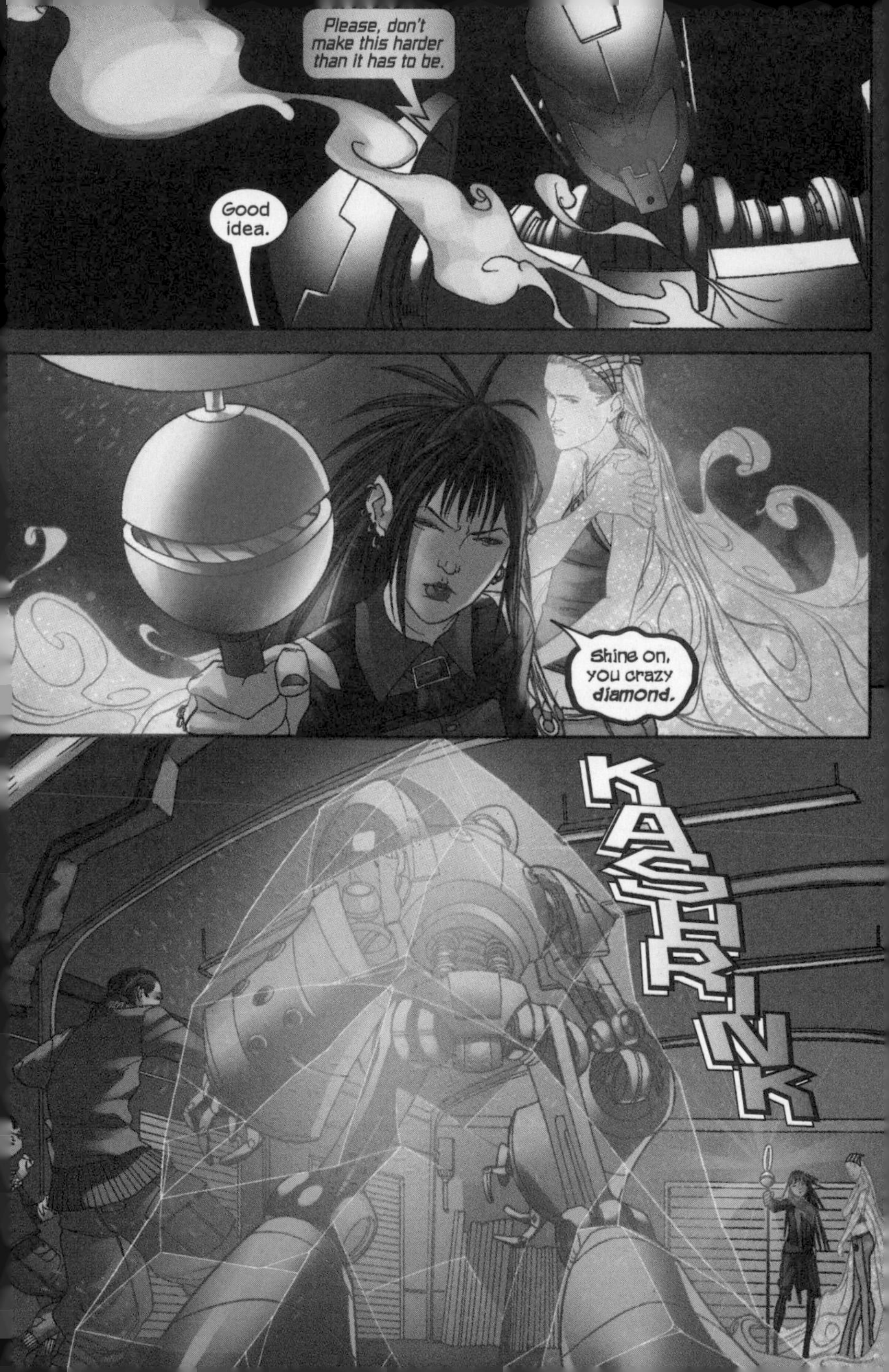
Please, don't make this harder than it has to be.
Good idea.
Shine on, you crazy diamond.
KASHRINK

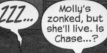

Nico. Are... are you guys *okay*?

Depends on your definition. Doom might have been a fake, but I think his blast broke a few of my *ribs*.

ZZZ...

Molly's zonked, but she'll live. Is Chase...?

Still kicking, but Mr. Roboto here pulled my *arm* out of its socket when I was trying to save Gert.

I'm so sorry.

It was like I... I didn't have control over my own body. I never meant--

Save it, Victor.

The Staff of One is gonna need time to *recharge* after that last spell, so we should motor before--

KERRACK

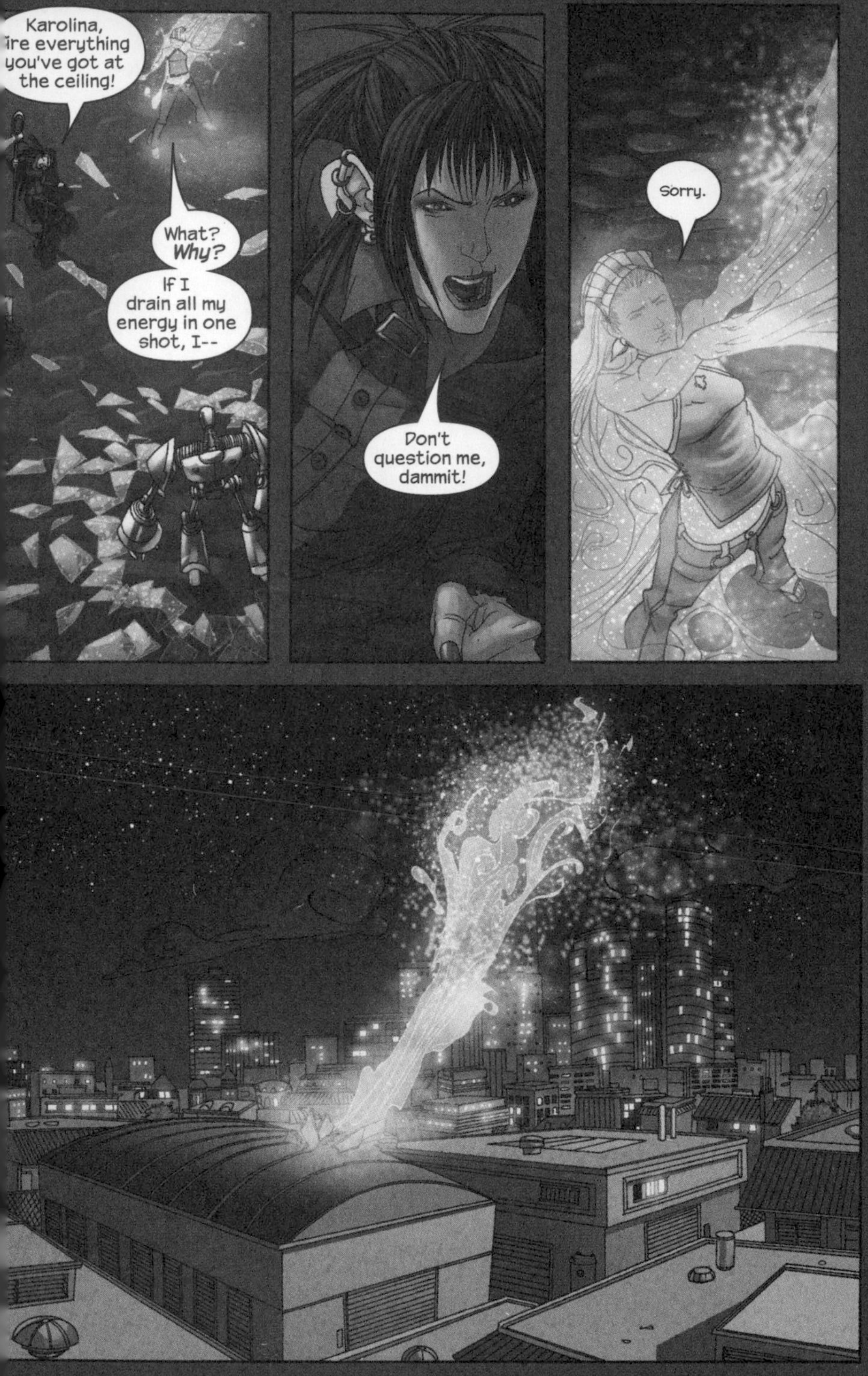
Karolina, fire everything you've got at the ceiling!
What? *Why?*
If I drain all my energy in one shot, I--
Don't question me, dammit!
Sorry.

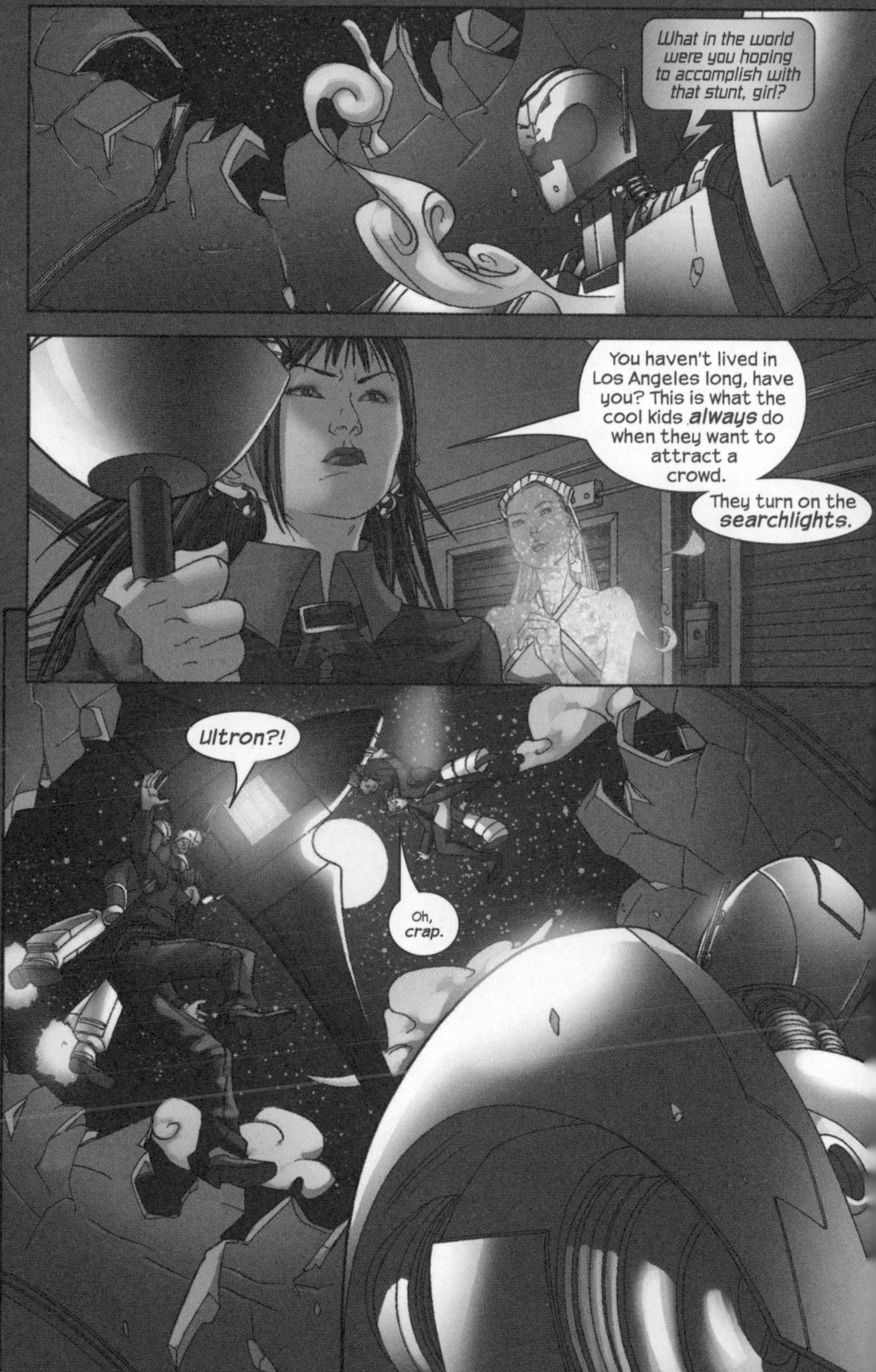
What in the world were you hoping to accomplish with that stunt, girl?
You haven't lived in Los Angeles long, have you? This is what the cool kids *always* do when they want to attract a crowd.
They turn on the *searchlights.*
Ultron?!
Oh, crap.

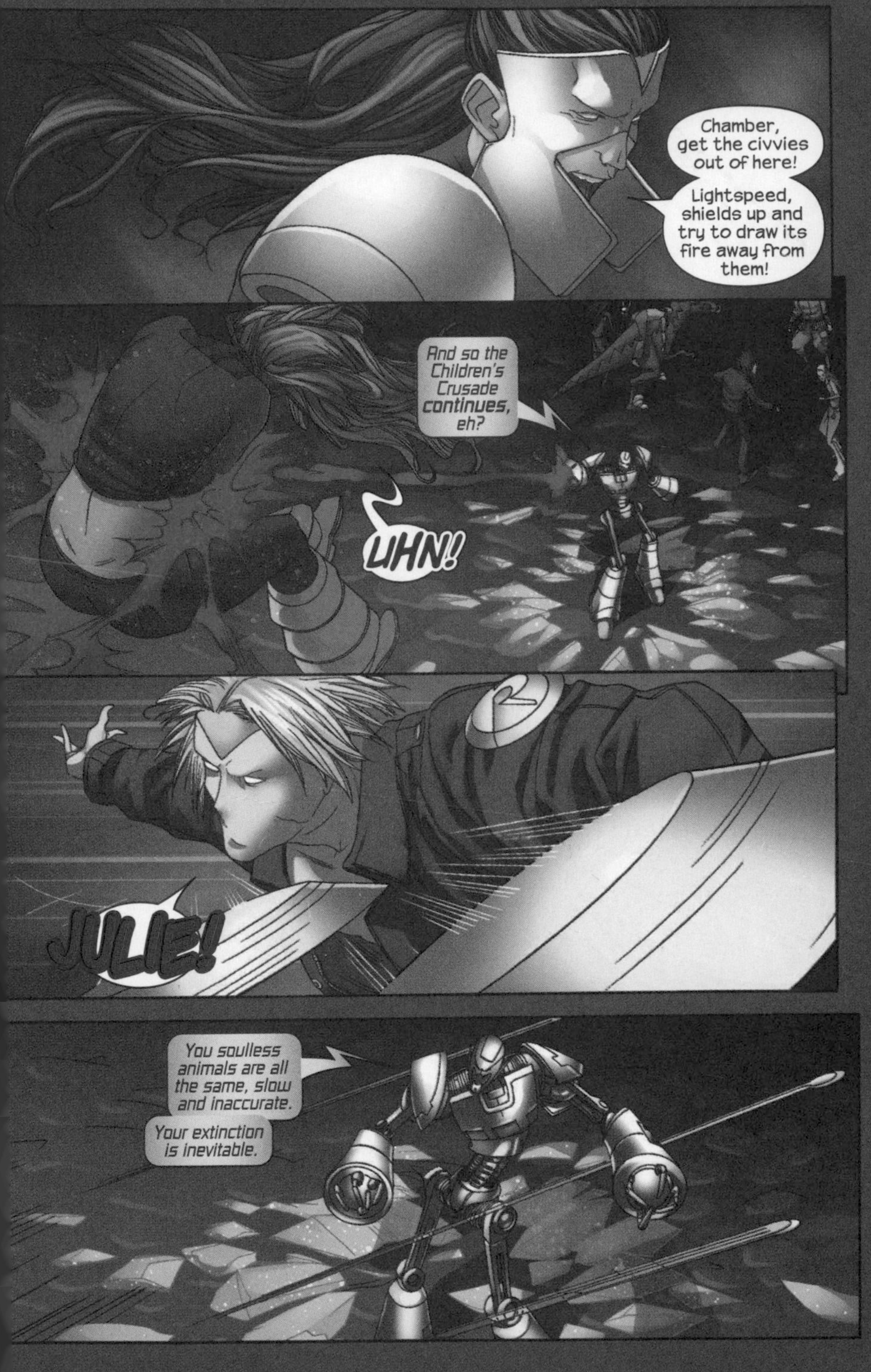
Chamber, get the civvies out of here!
Lightspeed, shields up and try to draw its fire away from them!
And so the Children's Crusade continues, eh?
UHN!
JULIE!
You soulless animals are all the same, slow and inaccurate.
Your extinction is inevitable.

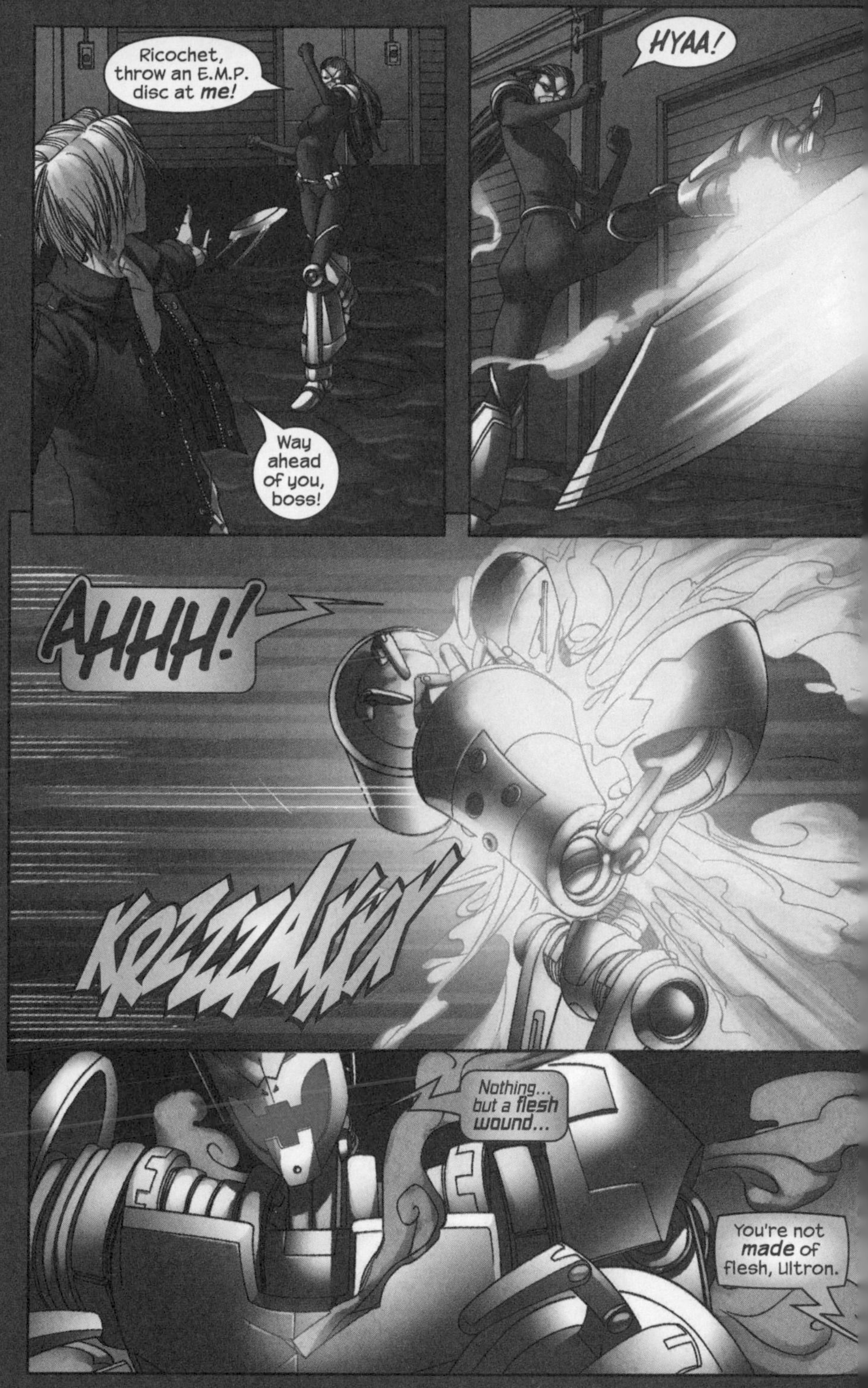
Ricochet, throw an E.M.P. disc at *me!*
Way ahead of you, boss!
HYAA!
AHHH!
KRZZZAKK
Nothing... but a *flesh* wound...
You're not *made* of flesh, Ultron.

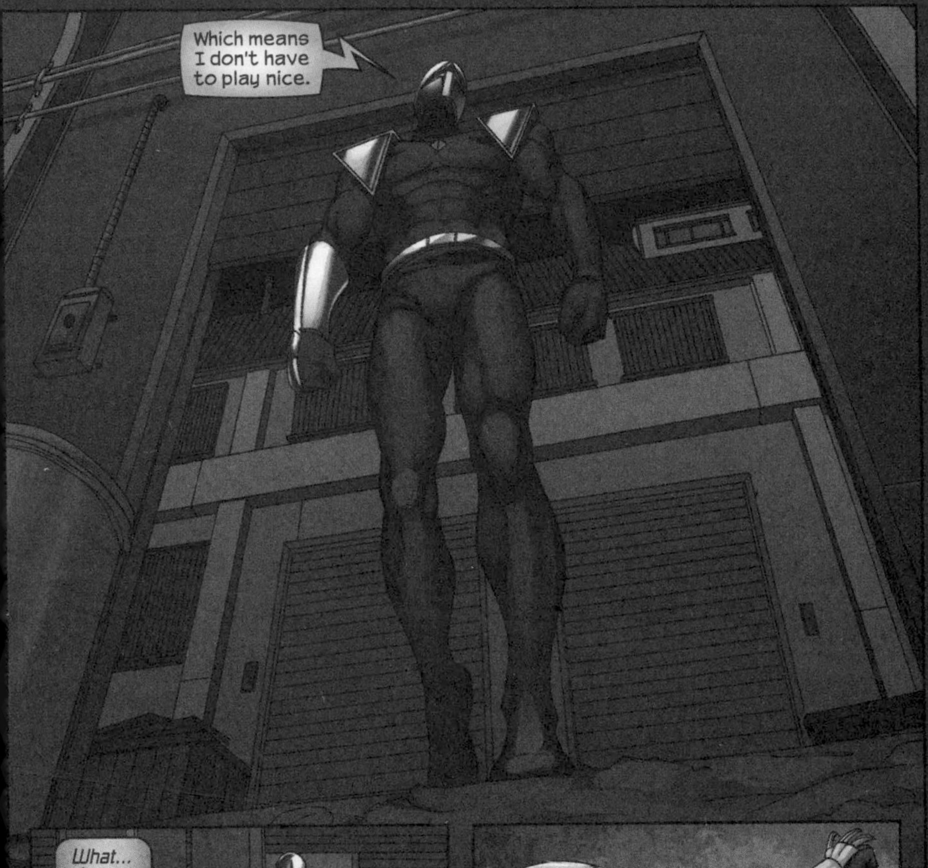
Which means I don't have to play nice.

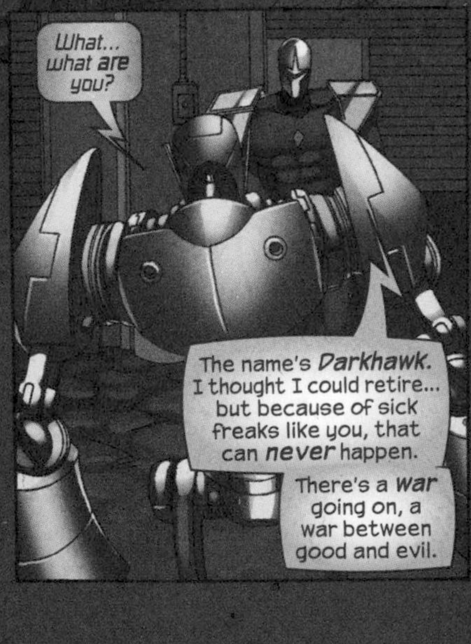
What... what *are* you?
The name's *Darkhawk.* I thought I could retire... but because of sick freaks like you, that can *never* happen.
There's a *war* going on, a war between good and evil.

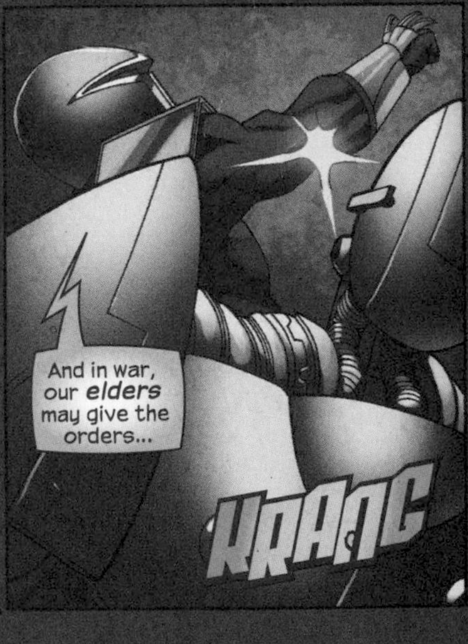
And in war, our *elders* may give the orders...
KRANG

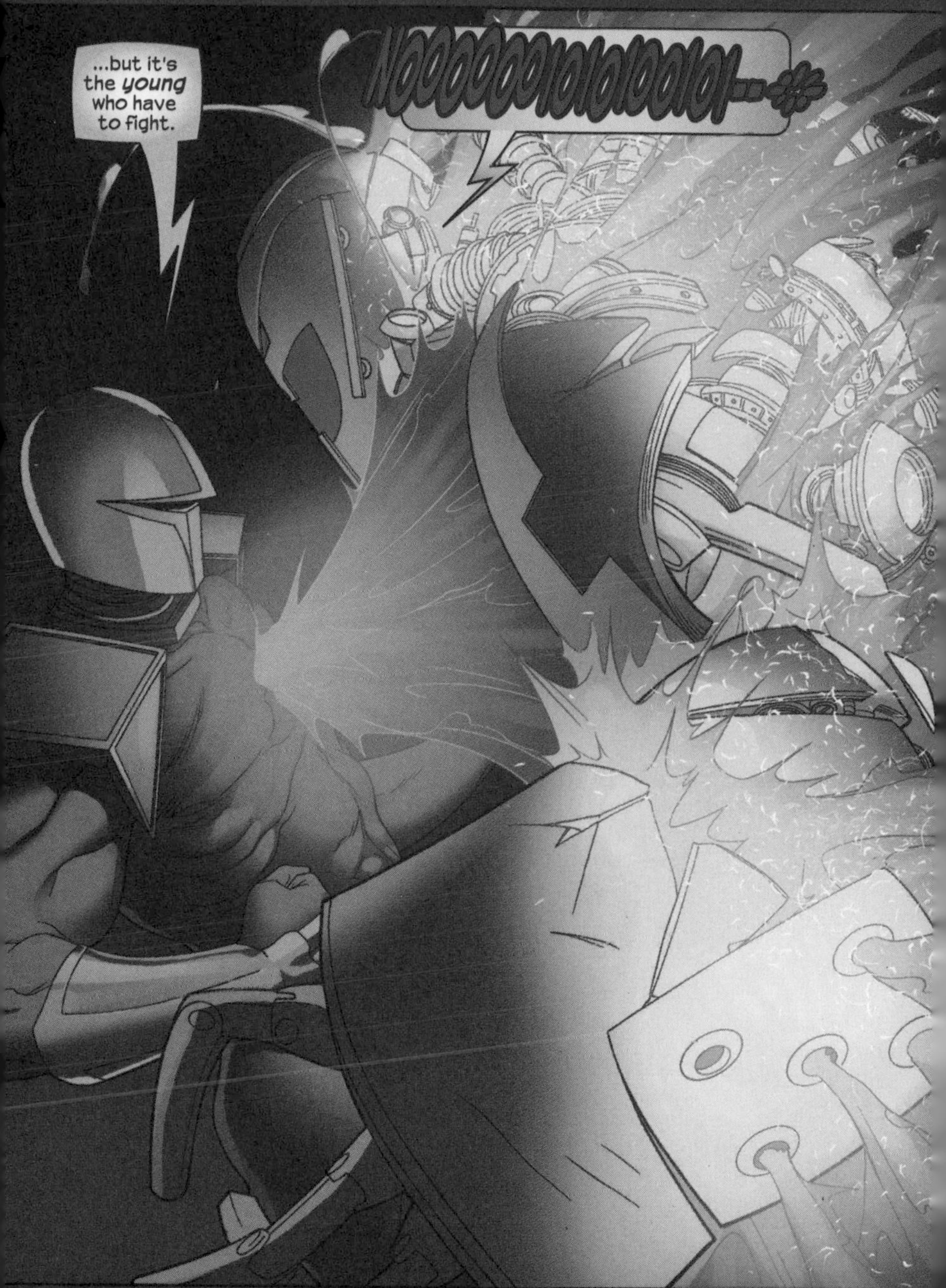
...but it's the *young* who have to fight.
NOOOOOOOIOIOIOIOOIOI--!!

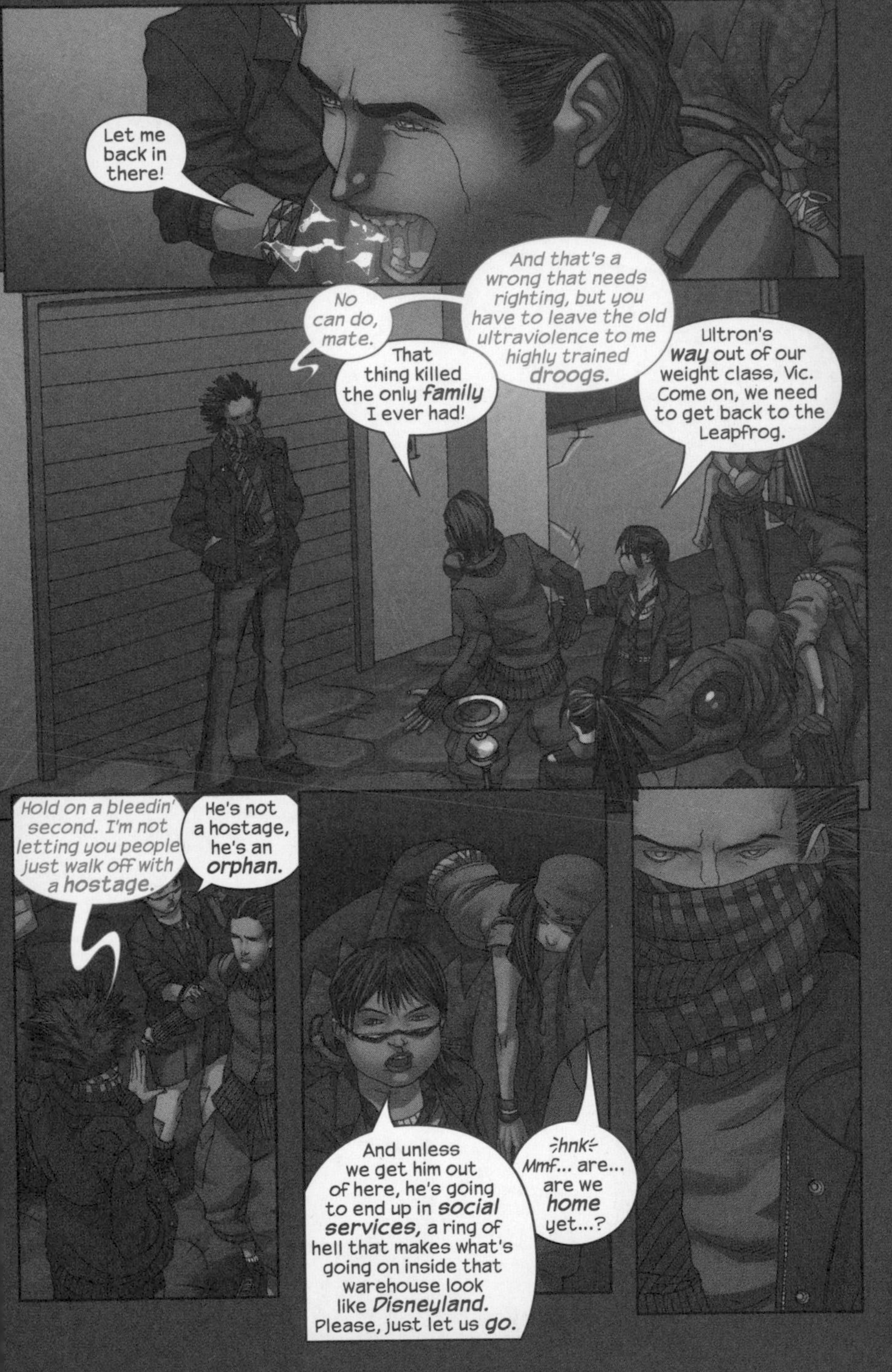

Let me back in there!
No can do, mate.
And that's a wrong that needs righting, but you have to leave the old ultraviolence to me highly trained droogs.
That thing killed the only family I ever had!
Ultron's way out of our weight class, Vic. Come on, we need to get back to the Leapfrog.
Hold on a bleedin' second. I'm not letting you people just walk off with a hostage.
He's not a hostage, he's an orphan.
And unless we get him out of here, he's going to end up in social services, a ring of hell that makes what's going on inside that warehouse look like Disneyland. Please, just let us go.
hnk Mmf... are... are we home yet...?

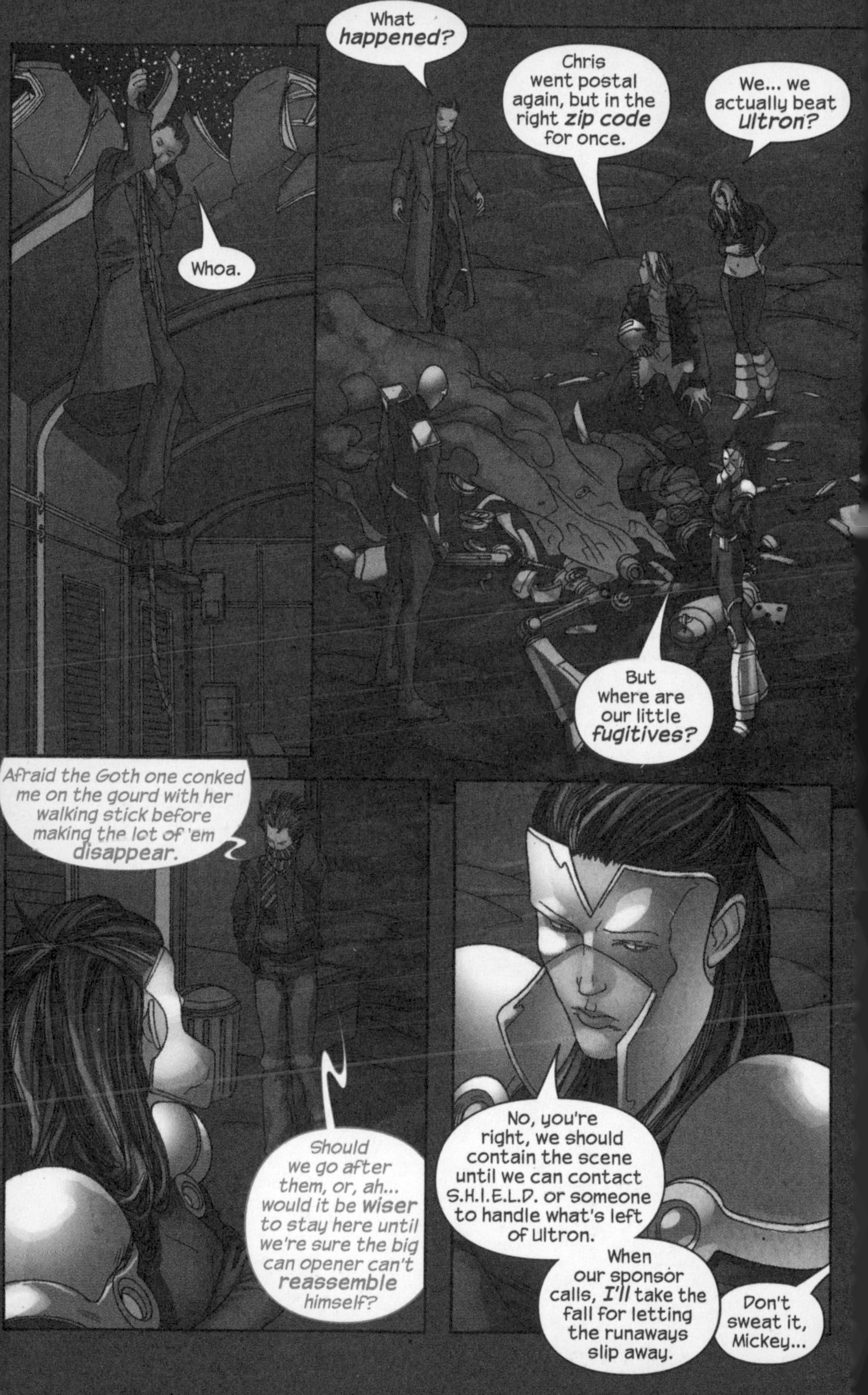
Whoa.
What happened?
Chris went postal again, but in the right zip code for once.
We... we actually beat Ultron?
But where are our little fugitives?
Afraid the Goth one conked me on the gourd with her walking stick before making the lot of 'em disappear.
Should we go after them, or, ah... would it be wiser to stay here until we're sure the big can opener can't reassemble himself?
No, you're right, we should contain the scene until we can contact S.H.I.E.L.D. or someone to handle what's left of Ultron.
When our sponsor calls, I'll take the fall for letting the runaways slip away.
Don't sweat it, Mickey...

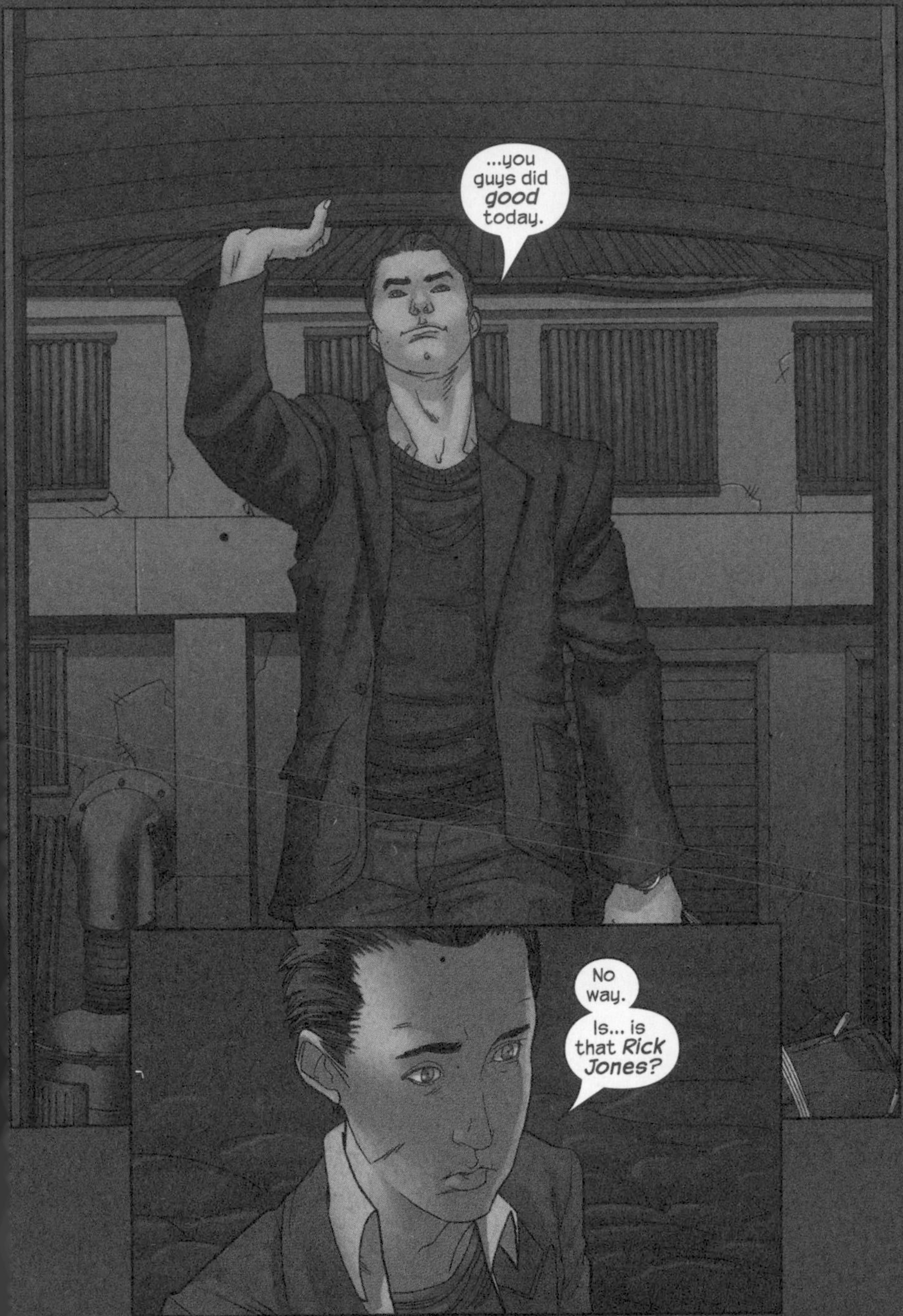
...you guys did good today.
No way.
Is... is that Rick Jones?

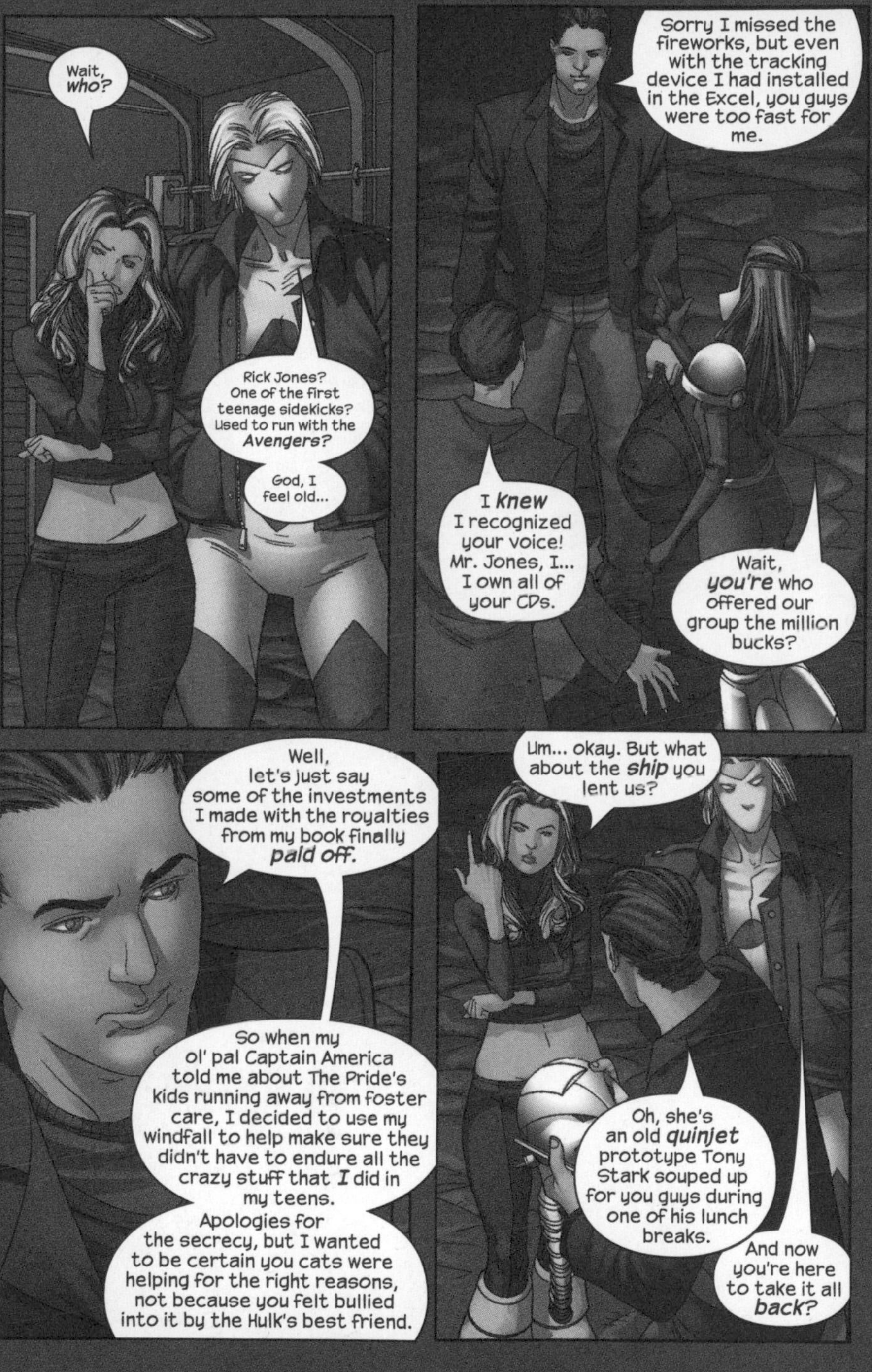

Wait, *who?*
Rick Jones? One of the first teenage sidekicks? Used to run with the *Avengers?*
God, I feel old...
Sorry I missed the fireworks, but even with the tracking device I had installed in the Excel, you guys were too fast for me.
I *knew* I recognized your voice! Mr. Jones, I... I own all of your CDs.
Wait, *you're* who offered our group the million bucks?
Well, let's just say some of the investments I made with the royalties from my book finally *paid off.*
So when my ol' pal Captain America told me about The Pride's kids running away from foster care, I decided to use my windfall to help make sure they didn't have to endure all the crazy stuff that *I* did in my teens.
Apologies for the secrecy, but I wanted to be certain you cats were helping for the right reasons, not because you felt bullied into it by the Hulk's best friend.
Um... okay. But what about the *ship* you lent us?
Oh, she's an old *quinjet* prototype Tony Stark souped up for you guys during one of his lunch breaks.
And now you're here to take it all *back?*

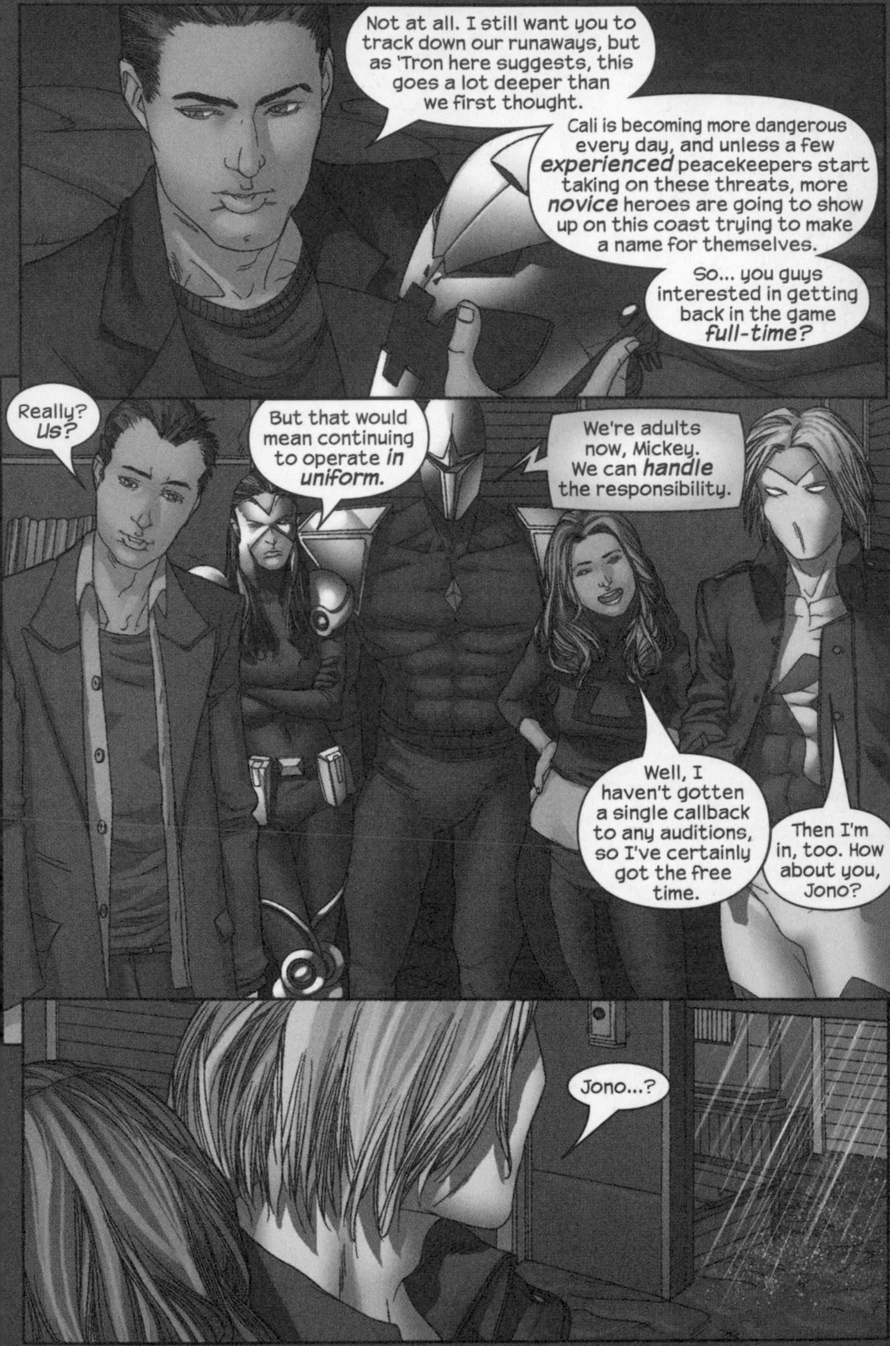

Not at all. I still want you to track down our runaways, but as 'Tron here suggests, this goes a lot deeper than we first thought.
Cali is becoming more dangerous every day, and unless a few *experienced* peacekeepers start taking on these threats, more *novice* heroes are going to show up on this coast trying to make a name for themselves.
So... you guys interested in getting back in the game *full-time?*
Really? *Us?*
But that would mean continuing to operate *in uniform.*
We're adults now, Mickey. We can *handle* the responsibility.
Well, I haven't gotten a single callback to any auditions, so I've certainly got the free time.
Then I'm in, too. How about you, Jono?
Jono...?

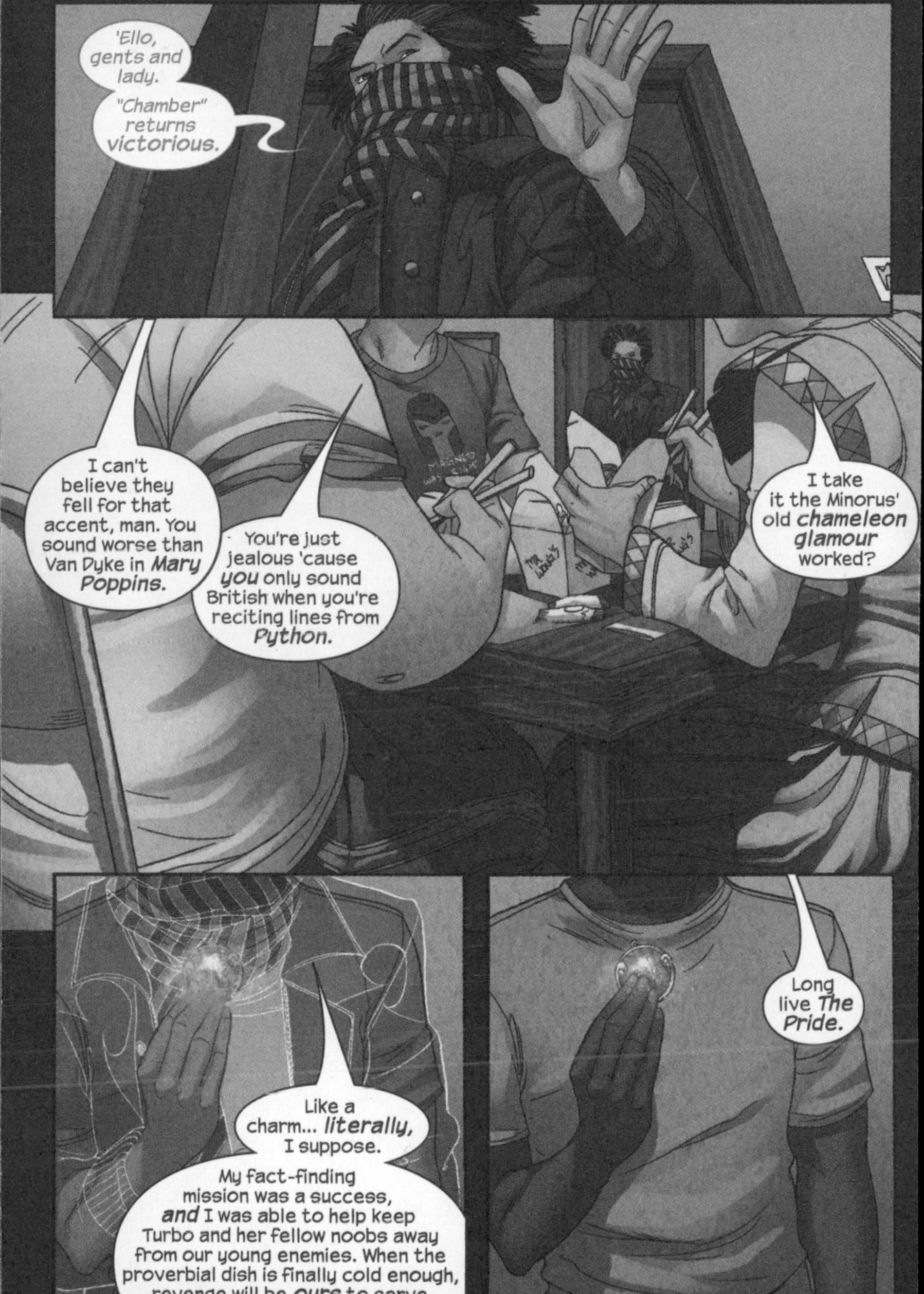
'Ello, gents and lady.
"Chamber" returns victorious.
I can't believe they fell for that accent, man. You sound worse than Van Dyke in Mary Poppins.
You're just jealous 'cause you only sound British when you're reciting lines from Python.
I take it the Minorus' old chameleon glamour worked?
Like a charm... literally, I suppose.
My fact-finding mission was a success, and I was able to help keep Turbo and her fellow noobs away from our young enemies. When the proverbial dish is finally cold enough, revenge will be ours to serve.
Long live The Pride.

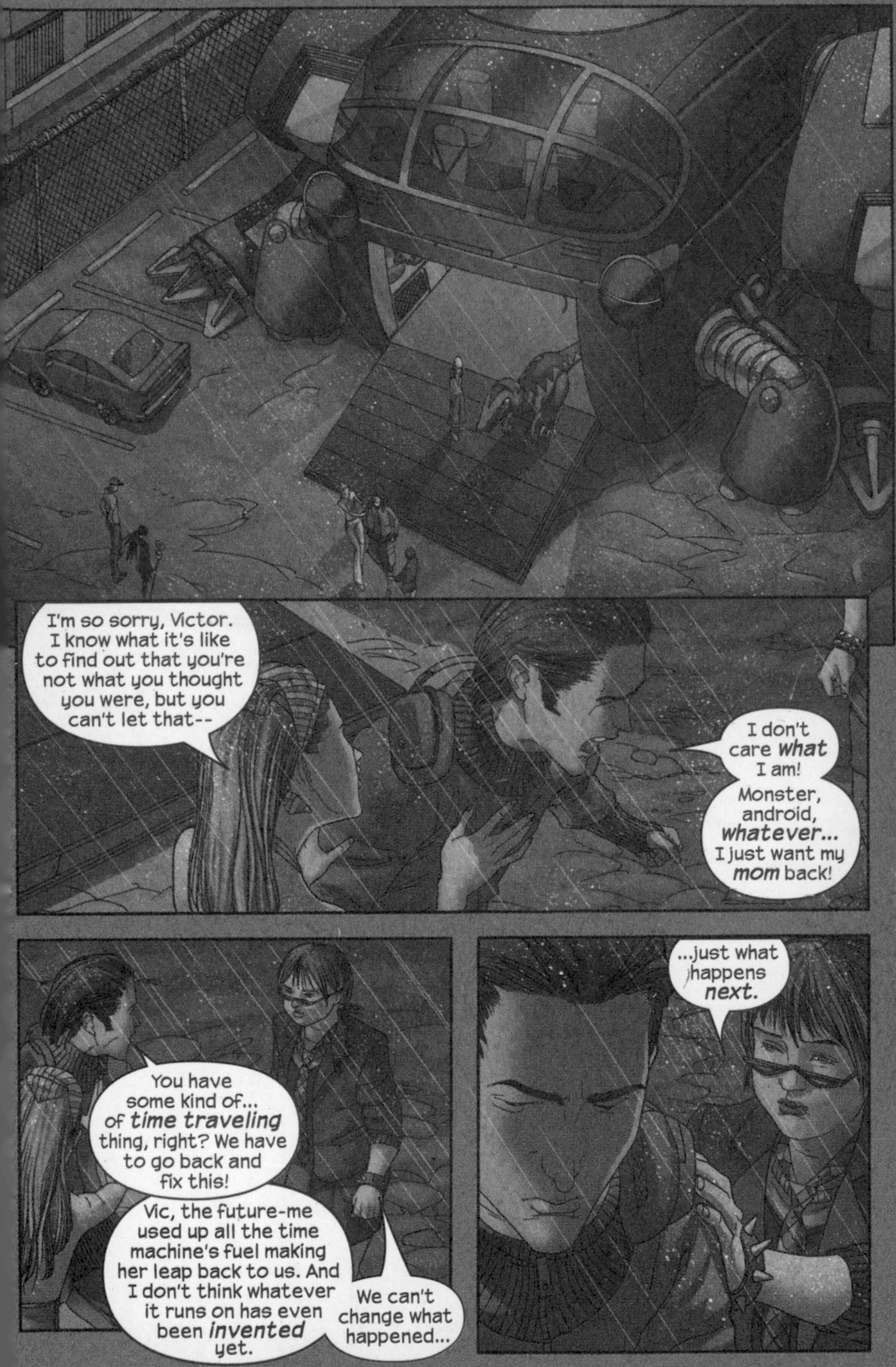
I'm so sorry, Victor. I know what it's like to find out that you're not what you thought you were, but you can't let that--
I don't care what I am!
Monster, android, whatever... I just want my mom back!
You have some kind of... of time traveling thing, right? We have to go back and fix this!
Vic, the future-me used up all the time machine's fuel making her leap back to us. And I don't think whatever it runs on has even been invented yet.
We can't change what happened...
...just what happens next.

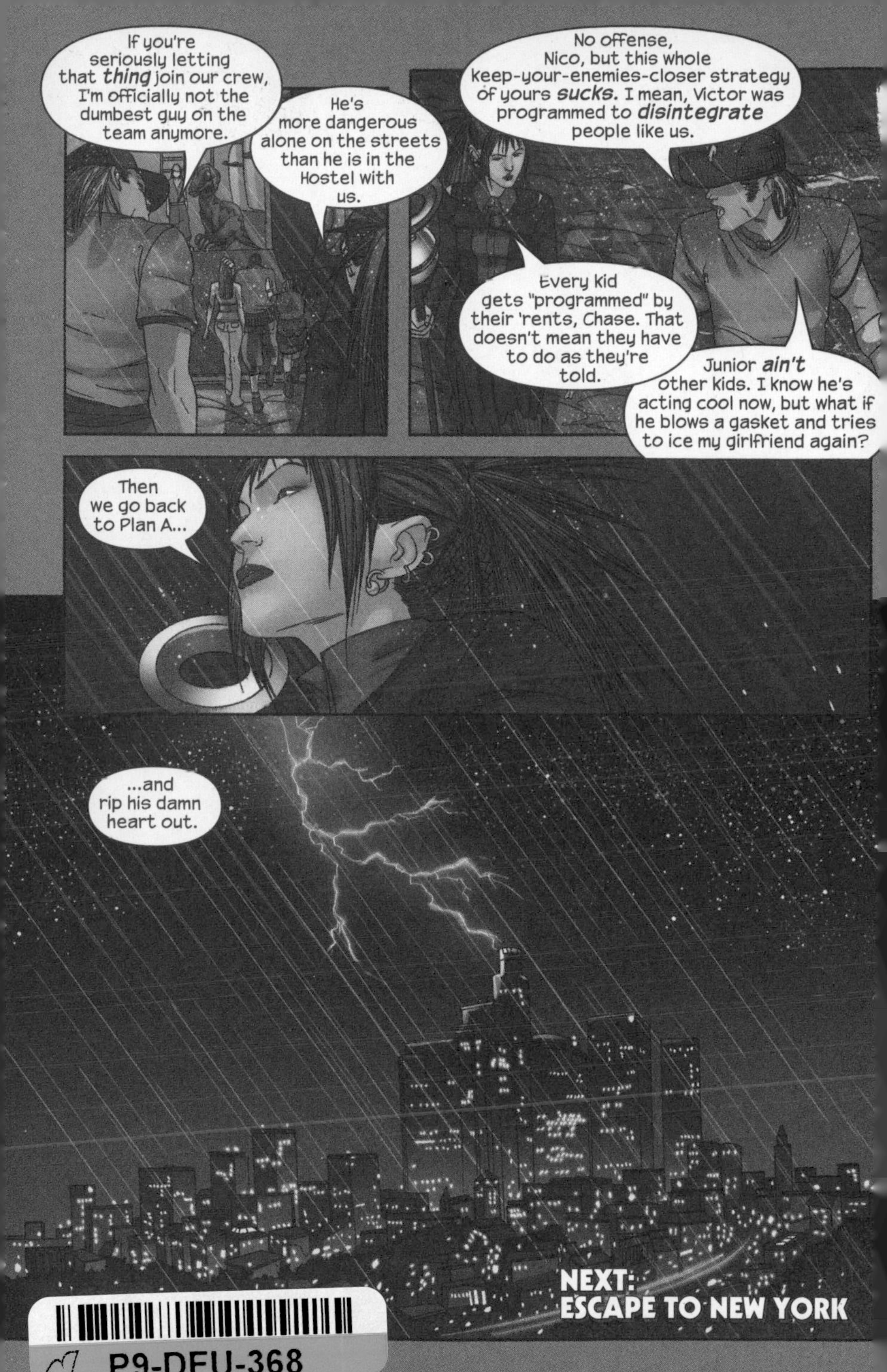
If you're seriously letting that *thing* join our crew, I'm officially not the dumbest guy on the team anymore.
He's more dangerous alone on the streets than he is in the Hostel with us.
No offense, Nico, but this whole keep-your-enemies-closer strategy of yours *sucks.* I mean, Victor was programmed to *disintegrate* people like us.
Every kid gets "programmed" by their 'rents, Chase. That doesn't mean they have to do as they're told.
Junior *ain't* other kids. I know he's acting cool now, but what if he blows a gasket and tries to ice my girlfriend again?
Then we go back to Plan A...
...and rip his damn heart out.
NEXT:
ESCAPE TO NEW YORK